Truth, Trust and Medicine

How should doctors resolve conflicts between their duty to be truthful and their other duties? What does the duty to be truthful actually involve? Is lying for the benefit of patients a betrayal of trust? Is the deliberate concealment of truth necessarily dishonest?

Jennifer Jackson investigates the notions of trust and honesty in medicine. She questions whether honesty and openness are of equal importance in maintaining the trust necessary in a doctor-patient relationship. The book begins with the assumption that doctors, nurses and counsellors have a basic duty to be worthy of the trust their patients place in them. Yet our understanding of what being trustworthy means, in the practices of modern medicine, is confused and uncertain. Doctor-patient relationships have recently come under serious scrutiny in ethical debates over issues such as: withholding information, obtaining consent, and employing covert practices in psychiatric, palliative and paediatric care contexts. This book boldly raises these questions which disturb our very modern notions of a patient's automony, self-determination and informed consent.

Truth, Trust and Medicine will be of interest to all those in medical ethics and applied philosophy, and a valuable resource for practitioners of medicine.

Jennifer Jackson is Senior Lecturer in Philosophy and Director of the Centre for Business and Professional Ethics at the University of Leeds.

Truth, Trust and Medicine

Jennifer Jackson

London and New York

First published 2001 by Routledge
11 New Fetter Lane, London EC4P 4EE

Simultaneously published in the USA and Canada
by Routledge
29 West 35th Street, New York, NY 10001

Routledge is an imprint of the Taylor & Francis Group

© 2001 Jennifer Jackson

Typeset in Times by Saxon Graphics Ltd, Derby
Printed and bound in Great Britain by Clays Ltd, St Ives plc

British Library Cataloguing in Publication Data
A catalogue record for this book is available from the British Library

Library of Congress Cataloging in Publication Data
Jackson, Jennifer C., 1939-
    Truth, trust and medicine/Jennifer Jackson.
        p. cm.
    Includes bibliographical references and index.
    1. Medical ethics. 2. Medicine–Philosophy. 3. Physician and
        patient–Moral and ethical aspects. I. Title.

    R725.5.J33 2000
174'.2–dc21   00-056027

ISBN 0–415–18548–3 (pbk)
ISBN 0–415–18547–5 (hbk)

To my son, Nicholas Coope (1980–98), who fell to his death climbing in Glen Clova: a brave and thoughtful lad, proudly remembered.

Contents

Preface

> When you get me a good man made out of arguments, I will get you a good dinner with reading you the cookery-book. That's my opinion, and I think anybody's stomach will bear me out.
>
> (Mrs Farebrother in George Eliot's *Middlemarch*)

Notwithstanding Mrs Farebrother's robust impatience with arguments, arguments influence for better or worse the choices people make and the principles they try to live by. It matters, therefore, that we are not seduced by bad arguments. I will argue that contemporary medical ethics is taking us in the wrong direction in so far as it conflates two distinct duties: the duty not to lie to patients and the duty to be open with patients. Although it might seem that the current emphasis on 'frank discussion', on openness, is an advance over the old Hippocratic toleration, even approval, of secrecy, I will argue that this is not a move that is entirely helpful in sustaining trust between patients and their doctors and nurses. Indeed, if the duty not to lie becomes entirely assimilated under the duty to be open, there is a danger that trust will be eroded as a result.

My book has three main aims:

1 to understand the importance of truthfulness in life generally, and in medical and nursing contexts specifically;
2 to explain why we need to adopt a very strict teaching repudiating the telling of lies: in life generally, and no less in medical and nursing practice;
3 to distinguish truthfulness from openness: defending secretive and concealing practices in life generally, and in *some* medical and nursing contexts.

The tendency to treat honesty in communication (truthfulness) and openness as one virtue is dangerous for the following reason. Whatever principle in the matter of truth-telling we adopt, it has to be a principle to which it is possible to commit sincerely. But a firm commitment to be truthful and open has obviously got to be qualified if it is sincere. It is neither possible nor desirable to be open about everything, all the time. Hence we have to understand the principled commitment to openness as a commitment that permits many accommodations: often other principles will supervene, necessitating less openness. That openness needs to be so qualified may be fine. But trouble arises, I will argue, if we adopt an equally flexible attitude towards truthfulness.

I will argue that concealment – pretence and secretiveness – is not necessarily dishonest. Take, for example, the way students may cheekily attach unflattering nicknames to their professors. Naturally they conceal these practices from the professors. Is this dishonest? Surely not. Nor is it dishonest to adopt different tones and styles of speech to fit in with different company (for example: with one's in-laws, friends or children). There are risks, of course: one may be overheard – like the patient being anaesthetised who happened to overhear the surgeon saying, 'Now, where's my lucky scalpel?' And, unforgivably, the patient who overheard her nurse grumbling: 'they always do this … They send the basket cases in a chair and the ones who can sit up, on a stretcher. I wish they'd get their signals straight!' – overheard by a 'basket case' (Cook 1981: 203).

Of course, in neither of these cases were the speakers expecting to be overheard. But their speaking thus does not show them to be dishonest (though in the latter example, it does show a lack of respect: inexcusable, whether or not it is openly displayed).

Whereas the duty on doctors and nurses to be open with their patients is one which quite rightly needs to be pursued alongside other duties (for example, to keep confidences), the duty not to lie to their patients is, I shall argue, one that needs to be treated as much more strictly binding. On this matter, I will part company with most contemporary commentators on medical ethics. To be sure, it is generally agreed that the duty not to lie is one that needs to be taken quite seriously: it is not to be lightly set aside. But the prevailing view is that there are bound to be rare occasions where doctors and nurses need to lie and do so justifiably. I hope to show that this is a mistake.

Acknowledgements

As I have been at work off and on for some years writing this book, I have garnered help from many sources. The initial planning and research was undertaken with the support of a Tennent Caledonian Visiting Research Fellowship at the Centre for Philosophy and Public Affairs at the University of St Andrews in the autumn term of 1992. This provided me with a very congenial environment in which to get the project underway. I am most grateful to the Centre for its support. There then followed an interlude of some years when I was busy with other duties. But as these included teaching for a taught MA on Health Care Ethics at the University of Leeds, I had many opportunities to test out some of my ideas and to listen to and learn from students and colleagues. I also had the benefit of comments on an early draft of part of the manuscript and on an early article of mine on the subject of lying and deceiving from my former colleague, Dr Piers Benn, and of comment on a more recent draft of some chapters from Dr David Stocks.

In the spring term of 1999 I was able to return to single-minded study with the help of a visiting research fellowship at the Center for Applied Ethics at the University of British Columbia and also with some financial support from my own University of Leeds. I am most grateful to all who made this visit possible: my hosts, the Director of the Centre, Professor Michael McDonald, his colleagues and the post-doc students there, my colleagues back at Leeds who took over my teaching duties while I was away, and my family who encouraged me all the way. While at UBC, I was most fortunate to become a member of Green College: which provided a very friendly and stimulating home from home. As always, the most constant and stalwart encouragement and guidance has come from my colleague and husband, Christopher Coope.

1 Truthfulness in medical and nursing practice

Truly, we are a truth crazed society

John Lantos, MD

A few years ago a hospital sister was suspended from her job and then given 'a final formal warning' for, on a consultant's instruction, having added haloperidol (a tranquillising medication) to the tea of a 91 year old who was attending a day hospital for the elderly. The patient had resisted all efforts to persuade him to be admitted to hospital. The team felt that he was hypomanic and unsafe to return to his old people's home without treatment. The consultant who had given the instruction to the sister was also upbraided: his medical director likened the action to having intercourse with a patient, 'it may not harm the patient but it is equally wrong' (Kellett 1996: 1250).[1]

The disciplinary steps taken (by the chief nurse and the hospital unit general manager) were bizarre in themselves, but equally baffling, surely, must have been the moral judgements that were thought to justify them. Were the managers sticklers for openness? Not exactly, it seems: the consultant was actually rebuked for having subsequently told the patient and the patient's nephew what had been done and why. The patient and the nephew were wholly satisfied with this explanation after the event. Not so, the management. Although the consultant was eventually found to be not guilty of professional misconduct, he was subsequently ordered 'to stop releasing information of this type [that is, an account of his clinical actions and the reasons for them] to relatives or patients' (White 1997: 299).

In the correspondence the report of this incident generated, doctors claimed that covert drug administration is quite common. In a questionnaire issued to a random sample of senior, middle grade and junior psychiatrists working in Heathlands Mental Health Trust, over a third of the doctors admitted to 'either having participated in surreptitious prescribing or having been economical with the truth when giving information to patients' (Valmana and Rutherford 1997: 300).

Of course, this is not the only setting in which doctors and nurses report that concealment, with or without deception, is routine practice. Parents and clinicians are said to collude in administering drugs surreptitiously to children (Griffith and Bell 1996: 1250). While many doctors and nurses admit to feeling particularly uncomfortable about lying, they may not feel so badly about other types of deception that do not involve outright lying, or that simply involve the withholding of information. Though, doubtless, they will agree that truthfulness is a duty, they may observe that this duty has to be balanced against other duties. It routinely and properly yields to other overriding concerns.

Maybe so. But how, then, are the different duties to be weighed up? Should the duty not to lie weigh more heavily than the duty not to deceive by other surreptitious tricks? By what measure or test are doctors or nurses to work out in this or that situation whether or not the duty not to lie, or the duty to be open, is properly overridden by some other duty? Is it possible at least to draw up guidelines on this matter? Will conscientious and experienced practitioners not need guidance? Are good intentions and common sense sufficient – sufficient to deal with the variety of challenges and predicaments that arise? Doctors and nurses can expect often to be faced with the questions what to tell, whether to tell, and how much to tell.

Should doctors inform their patients if Alzheimer's is diagnosed even if the patients' families want the information to be withheld? Should a nurse who discovers that she has accidentally given a wrong dose make a point of telling the patient that she has done so, even if the patient has suffered no ill effect in consequence? Should doctors always tell their patients if cost considerations prevent their being offered the best treatment for their condition? Is it ethically defensible to enter patients in a trial without telling them, provided that the treatment they receive in the trial is simply the standard treatment they would receive if they were not in the trial? Are there honest ways of using placebos on patients – as therapy? Is it unethical, in persuading an elderly patient to move into a nursing home, to withhold the information that no pets are allowed there, or to let the patient hold onto unrealistic hopes that the stay will be temporary? Is it unethical for the physiotherapist to persuade a patient to do exercises by giving unrealistic predictions (or by not correcting the patient's own unrealistic expectations) about the extent of recovery that these will achieve?

The brother of a young woman who is critically ill with cystic fibrosis comes forward as a potential donor – offering part of his lung. He is tested and found to be an excellent match. You are now explaining to him in detail what the operation entails – including the risks and possible complications for him and for the recipient, his sister. It becomes clear to you that he is changing his mind and wants to back off. But he cannot bring himself to do so unless you are willing to conceal from his family the reason for not proceeding. He wants you to lie to his family about why the transplant cannot go ahead. If you tell them that he has been found not to be 'medically suitable' is that a lie? Is it any way a defensible deception? If you aim to deceive does it matter morally how you do this, whether with an outright lie or with an equivocation?

You explain to your patient that there is a waiting list for the heart bypass operation of 6–9 months. You do not mention that 70 per cent of patients on the waiting list die before their turn comes up. You also omit to mention that those who can afford to go private can have the operation done immediately. It is obvious to you that this patient cannot afford to go private. You give accurate figures regarding the relative risks of alternative treatments, one of which involves surgery. But you omit to mention that the risk of surgery in *this* hospital is significantly higher than the national figures you have quoted. If a patient, dying of cancer, wants to know what the dying may be like, are you obliged to give details of every possibility, however grim or unlikely? Do all patients, if competent (and otherwise, their relatives) have a (moral) right[2] to participate in the making of a decision not to resuscitate should they arrest?

You are seeking permission from parents to remove tissue from their deceased child to use for research purposes. You do not make it clear that 'tissue' as you and your medical colleagues understand the term includes eyes and organs. You do not spell this out fearing that if you did, consent might not be forthcoming.

The relative wants to know whether the patient was in pain when she died. You do not lie. You evade. You describe the pain relief that was offered and omit to say that it was ineffective. If a mother whose baby is dying waits by the cot meaning to hold her baby in her arms as it dies, but falls asleep at the critical moment, is a nurse remiss if she wakes the mother and hands her the baby allowing the mother to think the baby is still alive though the nurse realizes that it is not? A mother asks what will happen to the baby she has miscarried and the nurse replies that it will be cremated. She does not add that the body goes into a skip along with other miscarried or aborted foetuses and is tipped into an incinerator. Nor does she volunteer the information that a neighbouring health authority has a policy of cremating separately boxed miscarried foetuses.

These are mostly examples of withholding information or of incomplete disclosure where the *intention* to deceive may or may not be present. There are also situations where patients or their relatives are routinely and deliberately tricked. The doors into Alzheimers' wards are deliberately designed so that the patients cannot work out how to open them. Pretences are adopted to trick patients out of their dependency on ventilators or drugs. Covert surveillance on relatives is used in paediatric wards where child abuse is suspected. If a patient dies suddenly, the relatives may be summoned with a lie or evasion to disguise the fact that the patient is already dead. Summoning relatives in this way may be the policy advocated to avoid what is considered worse: telling them the bad news over the telephone.

Deceptions in medical practice are not confined to doctors or nurses deceiving their patients: they may lie *for* them as well as *to* them. Is this always wrong? It is said that the first duty of doctors is to serve the best interests of their patients. What, then, if those interests are best served by lying on their behalf – to their insurers or employers or to a colleague?

Everyone can appreciate the prudential importance of being sparing with the lies one tells, in medicine, as in life generally. Lying is only useful where it is not suspected and if everyone lies, everyone suspects. That granted, is not truthfulness also something that can be overdone? If the reality in medical practice is that patients are often lied to, tricked with deceptions, and kept in the dark, is that necessarily a matter for surprise or condemnation? Are there not good and bad reasons for being untruthful or less than wholly truthful? Before condemning deceptive or secretive practices, we need to look into the situations in which they occur and the reasons why they are resorted to: these may or may not exonerate.

All the same, there does seem to be a rather blatant mismatch between what actually goes on in medical practice, the extent to which deceptions and secrecy occurs (naturally, one assumes that the extent is considerably wider than is admitted to) and the declarations and pronouncements on medical ethics which nowadays are so stridently in favour of truthfulness and openness. While there are many issues in contemporary medical ethics which are a source of continuing, often passionate, debate and controversy, one issue on which virtually everyone involved, professional associations of doctors and nurses, philosophers, patients' groups (in the 'Western' world) agrees, is the enormous importance of truthfulness in medical and nursing practice. Many of the debates in medical ethics nowadays address new challenges which the health professions and society have never faced in the past. How truthful doctors should be with their patients is not a new issue. What is new is the current insistence among ethicists and others that good medical (and nursing) practice eschews deception and aspires to be open.

Sissela Bok (1978) connects the change of attitude with the emergence of the notion of informed consent.[3] She and others also connect this change of attitude with the modern post-Kantian emphasis on the duty to show respect to patients by allowing them to make autonomous choices. Thus, for example, Sheila McLean declares that the 'fundamental characteristic' of showing respect is 'the honest provision of information which permits the patient to make a self-determining decision about the personal benefits attached to surgery'(1989: 81–2). This connecting of showing respect owed to patients with recognizing and supporting their 'autonomy,' their right to make their own choices in the light of their own personal values and 'life-plans' is echoed approvingly throughout the literature on medical ethics. Respect for autonomy, declares the BMA's practical guide to doctors, *Medical Ethics Today*, 'has become the core principle of modern medicine' (1993: 321). Attention to this principle is hailed as an advance over the less enlightened paternalist attitudes which prevailed in medical and nursing practice until recent times. Tom Beauchamp and James Childress remark: 'By contrast to this traditional disregard of veracity, virtues of candour and truthfulness are among the most widely praised character-traits of health professionals in biomedical ethics'(1994: 395).

Until quite recently, truthfulness has not featured in medical or nursing codes. It does not seem to have been any significant part of the Hippocratic tradition – unlike confidentiality, which has always been seen as a strict duty owed by doctors to their patients. But nowadays it gets explicit attention. The General Medical Council issues a card to all medical students in the UK stating the essential duties of a doctor. These include: 'be honest and trustworthy', 'give patients information in a way they can understand' and 'respect the rights of patients to be fully involved in decisions about their care'. The 1983 version of the International Code of Medical Ethics produced by the World Medical Association includes the statement: 'A physician shall deal honestly with patients and colleagues, and strive to expose those physicians deficient in character or competence, or who engage in fraud or deception'.

The United Kingdom Central Council for Nursing, Midwifery and Health Visiting issued an Advisory Document on 'Exercising Accountability' (UKCC 1989). It has a whole section on 'Consent and Truth' which includes the following:

> If it is to be believed that, on occasions, practitioners will withhold information from their patients the damage to public trust and confidence in the profession, on which the introduction to the Code of Professional Conduct places great emphasis, will be enormous.

So much for what is said. What actually happens may be rather different. Third year medical students at University College London are given practice through role-play in handling difficult patients.

> Judging by the scenarios I witnessed, the strongest reaction in students faced with a difficult patient was to obfuscate, and even lie. They protested that the doctors training them routinely lie to patients. 'My consultant never even tells the patients they have got cancer, let alone telling them that they are going to die' said one.
>
> *The Sunday Times* 30 April 1995

If there is a mismatch between what does happen and what it is said should happen in regard to truthfulness, which is it that needs fixing? Is it the declarations that are unsound, simplistic – maybe, because they are put about by ethicists who do not understand the realities of clinical practice and how patients' needs are best served? (Thurston Brewin blames what he calls 'fundamentalist ethics' for the unsound rhetoric which advocates an overly rigid tactless and insensitive insistence on telling 'the truth') (1993: 161–3). Or, is it bad practice that needs fixing – maybe because clinicians too casually assume that truthfulness is impossible – that other duties must often prevail? Or, are practice and pronouncements not all that far apart since the pronouncements, on closer inspection, are vaguely worded or hedged about with qualifications which allow practitioners ample scope for tailoring the extent to which they are truthful to the particular demands of the situations they encounter? Brewin claims that actual practice has not changed all that much: good doctors and nurses understand the need to convey information always with tact and sensitivity (1996: ix).

How important are honest communication and openness in medical practice? Why do they matter? Do they matter equally and for the same reasons? Are they just as important in medical practice as in life generally? And how important is that? How 'situationist' should doctors and nurses be about telling lies, condoning lies, deceptive tricks and ploys, withholding information or keeping secrets? How should the need to speak the truth and the need to be open be accommodated with the other needs that doctors and nurses are duty-bound to serve?

Should doctors heed truthfulness in one way if they are working under adverse conditions, for example, under a totalitarian regime which does not respect the basic rights of all people within its borders, and in another way if they are working within a stable democratic and liberal society? Thus, Christine Korsgaard (1996) argues that under non-ideal conditions truthfulness may have to be seen as a goal rather than as a constraint. The mountaineer ascending Everest who passed without stopping, a climber who had collapsed, said in self-defence: 'You cannot afford morality at 8000 metres'. Are there corresponding circumstances in which doctors cannot afford truthfulness – even as a goal?

If, as is so often claimed, patients can only trust those who are truthful and open with them, how did doctors and nurses manage to win their trust formerly in the days when truthfulness and openness were not seen to be requisite to good practice? Why is it that nowadays, notwithstanding the preaching, trust seems if anything more precarious, not less?

The mismatch between preaching and practice ranges beyond what is said or not said to patients (or for them). There is a mismatch, for example, between the official declarations which totally repudiate dishonest practices in research and publication – the use of fraudulent data, plagiarism, redundant publication, and actual practice.[4] The fact that there are charlatans and rogues in medicine as in every other profession comes as no surprise. Yet we should not too hastily assume that every type of deception is dishonest or otherwise ethically indefensible. Even the most vigorous enthusiasts for truthfulness and for openness with patients will concede that there are some occasions where deceiving a patient is justified. Should they be equally 'pragmatic' about recourse to fraudulent data in scientific research? If not, why not?

Is it always dishonest to pledge to act one way when you intend to act otherwise? Is it a dishonest pretence to 'respect' Jehovah's Witness patients' refusal of blood up until they lose consciousness and then proceed to transfuse them as emergency cases? Is it dishonest pretence to circumvent statutory regulations that restrict legal access to abortion, signing patients as needing abortion on 'social' grounds when they do not? Is such a ruse not dishonest if nobody is fooled, if it is an open secret that this has become the conventional way round a tough law?

Is it dishonest of doctors to invite pregnant mothers to undergo prenatal screening without making it crystal clear to them that if they test positive, they will be offered an abortion? One hears that women have sometimes been invited to undergo such screening as if it were a way of helping the baby – 'making sure it is doing well'. Should it not be made clear if the only help for the baby that might be forthcoming is being 'helped' to die?

Peter Singer (1995) complains of the mismatch between doctors' continuing firm insistence on the sanctity of human life alongside their adoption of a new definition of death that enables them to harvest vital organs from the living. Singer claims that this 'convenient fiction' that the brain dead are dead is a dishonest pretence.

There are thus a host of practices in medicine and nursing which compromise truthfulness (or may seem to), some of which many practitioners may defend as sometimes necessary and not unethical, others of which may be defended by some and denounced by others. Needless to say, there are also instances where the truth is compromised unjustifiably but understandably – where there are mitigating considerations.

Being truthful can be difficult for two quite different reasons:

1 it may be difficult because though it is obvious what being truthful requires, acting accordingly is costly (to oneself, to others)
2 it may be difficult because in a particular context what truthfulness allows or requires is not at all clear.

It is only the latter sort of difficulty that I want to explore in this book. Hence we will not be concerned with obvious skulduggery or venial lapses but with compromises with the truth that might seriously be defended: for example, on the grounds that these are necessary in the line of duty. In order to framework our reflections on truthfulness in clinical contexts we will need to explore more generally the nature of truthfulness: what it involves and why it matters.

Even if the general account of truthfulness that follows is sound, we cannot expect to be able to extrapolate guidelines directly from it in a way that will make truthfulness thereafter a problem free zone in clinical contexts. That would be a ridiculous ambition. My aim here is more modest: to shed some important light on truthfulness that will help those who encounter or anticipate such problems in their clinical roles to think them through more critically. Of course, much of the difficulty in applied ethics comes at the point where one moves from the more general enduring truths to the applications in particular fields, such as those explored in the study of health care ethics. But that is no excuse for not attempting to work towards a shared understanding of what are defensible and indefensible practices and policies. In working out their own guidelines doctors and nurses need to have one eye on the more general underlying issues: in this case, of what truthfulness involves and why it matters.

Before we proceed to analyse its nature, let us take a closer look at some of the pronouncements on the subject in medical and nursing ethics and at some of the history behind the current emphasis on these notions.

2 Noble lies and therapeutic tricks

If the appearance of doing something be necessary to keep alive the hope and spirits of the patient, it should be of the most innocent character. One of the most successful physicians I have ever known, has assured me, that he used more bread pills, drops of coloured water, and powders of hickory ashes, than of all other medicines put together.

Thomas Jefferson

Before we begin working out our own account of what truthfulness requires or permits in medical and in nursing practice, let us take some note of what others have said on this subject. We are not interested here in everything that has been said: not everything needs working out. We all agree that certain sorts of deeds are both dishonest and indefensible – the cashier who pockets cash from the till, for example. Naturally, there have been dishonest scamps and scoundrels in medicine and nursing as in all other occupations: quacks peddling bogus cures, doctors or nurses attempting to hide their mistakes by falsifying the records, or stealing drugs and selling them on the black market. Let us label such obvious dishonesty as 'hands in the till' dishonesty. Our interest here is not in such undisputed, glaring examples of dishonesty but in the more problematic aspects of what honesty, primarily in communication, requires or permits. Our interest is in the 'noble' lie, so-called, not the scurrilous. The lies, deceptive tricks and concealments that I have described in the last chapter may be used by conscientious, well-meaning practitioners who think that in some circumstances such conduct is justified. Which, if any, and why, are indeed justifiable is the object of our enquiry.

Our review of what others say or have said does not pretend to completeness. It will serve, though, to remind us that some of our uncertainties and confusion about lying, deceiving, concealing, and not revealing in the context of medical and nursing practice are not new. While doctors' benevolent lies, deceptive tricks and secretive ways have long been subject for debate, our enquiry into the matter now is timely: for two reasons, one practical and the other theoretical.

The practical interest of this study

The topic (truthfulness in medicine and nursing practice) has acquired a new practical urgency for practitioners because nowadays their conduct is more exposed to challenge from patients, their relatives and even from colleagues. Roughly speaking, up until the 1960s, individual doctors could often make up their own minds as to when if ever they should lie to their patients or trick them or conceal matters from them; and quietly go about their business, restricted only by the law and their own consciences. Nowadays, though, there are further restrictions: the profession makes public pledges; so may the health authorities who pay doctors' salaries. The law itself has become more meddlesome: especially in policing the adequacy of information given to patients when consenting to invasive treatments. Those who practice as members of teams, pooling their different specialisms, need to have a shared stance in respect of lying or concealing.[1] Hence the need not only to have one's own view but to be able to explain and defend it to colleagues in the team.

Similarly, the issue of when, if ever, lying or tricking or concealing is defensible arises more starkly nowadays for nurses than it did in times gone by. They are no longer able to pass off their own actions as 'Doctor's (or Sister's) orders' (not that this would ever have excused wrongdoing). They are each (however junior) bound by their own professional codes and by the pledges made to patients by the organizations which employ them. Like many doctors, nurses too often work in teams and relays, and need to have a shared stance in respect of lying and concealing. They need not only to have their own personal view but to be able to defend it against, or square it with, whatever policy is generally proposed.

Lying or concealing is only feasible if the strategy is supported by all those with access to the truth that is being suppressed. It is not an aspect of practice on which team members can agree to disagree: it is a co-operative strategy (as in football: the tricks to be tried are whispered to all members in the huddle). Whereas junior doctors and nurses used to put up with practices of their seniors that they did not personally approve of, nowadays it is no longer safe to count on their submissiveness or 'loyalty'. Whether a doctor or nurse is challenging, or being challenged, about a proposed deception or concealment, the challenge can only be met by appeal to agreed understandings of what is ethically defensible. If there are no agreed understandings, these need to be achieved. As we will see, codes and custom are a meagre and inadequate resource for resolving the disagreements.

The theoretical interest of this study

The contours and shape of discussion of truthfulness in medicine and nursing have been altered by recent developments in the study of applied ethics: above all, with the importance now attached to autonomy and the implications this has for our topic. For present purposes, it is useful to draw a line between medical and nursing practice before and after the 1960s: before that we will refer to 'traditional' practice, and subsequent events, as 'modern'. Obviously, what I'm labelling here as 'traditional' spans huge variations in practice. But the 1960s were a kind of watershed after which concerns about truthfulness took on a different tone and perspective. Prior to this, discussion about what was or was not defensible deceiving or concealing in medical and nursing practice turned on questions about what helped or harmed patients and the nature and scope of the duty not to lie. After the 1960s a new concern entered and dominated the discussion: what information was owed patients out of respect for their right of autonomy: their right to decide or at least participate in deciding, questions of treatment and care. Deceiving patients, even keeping information relevant to the decisions they were taking from them, hindered their exercise of rightful autonomy. Thus, deceiving and concealing have come under a cloud indirectly, not because of a sharpened antipathy for untruthfulness as such, but mainly as a knock on effect of the new enthusiasm for patients taking more control and having more of a voice in, decisions about their treatment and care.

Let us not exaggerate the extent to which patients used to lack control over their treatments. Dorothy and Roy Porter point out that though in seventeenth century England patients were 'under doctor's orders', at the same time doctors were 'sent for', 'summoned' (1985: 228–9). They describe how in the nineteenth century patients would often seek multiple consultations and choose whose advice to follow: 'On occasions, whole tribes of doctors were called in, thereby giving the customer elbow-room to accept whatever diagnostic suggestions most gratified the ears' (1989: 79).

Traditional practice did not force patients to take medicines or undergo surgery. Treatment has always been subject to consent. There can be no consent unless one knows at least in broad terms what it is one is consenting to. The difference that has arisen from the 1960s onwards is not that a new right has been created out of the blue, according to which patients are now not treated against their will. That right has always been recognized (in principle, at least). What is new is the idea that patients should be encouraged to participate in reaching decisions as to what treatments or procedures are appropriate for them. It is this right to participate in deciding what is appropriate that spurs the call for full and frank information-giving. Since the idea of patients' rights to be involved in deciding what treatment is appropriate has emerged and has taken hold, the duty of doctors and nurses to speak and act truthfully has been largely perceived as derivative from the duty to respect autonomy. Consequently, concerns over how to proceed when revealing a truth might worsen a patient's health have been wrapped up in the more general issue of how to balance duties to respect autonomy and duties to cure and care.

The focus on shared decision-making and the attention to the duty to inform have influenced thinking about truthfulness and have reshaped the debate; whether in ways that are enlightening remains to be seen. At any rate, we need to pay attention to the change and reflect on its impact. Two consequences especially need to be reckoned with:

1 it may divert our attention from instances of deception or secrecy in medical and nursing practice where choice of treatment is not at issue;

2 it may lead us to assimilate the duty not to lie to the duty to inform so that when the latter does not apply we neglect to examine separately whether the former still does.

As to the first consequence, it is, of course, true that one powerful motive for deceiving or withholding information has been to engineer a patient's consent. But it is not the only one. Many of the examples of problematic secrecy or deception in the previous chapter do not involve attempts to bypass informed consent. However impeccably the procedures of consent-seeking are conducted, there are many other occasions where, rightly or wrongly, patients feel aggrieved if they find or suspect that they have been deceived or denied information.

As to the second consequence, while it is true that wherever doctors or nurses are under a duty to inform, they are under a duty not to lie; it does not follow that wherever they are not under a duty to inform, they are entitled to lie. Because of the first consequence we will need to cast our survey over other contexts besides the consent-getting one. Because of the second consequence, we will need to pay attention to the difference between truthfulness and candour (between honesty in communication and openness).

Truthfulness in traditional practice

Hippocratic teaching

Hippocratic writings ignore the matter of doctors' lies although mention is made of patients' lies: doctors are warned to be on the look out. As to openness with patients, that is strongly discouraged. Doctors are advised to be secretive – *towards* their patients, not just on their behalf (keeping their confidences): 'concealing most things from the patient, while you are attending to him ...turning his attention away from what is being done to him; ... revealing nothing of the patient's future or present condition'. (Hippocrates, *Decorum* XVl: 296–7, 298–9.)[2] The reason for such secretiveness is simply a concern to act in the way most helpful to patients – whether to give them the best chance of recovery or to ease their distress if they are dying. Of course, just because the Hippocratic teaching does not explicitly denounce doctors' lies, it does not follow that these were condoned. After all, lying is not the only way of concealing unhelpful truths. That this method is not mentioned could indicate that it was simply assumed that lying was not on. Yet the fact that Plato assumes that doctors must tell benign lies suggests otherwise.

Plato[3]

The ready and frequent references Plato (427–347BC) makes to doctors' benign lies and deceptive tricks suggests not only that their doing so was common knowledge, but also that the practice was generally approved. Otherwise, Plato would hardly have relied on this analogy as he does to justify similar behaviour on the part of wise rulers. He characterizes these wise rulers as the doctors of our souls as physicians are doctors of our bodies. Just as physicians often put us through grim treatments and procedures and even deceive and trick us into submission – all for our own good – so too will our rulers have to impose upon us in ways that are immediately troublesome and to win our willing obedience they may need to charm us with noble lies (Cooper 1997: *Rep.*V.459c, cf. *Theaetetus* 167a, *Laws* ll.659e).

Plato also speaks approvingly of doctors who take the trouble to explain the whys and wherefores to their patients. He contrasts the slave doctors who simply issue orders without explanations with the kind of conversation free doctors are wont to initiate with their educated patients. If patients understand why they need to alter their eating and drinking habits or whatever, they will be much more likely to comply than if they are simply ordered to do so without discussion. The free doctor listens to his patients' histories and then 'gives all the instruction he can': 'He gives no prescription until he has gained the invalid's consent; then, coaxing him into continued co-operation, he tries to complete his restoration to health.'(Cooper 1997: *Laws* Vl.720d).

There is no suggestion in Plato, though, that this way of proceeding is better because it shows respect for patients' autonomy; it is simply that persuasion *works* better than compulsion on patients whom doctors are seeking to restore to health, and to re-educate into healthier habits. Information is given merely as a means to ensure intelligent compliance; it is expedient to persuade rather than coerce. But withholding information is sometimes necessary and justified provided the doctors know what they are about and are intent simply on achieving better health for their patients:

> We believe in them [doctors] whether they cure us with our consent or without it, by cutting or burning or applying some other painful treatment, and whether they do so according to written rules or apart from written rules, and whether as poor men or rich.
>
> (Cooper 1997: *Statesman* 293b)

What Plato has in mind here as curing 'without consent' we may take to be curing without specific consent – as opposed to general consent.

Plato's various observations on what is good medical practice suggest that doctors have two definitive and essential duties. One is that they should ground their practice on knowledge – study of the nature of the body. He deplores the merely 'empirical and artless' style of doctoring in which treatments are dispensed which are observed to work, where the dispenser has no notion of, or interest in, why they work (Cooper 1997: *Phaedrus: 270b, Lysis: 210a*). The other is that their sole aim in all their advising and treating should be to restore the patient's health. Someone who knew how to bring about changes in the body (for example, how to raise or lower the temperature) but did not understand that the point of all treatments is to achieve health, would have only the 'preliminaries' to medical knowledge (*Phaedrus: 268a+*). As to speaking truthfully or deceptively, volunteering information or suppressing it: doctors should do whatever in the light of their knowledge is best calculated to help the patient recover health. True words and false words are likened repeatedly to drugs: sometimes plain speaking is therapeutic, sometimes, soothing falsehoods.

It is noteworthy that Plato, notwithstanding that he upholds the pursuit of knowledge as the highest and noblest activity, does not hesitate to approve lying on the part of the wise – wise rulers or wise doctors. Lying, though, is not to be recommended to private citizens because they are ignorant and if they lie they probably compound their troubles – like the foolish patients who lie to their doctors (Cooper 1997: *Republic* lll: 389b).

Medical ethics in Roman times and the Middle Ages

The Hippocratic tradition continued to govern ideas of doctors' duties to their patients. The essential duties were still to be competent (studious and diligent in learning the art of medicine) and to be conscientious (always advising and acting solely with a view to the patient's health needs). Comments on the matter of truthfulness and openness are all of a piece with this understanding of the kind of trust reposed in doctors. Cassiodorus advises the supervising physician to the royal household in the Ostrogothic kingdom of Italy (in sixth century AD): 'let the patient ask you about his ailment, and hear from you the truth about it … To make things easier, do not tell the clamoring inquirer what these symptoms signify…' (MacKinney 1952: 4). Henri de Mondeville (c. 1260–1325) advises: '[P]romise a cure to every patient, but … tell the parents or the friends if there is any danger' (1977: 15).

In the late middle ages moral theologians discussed the dilemma doctors could face over whether to warn dangerously ill patients they might die. On the one hand it was felt that such warnings could be self-fulfilling – damaging. On the other, patients might need warning so as to put their affairs in order or to make their peace with God (Amundsen and Ferngren 1983: 35).

John Gregory(1725–73)[4]

John Gregory taught and wrote generally on topics in medical ethics, including questions about honest communication and openness. He advocates candour – but not with patients, only with one's colleagues. He deplores the 'bad pride' that sometimes prevents doctors from confessing their faults to one another. Frank admission of having made a mistake to one's patients is not advised: 'A prudential regard indeed for the patient's safety may make it necessary to conceal any embarrassment or mistakes from him, lest it alarm him and lose his confidence …'(McCullough 1998: 106, cf. 75). If the patient's situation is dangerous this should always be explained to the relations, and sometimes should even be explained to the patient – where the patient needs to know (McCollough 1998: 175). But sometimes doctors ought to lie:

It would be very wrong to acquaint the patient that he was really on the point of death, as this would hasten his death so much the sooner, now this may be a very important time for to acquaint his friends, as some minutes longer in life, might do a deal of service to the family, therefore a lie in this case may be excusable.

(McCullough 1998: 75)

Gregory repeats that a 'small deviation from the truth' when talking with the patient about the 'true state and hazard he is in' is sometimes required – where telling a patient in a 'harsh and brutal manner' that he is dying is 'acting the part of one giving the sentence of death rather than a physician' (McCullough 1998: 87). Sometimes, though, the patient needs to be warned, so as to be able to put his affairs in order (McCullough1998: 108).

Gregory urges the necessity of a doctor preserving 'composure, steadiness and resolution in acting, even in cases where, in his private judgement, he is extremely diffident'. He adds that 'it is also necessary to acquire such command of temper, as may enable him to conceal his diffidence or embarrassment, both for the patient's sake and for his own' (McCullough 1998: 102).

On the matter of truthfulness there is not then much difference between Plato (speaking from within the Hippocratic tradition) and Gregory. Both take the over-riding aim to be doing what is best for the patient's health. Both recognize that dissimulation, secretiveness and even lying is sometimes necessary. Gregory's tone is perhaps more agonized over the necessity of deviating from the truth. There is more of a suggestion that lying goes against the grain and is hard upon the liar (McCullough 1998: 80). But, at any rate, if it really is better for the patient to be lied to, that may be precisely what the doctor should do.

Benjamin Rush (1745–1813)[5]

Rush, who was one of the signatories of the American Declaration of Independence, studied under Gregory. He too wrote on medical ethics, including the matter of truth-fulness. Like Gregory, he is emphatic about the duty of candour owed to one's colleagues. Rush accepts the need for reserve in front of patients, but he does not condone it if put on for merely self-serving motives. He objects to doctors putting on airs of 'affected gravity and taciturnity' in conversing with their patients where this is done merely to conceal their own fallibility (Runes 1947: 310). Guardedness before patients for their benefit, is another matter: 'Preserve, upon all occasions, a composed and cheerful countenance in the room of your patients, and inspire as much hope of a recovery as you can, consistent with truth, especially in acute diseases' (Runes 1947: 313). Rush recognizes the placebic inspirational value of the cheerful and composed manner – the power imagination has over the course of a disease.

Unlike Gregory, Rush firmly repudiates lying to patients:

Equally criminal is the practice among some physicians of encouraging patients to expect a recovery, in diseases that have arrived at their incurable stage. The mischief that is done by falsehood in this case, is the more to be deplored, as it often prevents the dying from settling their worldly affairs, and employing their last hours for their future state.

(Runes 1947: 124)

Since Rush says lying is *more* to be deplored for these reasons, he implies that it is not *only* to be deplored on their account. But he does not comment on what other reasons he has in mind. Is he thinking here of other bad effects this practice has on the patients, or on others who collude or observe, or on the doctor, or is he thinking of the inherent wrongness of lying, not just the harmfulness of it?

Thomas Percival (1740–1804)[6]

Percival, who had also studied under Gregory, wrote a book on medical ethics at the request of Manchester Infirmary, which was being troubled by a succession of intra-professional quarrels. Percival's *Medical Ethics* (first published in 1803) was heavily borrowed from in the composition of the first American Medical Association Code in 1847. Among the subjects discussed by Percival is truthfulness.

What he has to say follows very much in the footsteps of Gregory. Patients need to have their spirits kept up. 'Gloomy prognostications' are bad medicine, sometimes, even self-fulfilling. Relatives should always be warned. Patients too 'if absolutely necessary'(Leake 1927: 91) – though preferably this duty should be assigned to someone else:

> For the physician should be the minister of hope and comfort to the sick; that, by such cordials to the drooping spirit, he may smooth the bed of death, revive expiring life, and counteract the depressing influence of those maladies which rob the philosopher of fortitude and the Christian of consolation.
>
> (Leake 1927: 91)

(Much of this turns up verbatim in the AMA Code slightly reduced – omitting the philosopher and the Christian.)

Percival defends lying to patients – though only in real emergencies. And he goes into the question in some depth. He had received a letter from Thomas Gisborne commenting on his statement: 'A physician should be the minister of hope and comfort to the sick'. Gisborne suggested adding the words: 'as far as truth and sincerity will admit'. Gisborne surmised that

> There are few professional temptations to which medical men are more liable, and frequently from the very best principles, than that of intentionally using language to the patient and his friends, more encouraging than sincerity would vindicate, on cool reflection. It may be right scrupulously to guard against such error.
>
> (Leake 1927: 186–7)

Percival notes that the question whether lying is always wrong has been a matter of debate in ancient and in theological writings. He appeals to the philosopher, Francis Hutcheson,[7] a contemporary, who defends lying in some circumstances – explicitly singling out doctors' lies as obviously defensible:

No man censures a physician for deceiving a patient too much dejected, by expressing good hopes of him, or by denying that he gives him a proper medicine which he is foolishly prejudiced against: the patient afterward will not reproach him for it.

(Fabian 1969: Vl.33)

Hutcheson adds, 'Wise men allow this liberty to the physician in whose skill and fidelity they trust. Or if they do not, there must be a just plea of necessity' (Fabian 1969: Vl.33).

Hutcheson defends departing from the ordinary rules of morality 'in great and manifest exigencies' (Fabian 1969: Vl.135) where that is necessary for the public good. 'To deny all exceptions, upon pleas of necessity, contradicts the sense of mankind' (Fabian 1969: Vl.123). Against the Pauline teaching that we must not do evil that good may come, Hutcheson instances circumstances where we see fit to expose people to pain, suffering, and risk of death, for a good end – for example, the amputations of the chirurgeons; and exposing good men to danger, defending their country. If these means are not to be counted as 'evils', Hutcheson asks, what kinds of actions are supposed to be so evil that they may not be done for a good end, and what argument is there to support the bare assertion that there are any such kinds of actions which can never be necessary. Percival relays the views of Hutcheson, and mentions Dr Johnson's vigorous opposition to benevolent deception *as practised by doctors* – Johnson singles this out as especially offensive but *not* on the grounds that the duty not to lie is exceptionless.

Percival then sums up his own views on the 'contending obligations of veracity and professional obligation'. The former duty, he suggests is owed to one's patients and to oneself. To one's patients, he says, it is a relative duty, properly regulated by the 'rule of equity prescribed by our Saviour to do unto others as we would, all circumstances duly weighed, they should unto us' (Leake 1927: 194). Thus there is no tension between this part of the duty of veracity and the professional duty to do what is best for the patient. If a truthful reply would harm the patient, the patient is not owed it. The patient, he says, 'has the strongest claim, from the trust reposed in his physician, as well as from the common principles of humanity, to be guarded against what is detrimental to him' (Leake 1927: 195).

The other aspect of the duty of veracity, as it is owed to oneself, Percival suggests, is a personal rather than a professional duty. It is only this personal aspect of the duty that sets up a conflict: between veracity and humanity. Percival observes:

In such a situation, therefore, the only point at issue is, whether the practitioner shall sacrifice that delicate sense of veracity, which is so ornamental to, and indeed forms a characteristic excellence of the virtuous man, to this claim of professional justice and social duty.

(Leake 1927: 195)

In this painful kind of conflict, Percival expects that the wise and good will put the duty to another before the duty to himself (1927: 195). Percival, being an admirer of Hutcheson, would readily suppose that obligations to oneself must yield to obligations to others.

Hutcheson observes:

> But, although private justice, veracity, openness of mind, compassion, are immediately approved, without reference to a system; yet we must not imagine any of these principles are destined to controll or limit that regard to the most extensive good which we shewed to be the noblest principle of our nature. The most extensive affection has a dignity sufficient to justify the contracting any other disposition: whereas no moral agent can upon close reflection approve himself in adhering to any special rule, or following any other disposition of his nature, when he discerns, upon the best evidence he can have, that doing so is contrary to the universal interest or the most extensive happiness of the system in the whole of its effects.
>
> (Fabian 1969: V.255–6)

> But where a publick interest is at stake, and founds a just exception, a good man is not at liberty to sacrifice it to any false notion of his own honour or character. He must be deficient in his extensive affections, or mistaken in his moral notions, if he follows in such cases some lower species of goodness in opposition to the publick interest.
>
> (Fabian 1969: 139)

Thomas Gisborne (1758–1846)

As we have seen, Gisborne objects to the practice of benevolent lying and of insincere encouragement. He does, though, agree with the common rule that if an illness is dangerous, relatives should always be forewarned; patients, only sometimes – if necessary. He approves doctors maintaining a 'prudent reserve':

> In attending upon a patient, the physician, while he omits not the reserve which prudence dictates, will shun all affectation of mystery. He will not alarm the sick man, by discussing his case openly and unguardedly before him; nor will he put on a countenance of profound thought, and gestures of much seeming sagacity, either to augment his importance or to conceal his ignorance.
>
> (1797: 159)

Where he takes issue with Percival and Gregory is on the matter of lying. He puts the impulse to lie down to 'mistaken tenderness'. He maintains that lying is both wrong (doing evil that good may come) and that it does not work (at most it achieves only a temporary advantage). In support of his principled objection to lying he says: 'Truth and conscience forbid the Physician to cheer him'[the patient] by giving promises, or raising expectations, which are known or intended to be delusive'(1797: 160). He adds: 'The physician is at liberty to say little; but let that little be true'(1797: 161) – and he appeals to the Pauline teaching. In support of the objection based on grounds of efficacy he claims that lies are soon discovered and thereafter any assurances are rendered useless (1797: 161).

Worthington Hooker (1806–67)

Hooker, like Gisborne, objects to doctors' benevolent lies. He takes issue with the AMA code's stance on truthfulness (which was based on Percival's *Medical Ethics*). Like Gisborne and Rush, Hooker is quite prepared to approve reserve before patients. Concealing things from patients might be necessary. He stresses patients' needs for quiet and peace of mind (1849: 298, 302). He also warns against careless talk in front of children who, he says, have much more understanding than they are usually credited with (1849: 300). But in his view lying is never justifiable, however kindly meant. Like Gisborne, Hooker objects to lying both on grounds of experience (what works) and of principle.

On the basis of his own professional experience, he argues that lying does more harm than good. He argues that doctors exaggerate the damage that bad news does to patients – if communicated sympathetically; he argues that concealment is often a failure, even with children; he claims that the effect of discovery is worse than the effect of being told the truth: once patients find they have been lied to they lose all confidence and there is no way to restore it. And all these considerations, Hooker says, apply no less to the lies told to children or the insane than to anyone else. Even if the patient never finds out, others who are aware of what is going on have their trust in doctors undermined. Nor does Hooker attach any confidence to a policy which permits lying only where it will not be discovered and the case is urgent: 'Once open the door for deception, and you can prescribe no definite limits. Everyone is left to judge for himself' (1849: 376).

As a matter of principle, Hooker observes: 'Men often do as physicians what they would be ashamed to do as men. The strict morality of common intercourse is relaxed in professional intercourse. But the man and the physician cannot be thus separated' (1849: 402). He takes issue with Hutcheson's rebuttal of St Paul (quoted at length by Percival). Against St Paul's teaching that we must not do evil that good may come, Hutcheson notes that we condone the use of terrible means simply because they are necessary to achieve important and good ends: we send good men to fight for their country; we let surgeons amputate limbs and do other fearsome things to their patients. But, argues Hooker, inflicting pain or risking life that good may come does not involve any sacrifice of *principle*. Lying is not just doing harm that good may come, it is doing evil or wrong that good may come. Hooker does not object to doctors being at pains to hide the truth where the truth might hurt, only they must not, he insists, use lies. The hiding must be done by fair and honest means. Questions must be answered without falsehood or equivocation (1849: 381–2).

Hooker suggests a way of testing whether the hiding and deceptive tricks doctors use are dishonest: whether they can be publicized without shame in a general way, and without undermining people's trust in their doctors. He maintains that there are times when patients can only be helped if certain things are kept hidden. For example, he notes how sometimes patients need some kind of diversion to jog them into better spirits. 'All direct and palpable efforts to make the gloomy invalid cheerful, are almost always unsuccessful...'(1849: 313). In such cases, though, getting the patient away from disagreeable associations, say by having a change of scene, can help them recover (1849: 307). This is a policy that can be made known to the public at large, though not of course directly to those on whom it is applied. Owning up to this policy does not render it useless or demonstrate that doctors cannot be trusted. Patients might suspect it is being tried on them, but not know.

Richard C. Cabot (1868–1939)

Cabot also objects to doctors' lies. He reports that as a medical student at Harvard he was advised that provided doctors lied solely for their patients' benefit and never with a self-serving motive, they should 'go ahead with a clear conscience'(1903: 344). He recalls occasions in his own practice when he was challenged by patients wanting the truth, and how he gradually came round to the view that doctors should never lie. Many of his objections to lying echo Hooker's: 'a lie saves a present pain at the expense of future greater pain' (1903: 346). He claims that 'Doctors make a great mistake when they think their deceits really deceive' (1903: 345). He says that he has found patients and relatives to react surprisingly well when told the truth – not that he advocates *volunteering* information, if a patient does not ask and does not need to know. All he insists, in medicine, as in life generally, is that one does not lie to save people's feelings:

> So in medicine, if a patient asks me a straight question I believe it works best to give him a straight answer, not a rough answer, but not yet a lie or a prevarication. I do not believe it pays to give an answer that would justify a patient in saying (in case he happened to find out the truth): 'that doctor tried to trick me'.
> (1903: 347)

Cabot also objects to placebos – 'bread pills'. He remarks, 'It is only when we act like quacks that our placebos work'. He urges that rather than handing out such pills, doctors should be prepared to teach patients that they do not need pills for every symptom that arises (1903: 348).

Cabot's argument is explicitly based on his own professional experience – what he has found works best. He suggests that those who doubt his findings, should try out for themselves the advantages of being truthful. He is confident that his policy will stand the test:

> Everything seems to conspire to help you out when you are trying to tell the truth, but when you are lying there are snares and pitfalls turning up everywhere and making your path a more and more difficult one.
> (1903: 349)

Unresolved questions

What do we learn from this survey of views? There seems to have been much wider agreement on the need for reserve towards patients than on the need to avoid lying. That at least suggests that doctors distinguished the question of how open they should be from the question of how truthful they should be. On the matter of openness with patients, all the writers in our survey recommend guardedness, and for the same kinds of reasons – on grounds of expedience – what works. All recognize the 'psychological dimension' in illness: the importance of sustaining the patient's morale and spirits. Of course, these doctors did not have wonder drugs to effect cures. In some cases the best they could do to swing the course of a patient's illness towards recovery might be to boost morale: that sometimes seemed to make a difference (Shorter 1993: 791). Gloomy prognostications, on the other hand, might be self-fulfilling. There was also the possibility that the doctor's expectations would prove mistaken: what they were withholding was usually not knowledge but speculation.

On the matter of lying to patients, the writers in our survey disagree: some defending its use – though only sparingly, others repudiating its use totally. Naturally, all deplore the use of lies from bad motives. Those who defend occasional use have in mind situations where a patient's life is in danger, where a lie might be effective in rallying the patient's spirits and preventing or delaying death, or situations where the patient is at the point of death where it is assumed that knowing this would only cause distress, make the dying more wretched. But Hooker comments (disapprovingly) on the commonness of lying to children and the insane – and not just in situations where their lives are in danger. If defensible lying is widened to include routine management of patients in these two categories, its use will not be so sparing. The purpose behind such lies is no longer to sustain the patient's spirits, but to obtain the patient's co-operation.

Those who repudiate lying totally object mainly on the basis of their own professional experience. They argue that patients are not fooled by lies, or are fooled only temporarily – and when they discover, are much more wretched than if the doctor had been honest. Lying to children, in order, for example, to persuade them to take their medicine, is inexpedient for the very same reasons: 'Many a parent has thus in a moment, for the sake of a slight temporary advantage, sown the wind to reap the whirlwind' (Hooker 1849: 367). Hooker insists that lying to the insane is also inexpedient:

> Let the insane man once see that you have deceived him, and you lose the principal, perhaps we may say the only, moral means you have for curing his malady. Confidence is essential to any good moral influence that you may exert upon him.
>
> (1849: 367)

Quite aside from the harm lying may do to patients, there is also the collateral damage: how it undermines confidence in doctors by those who observe the lying or are party to it.

While most of the debate about the practice of lying to patients is conducted with reference to what works – what is best for the patient – Percival also grounds his own stance on considerations of the duty of veracity and how it should be weighed against the doctor's professional duty to help the patient. Gisborne and Hooker, in taking issue with Percival, likewise appeal to considerations of principle. Of course, none of these writers is engaged in writing philosophical treatises and they do not take their argument very far. The principled objection to lying made by Gisborne and Hooker appeals to St Paul's 'thou shalt not do evil that good may come'. But Percival, quoting Hutcheson, asks why we should agree with the Pauline teaching. Even if we do agree with it, should we include lying among the evils? Don't we allow lying when we are at war? If that is defensible, why not permit doctors to lie in their war against disease?

On the other hand, Hooker, as we have seen, claims that Percival (following Hutcheson) misapplies the Pauline teaching: he fails to distinguish doing an evil (for example, lying) from doing a harm (for example, going to war or performing a surgical amputation). Furthermore, doesn't Percival dismiss the duty of veracity we owe to others too lightly when he subsumes it under the duty to do unto others as you would be done to? And does he make too light of the other 'personal' aspect of veracity, how it is a duty to oneself? He refers to it as 'that delicate sense of veracity.' It is 'ornamental' to the virtuous man. One should be willing to give up parading one's ornaments where patients' needs depend on it. Otherwise, Percival suggests, one would be putting self before others.

On both sides of the debate about truthfulness with patients, appeals are made to experience: what are the effects of being guarded or unguarded, of lying or not lying. Thus it is more usual to reject lying to patients because it is found not to work than to reject it because lying is 'wrong' *per se*. Cabot, for example, relies entirely on his own observations of the consequential harms in his objections to lying to patients. We need not suppose that he did not also have objections on grounds of general principle. But it stands to reason that medical people will prefer to support their arguments from the evidence they have gathered through their own working experience. Here, they speak with professional authority. They have first hand knowledge of the consequences, good and bad: of being open and of being reserved; of being scrupulously straight with patients and of being deliberately devious.

Cabot speaks in this vein: 'My method is experimental, the only one in which reasonable men place confidence, the only sound scientific method ...'(1903: 344). He recounts:

As a young physician I tried the usual system of benevolent lying from 1893–1903. About that time a bitter experience convinced me that I could not be ... an occasional, philanthropic liar in medicine or in any other part of my life. I swore off and have been on the wagon of medical honesty ever since.

(1938: 134)

Even doctors who distinguish arguments based on their own clinical experience from arguments based on considerations of more general principle will prefer, if they can, to rely on the former. There they are on home ground.

Truthfulness in modern practice

None of the opponents of the practice of lying to patients so far discussed were opposed to concealing things from patients *per se* – not so long as it could be done without dishonest words or tricks. But in the last half of the twentieth century, secrecy and concealment have been attacked both on the basis of experience – their effects on patients, and on the basis of principle – how they violate patients' rights. In both cases, it is openness that is directly held to be a duty; honest communication, only indirectly, in consequence. Concealment (of information about the patient from the patient), some take to be prima facie wrong, however it is achieved – with or without telling lies.

Patients need information

It used to be assumed that people who were dying were better off being protected from the knowledge – though sometimes they had to be told so that they could put their affairs in order. With the development of the hospice movement and the emergent specialties of palliative medicine and nursing has come a new appreciation of the burdens reserve itself may impose on patients and their relatives: the barriers that reserve creates, the loneliness of the dying if they are inhibited by other people's reserves and pretences. While it is not now claimed that everyone who is dying is better off being 'helped' to face the facts, it is at least held that doctors and nurses should not try to prevent patients from doing so. The current teaching in palliative care ethics, say Fiona Randall and Robin Downie, is: 'Patients should be given as much information as they want to know' (Randall and Downie 1996: 80). Sometimes, of course, they need to know more than they want to hear. They give the example of a patient with breast cancer who is found to have bone metastases in her spine. She may need to be forewarned of the risk of quadriplegia as there may be precautions she can take to lessen the risk (1996: 82).

Because there are many options nowadays in the treatment of patients who are terminally ill, patients cope better if these are all explained and discussed. Such discussions necessitate openness:

> Decisions concerning appropriate as compared with possible treatments need to be discussed with the patient and the family after due consideration by the professional team ....A competent patient can refuse any or all treatments but needs to be suitably informed and choices respected.
>
> (Saunders 1994: 776)

As Sissela Bok has pointed out, dying patients who have been 'protected' from information have not been able to take part in decisions affecting procedures on them. In consequence, they

May slip unwittingly into subjection to new procedures, perhaps new surgery, where death is held at bay through transfusions, respirators, even resuscitation far beyond what most would wish. Seeing relatives in such predicaments has caused a great upsurge of worrying about death and dying.

(1978: 232)

These new insights into the needs of the dying – the importance to them of being able to have open conversations – make concealment and deception often ill-advised. If patients need their questions answering and need to be offered the opportunity to discuss fully their circumstances and prospects, then doctors or nurses who hinder this are failing in their duties to provide good standards of care. But notice here that it is openness that is the basic duty from which, of course, it follows that doctors and nurses should not lie. The duty not to lie may not here be seen to have any independent standing.

Patients' autonomy and right to information

Ruth Faden and Tom Beauchamp observe that 'Autonomy is almost certainly the most important value "discovered" in medical and research ethics in the last two decades…'(1986: 18). The new emphasis on patient autonomy, the right to be involved in the choice of treatment, and hence, the right to information, arose mainly through legal landmark cases in the US: *Canterbury* v. *Spence*, *Cobbs* v. *Grant* and *Wilkinson* v. *Vesey* – all of which were decided in 1972.[8] The notion that doctors must obtain *informed* consent swiftly graduated from the status of 'legal nuisance' to moral duty (Faden and Beauchamp 1986: 88). Of course, as we have already noted, consent-getting must always have involved the sharing of some information with patients. What was new was the amount of specific information it became necessary to share – if patients were to be involved not just in accepting or rejecting their doctor's advice but in deciding what among the options would be appropriate. In 1973, the American Patients Bill of Rights was published. It includes the following: 'The patient has the right to obtain from his physician complete current information concerning his diagnosis, treatment, and prognosis in terms the patient can reasonably be expected to understand'[9] (American Hospital Association 1973: 41). By the time the President's Commission was published ten years later, the principle of self-determination had come to be treated as 'bedrock' (President's Commission 1982: 50–1).

Recognition of patients' moral right to fuller information took on fresh urgency after a series of shocking cases came to light, in which patients had been subjected to research to which they (or their relatives) would hardly have agreed had they realized what was involved (for example the Jewish Chronic Disease Hospital Case in the 1960s and the Tuskegee Study, begun in the 1930s, but which only came to public notice in the 1970s). The publications of Henry K. Beecher's *Experimentation in Man* in 1959 (and follow up articles) in the US and of M.H. Pappworth's *Human Guinea Pigs* in 1967 in the UK demonstrated that the scandals were not isolated incidents, but indicative of a culture in which doctors either did not get very specific consent, or did so in a way that failed to yield significant decision-making control to their patients.

'Truth-telling' surfaced as a matter of importance in medical ethics, though not mentioned in codes before the modern period, largely in consequence of the ferment over the newly discovered rights of patients to information:

> It is with the working out of all that informed consent implies and the information it presupposes that truth-telling is coming to be discussed in a serious way for the first time in the health professions.
>
> (Bok 1978: 233)

The term 'truth-telling' itself straddles notions of honest communication and openness confusingly. Sometimes 'Tell the truth!' means no more than 'Do not lie!' other times we mean more than this. Thus when it is said that doctors and nurses ought to tell the truth it is not always clear just what obedience to this stricture entails.

Because of the way in which the topic has arisen in modern medical ethics – partly because patients are seen to need information – even (maybe especially) those who are terminally ill, and partly because patients are now held to have a right to information, the distinct duties not to lie, not to deceive and not to conceal tend to get conflated: 'much of the literature treats them as a single obligation'(Beauchamp and Childress 1994: 397). But as Beauchamp and Childress observe, these are not all of a piece. It may be that in some circumstances, where information is owed, it is no excuse that a doctor or nurse who conceals takes care not to lie. In other circumstances, though, concealing might be justified, lying not. As Beauchamp and Childress observe, the legal focus on disclosure in the context of consent getting is, from an ethical standpoint, 'too narrow'(1994: 397).

Yet according to Beauchamp and Childress it is identical considerations that make lying, deceiving by other means, or underdisclosure to patients, wrong. The difference they draw attention to is simply in the relative difficulty of justifying setting aside these duties: it is easier to excuse underdisclosure than deceiving and easier to excuse deceiving than lying. But actions of these kinds are morally objectionable, when they are objectionable, for just the same *sorts* of reasons: typically, they show a lack of respect (for the patient's autonomy); they violate promises that are implicit in the contract between doctor and patient; and they undermine trust. Beauchamp and Childress maintain, though, that there are some circumstances in which even lying is justified: 'like the other obligations in this volume, veracity is prima facie binding, not absolute' (1994: 397).

Truth, trust and patients' rights

Beauchamp and Childress remark: 'Surprisingly, codes of medical ethics have traditionally ignored obligations and virtues of veracity' (1994: 395). Are they right to suppose that since the duty not to lie got no mention in codes, that duty was ignored? After all, theft got no mention either. This hardly suffices to show that doctors thought it all right to steal from their patients. All the same, as we have seen from our survey, the acceptability of lying to patients was a subject of debate – unlike stealing. At any rate we should not just assume that doctors who often felt justified in being secretive and reserved were similarly relaxed about lying.

Given the importance Beauchamp and Childress attach to 'obligations and virtues of veracity', their alleged neglect until recent times is not just surprising, it is astonishing. If trust is vital between doctors and patients and both lying and concealing information destroy trust, how have doctors got away with their habits of deceitfulness and reserve for so long? If it is only nowadays that respect for autonomy and the duty to inform have come to be seen to be the bedrock of medical ethics, should we not expect to find that patients have lately become much more trusting in their doctors than in times gone by? Is that what opinion surveys show?

Let us examine more closely the three 'arguments' that Beauchamp and Childress adduce to explain the (presumptive) wrongness of lying and of under-disclosure. The first argument makes out that for health-professionals keeping information from patients shows disrespect. Patients are owed respect and showing respect requires obtaining consent – informed consent. Yet we have seen that discussion of consent is missing from medical ethics until recent times. Are we to suppose that hitherto, before the relevance of autonomy to patients' rights was 'discovered', health professionals did not show respect in how they behaved towards their patients? Presumably, it used to be assumed that patients gave tacit consent in so far as they sought the help of doctors – put themselves in their hands. And in the Hippocratic tradition doctors are seen to be duty-bound to be trust-worthy – which implies that trust is placed in them. Patients, then, can be assumed to have consented, albeit tacitly, to being treated.

This is not what is nowadays meant by 'informed' consent. Beauchamp and Childress observe that 'consent cannot express autonomy unless it is informed' (1994: 396). It is this concern that patients 'express autonomy' when they consent which lies behind the requirement that they be given information. Otherwise, patients could consent simply by trusting to the doctors, believing them to be competent and conscientious. We often consent to things in this way, trusting to others' expertise without bothering to find out details of what they propose to do. In this spirit you may happily hand over your car for servicing and if you trust the garage you may simply ask the mechanics to do whatever they find needs attending to. If patients have ceased (or should have) to be minded in similar fashion to put themselves in the hands of their doctors, this cannot simply be because of the need for consent *per se*.

Indeed, as Beauchamp and Childress themselves observe, seriously ill patients used to hand over decision-making to their families – they still do, in some countries. Where such is the custom, patients who follow the custom need not be failing to exercise their autonomy: 'Autonomous patients may choose to delegate decision-making to others' (1994: 401). Quite so! But doesn't this show that consent does not have to be informed after all? The idea that patients who consent must at least in a broad sense grasp what they are consenting to, is nothing new or peculiar to 'Western' contemporary cultures. Patients in other cultures who delegate the decision-making to their families may be kept broadly in the picture of what they are asked to consent to and still be spared the full discussion of alter-natives, possible and probable outcomes of treatments, risks, etc. Hence, though showing respect requires obtaining consent (from patients who are able to give it), it does not necessarily require obtaining informed consent – not, for example, if the patient backs off frank discussion.

The second argument Beauchamp and Childress use to underpin the duties of veracity derives these from the *promise* which they say is implicit in serious communication, and particularly, in communications of health professionals with their patients. But this underpinning seems to provide at best only a pretty weak restraint on doctors' lies, let alone on their reserve. It assimilates our taking assertions in 'serious communications' to promises. The law differentiates. Whereas breaches of contract are often actionable even if the promisee has suffered no loss (disappointed expectations aside) telling an untruth is not actionable 'unless and until it has been acted upon to the loss of the agent' (Atiyah, 1981: 105). Atiyah suggests that the differences marked by the law 'reflect real differences' not just 'technical idiosyncracies' of the law:

> The fact is that an explicit promise, at any rate, does differ from an ordinary assertion in that the former invites reliance and expectations in a way which the latter does not. Statements are often made in the course of ordinary discourse, and these may in fact be relied upon; but statements do not, as explicit promises do, plainly invite reliance.
>
> (1981: 105)

Even supposing there is such a promise implicit in 'serious communication', it is in the nature of tacit promises that their boundaries are often quite uncertain. In ordinary serious communication, it is surely quite unpredictable whether people feel that they have promised not to lie – if talking with strangers, with children, with inquisitive people prying into matters that are none of their business, with people who themselves are (probably) not being honest. Even in serious conversation between health-professionals and patients it is surely very uncertain if and when participants have tacitly promised not to lie, or to fully inform.

The third argument points out how crucially important trust is between health-professional and patient. Lying and failing to disclose information undermine trust. Those who opposed lying to patients in earlier times also made this claim – in regard to lying. But they did not see that failure to disclose information was necessarily subversive of trust. Why should it have been – unless disclosure had been promised? Nowadays, non-disclosure does often violate promises – the promises made, for example, in the above-quoted Patients Bill of Rights offering patients 'complete current information'. If health professionals practice under such banners and do not intend to abide by them, they are acting dishonestly – making false promises.

Still unresolved questions

Our survey of what has been said and is being said about truthfulness in medical practice raises a number of unresolved questions. Beauchamp and Childress say that lying is more damaging to trust than is deceiving by other means, and deceiving by any means is more damaging than is underdisclosure or nondisclosure (1994: 397). Why is this true, if it is? Was the traditional reserve of doctors always wrong – or has it become so? How strictly should we regard the duty not to lie in medical and nursing contexts? Is this duty merely presumptive as Beauchamp and Childress claim? If so, how should we answer the principled objection to lying made by Gisborne, Hooker and Cabot? Should we agree with Hooker that any policy which cannot be pursued openly is dishonest and indefensible? What are the implications of the Beauchamp and Childress account of what is wrong with lying and underdisclosure in regard to communication with patients who are children or who are mentally impaired or confused? What counts as disrespectful where *they* are concerned? If what is said in serious conversation between doctors, nurses and patients involves the making of tacit promises, what about conversation with child patients, or patients with Alzheimers: is it also 'serious'? Finally, while nobody denies the importance of preserving trust, whose trust is more important: the relative's or the patient's? Why? What guidance for deliberations and discussions might be helpful to practitioners who want to be truthful, but are uncertain in the face of dilemmas that can arise what truthfulness requires or allows?

We will not make much headway in answering these questions until we have a clearer view of what truthfulness is and why it matters. To this end it is necessary to reflect on obligations of truthfulness not just as these arise in medical or nursing contexts, but also as they arise in ordinary life. Plato often observes how in order to answer a specific question we need to explore more general and fundamental questions:

> You have probably heard this about good doctors, that if you go to them with a pain in the eyes, they are likely to say that they cannot undertake to cure the eyes by themselves, but that it will be necessary to treat the head at the same time if things are to go well with the eyes. And again it would be very foolish to suppose that one could treat the head by itself without treating the whole body. In keeping with this principle, they plan a regime for the whole body with the idea of treating and curing the part along with the whole.
>
> (Cooper 1997: *Charmides*: 156)

In this spirit, we will examine truthfulness outside the special context of medicine and nursing first, and then come back to this special context and to our unresolved problems about lying or using deceptive or secretive strategies in dealing with patients.

3   Why truthfulness matters

The aspects of things that are most important for us are hidden because of their
simplicity and familiarity.

Wittgenstein

Judith Shklar ranks dishonesty among the 'ordinary vices': 'the sort of conduct we
all expect, nothing spectacular or unusual' (1984: 1). Our interest here is in
dishonesty in communication – untruthfulness. Is untruthfulness one of the
'common ills we inflict upon one another every day' (1984: 1)? How we answer
will depend on what we count as 'untruthful': is every instance of pretence or
concealment an instance of untruthfulness (even if not done *in order to* cause
anyone to believe what is false)? For all our familiarity with the vice of untruthfulness, deciding what to count as untruthful is by no means easy and
uncontroversial. Nor is it altogether easy to show why untruthfulness is a vice,
even if everyone agrees that it is. What to count as untruthful – whether, for
example, all lies are untruthful or whether there are 'honest lies', we will take up
in the next chapter. Here let us consider why truthfulness matters – what makes it
a virtue.

What makes untruthfulness a vice

We attend here more to the vice than to the corresponding virtue, because vices are
more fundamental. Truthfulness is good just because untruthfulness is bad. Moral
virtues are essentially corrective and protective traits of character. Thus to understand the virtues, what they are and why they matter, we need to examine what it is
they protect us against.

Vices are traits of character that diminish our prospects of doing well or faring
well in life. Cowardice and recklessness prevent us from coping effectively with
things that are fearful. Everyone needs to learn how to handle fear. Similarly, we
can see that everyone needs to learn how to handle anger. How does untruthfulness

prevent our doing well, if it does? There does not seem to be any particular emotion – like anger or fear — or even a type of desire, which truthfulness equips us to handle. Philippa Foot makes this same observation in regard to unjust actions generally (by which she means actions which fail to give people what they are owed by way of help or forbearance). She observes that 'Almost any desire can lead a man to act unjustly, not even excluding the desire to help a friend or save a life' (1978: 8). What Foot says of unjust acts in general applies, unsurprisingly, to untruthful acts, untruthfulness being one kind of injustice. Truthfulness can prevent a person from helping a friend – even from saving a life. (So, do we always want our friends to be honest – for us, as well as to us?) David Lloyd-George, while Chancellor of the Exchequer, was accused, correctly, of having an affair with a married woman. He decided to sue and implored his wife to perjure herself on his behalf. Luckily for him (some would say)[1], she obliged. 'A friend who cannot at a pinch remember a thing or two that never happened is as bad as one who does not know how to forget', says Samuel Butler.

David Hume says that a trait of character must be either amiable or useful to qualify as a virtue. Truthfulness hardly seems a particularly amiable trait. It is not like generosity or kindness, something which wherever it is manifested is found to be agreeable. Every individual act of meanness or cruelty is abhorrent, whereas not all untruthful deeds considered in themselves seem so. Truthfulness can be an uncomfortable, unlovable, and often troublesome trait. It can frustrate our worthy aims as well as our unworthy aims. Is it a virtue despite this? Is it useful, in fact, indispensable, even if sometimes disagreeable?

'Indispensable', though, for whom? Peter Geach has observed that 'we need virtues as bees need stings' (1977: 17). This certainly seems apt in regard to justice, hence, truthfulness. As Thrasymachus (in Plato's *Republic*) observes, justice is 'another man's good'. If we benefit personally by our own just ways, it is at best only *indirectly*. Actually, though, single acts of justice do not even always benefit others, either individually or collectively.

> When a man of merit, of a beneficent disposition, restores a great fortune to a miser, or a seditious bigot, he has acted justly and laudably, but the public is the real sufferer. Nor is every single act of justice, consider'd apart, more conducive to private interest, than to public; and 'tis easily conceived how a man may impoverish himself by a signal instance of integrity, and have reason to wish, that with regard to that single act, the laws of justice were for a moment suspended in the universe.
>
> (Hume 1888: 497)

Yet, Hume goes on to say, it is all the same evident, that 'the whole plan or scheme is highly conducive, or indeed absolutely requisite, both to the support of society, and the well-being of every individual'. He adds that ' 'Tis impossible to separate the good from the ill' (1888: 497).

What is this 'whole plan or scheme' that is so indispensable to any society? For our purposes it is useful to compare two of its essential components: the practice of promising and the disposition to be truthful. The former is a device that enables us to co-operate with one another and which we rely on both formally and informally in our daily dealings. The latter, the disposition to be truthful, is a prerequisite for the device of promising to be workable. We could not sensibly rely on promises if we could not rely on people (in general) to be truthful (most especially, to be true to their word). That is to say, we need to know that people recognize some obligation to be truthful with one another – that they understand that they are supposed to be truthful, that truthfulness is expected, and that they are generally minded to conform. Without that underlying reasonable expectation (hedged about as it may be by various qualifications – which we will come to shortly) there would be no sense in exchanging promises, and co-operation would be fragmentary and minimal. In short, truthfulness matters because it is necessary to support trust and co-operation, without which social life would be radically impoverished – in Hobbes' memorable words: 'nasty, poor, brutish and short'.

Truthfulness is useful, indispensable even. But that is not to say that each instance of untruthfulness does harm. To understand the value of individual acts of truthfulness one needs to think not of the consequences of that particular act (which may result in more harm than good) but of the value of people being committed to the rules of justice – which require promise keeping and truthfulness. Hume contrasts the value of individual acts of benevolence and individual acts of justice by drawing on the following analogy:

> The happiness and prosperity of mankind, arising from the social virtue of benevolence and its subdivisions, may be compared to a wall, built by many hands: which still rises by each stone, that is heaped upon it, and receives increase proportional to the diligence and care of each workman. The same happiness, raised by the social virtue of justice and its subdivisions, may be compared to the building of a vault, where each individual stone, would, of itself, fall to the ground; nor is the whole fabric supported but by the mutual assistance of the combination of its corresponding parts.
>
> (1975: 305)

Whereas benevolent acts are incrementally beneficial and each such act does good, acts which justice requires considered in themselves may do no good, though the practice of following the rules of justice is still a benefit. But the practice of rule-following demands that we do not treat the rules as mere rules of thumb. Promising works only if people (in general) consider themselves bound to act in a certain way simply because they have promised. Of course, promises vary in their seriousness and we do not expect or require people to keep them come what may. But we do expect the mere fact that one has promised to signify an honest intention to act accordingly.

Is justice, and hence truthfulness, a core virtue?

By core virtues I mean virtues that are pervasively relevant and needed by people whoever they are and whatever society they live in. If we define courage as the disposition to face things difficult, dangerous or painful that need to be faced, it seems to be a core virtue since everyone is subject to fear in such circumstances and needs to learn how to handle it wisely. Any individual – rich or poor, young or old, healthy or sickly, has better prospects of faring well in life if equipped with this disposition. Contrast tidiness: if it is a virtue at all, it is only a minor, peripheral, virtue. It is not a core virtue. Tidiness is more important for some kinds of life and in some roles than for others, but it hardly seems to be essential for everyone. If you are not yourself tidy, you might hire someone to tidy for you. A friend might tidy after you for love. But core virtues are traits that we each of us need to graft into our own personality whatever roles we have, whoever, wherever, we are. You could not hire someone to be courageous for you – although you might, of course, *occasionally* manage to avoid facing something fearful by getting someone to take your place for pay or for love – for example, paying someone to take your place as a conscript if that were allowed. But while you may in this way fend off some fearful encounters, many cannot be dodged: if you need to undergo a serious operation or cope with a bereavement, you cannot pay someone else to face this in your stead. Not even your best friend can stand in for you.

What then of justice (and that aspect of justice which is truthfulness)? Is it a core virtue? Hume observes: 'encrease to sufficient degree the benevolence of man, or the bounty of nature, and you render justice useless, by supplying its place with much nobler virtues, and more valuable blessings' (1888: 494–5). But in so saying isn't Hume forgetting his own observation that neither self-love nor benevolence towards the recipient of just treatment nor universal benevolence towards society gives reason for many individual acts of justice (1888: 497). Justice, then, is a corrective to more than self-love. Take away self-love and we would still need justice. Foot observes:

> If people cared about the rights of others as they care about their own rights no virtue of justice would be needed to look after the matter, and the rules about such things as contracts and promises would only need to be made public, like the rules of a game that everyone was eager to play.
>
> (Foot 1978: 9–10)

But caring about (respecting) people's rights is not the same as caring for their welfare or happiness. Hence, in a close community whose members are already kindly-disposed to one another, the virtue of justice would not be superfluous.

Far from charity or generosity making justice superfluous, they would not be virtues if not exercised with an eye to people's rights. As Foot herself says, 'if natural virtue cannot be the whole of virtue this is because a kindly or fearless disposition could be disastrous without justice and wisdom, and these virtues have to be learned' (1978: 11). John Tomasi maintains that justice – respect for people's rights – is no less important in close communities or between friends than it is in other social settings. Generosity, for example, presupposes recognition of rights: 'You cannot most properly be generous with what you do not know is yours; you cannot truly forgive without first recognizing a debt'(1991: 525). Against Hume's idea that 'the nobler virtues' could 'supply' the place of justice, Tomasi emphasizes the value of our being respectful of each other's rights in all our dealings with one another. Being respectful need not involve asserting one's rights, it may involve deliberately not doing so: 'When voluntarily withheld, liberal individual rights offer the opportunity for profound expression of community' (1991: 536). Thus, says Tomasi, even 'within close communities, there is art in exercising rights properly' (1991: 527).

Truthfulness and 'respect'

It is usual to explain why untruthfulness is a vice by dwelling, as I have done, on how untruthfulness undermines trust and on how we need to act in ways that maintain trust. When we take note of how reliant we are on trust in our dealings with one another and of how fragile trust is (easily shattered and hard to mend), we need probe no further to establish that untruthfulness is a core vice and truthfulness a core virtue. That is the Humean and commonsensical story. It is the story reaffirmed by Sissela Bok. There is more, to be said however, in explaining the virtue and the vice.

This more, though, is hard to grasp and explain. It requires us to pay attention to some of the things that Kant says about lying. Kant does not dispute the idea that lying is destructive of trust. He says himself that a liar destroys fellowship and conversation (1930: 224). If lying were a universal practice, he observes, society would be impossible. But Kant also says that the wrongness of lying is to be located not just in the harm done to others but in the harm liars do themselves. Kant is not here thinking of the risk liars take of becoming habitual liars (the risks Bok says liars tend to underestimate). Bok's point is that lying is both unjust (to others) and imprudent. Kant, in claiming that we have a duty to ourselves not to lie, is not thinking of this sort of harm – the imprudence, the risks – but of the violation to self-respect (1964: 93). We have seen that Percival also thought that we have a duty to ourselves not to lie, but in Kant's view this is something much more imperiously binding than Percival supposes: it is not just a fashion item for gentlemen.

What is this notion of 'duty to ourselves'? Kant complains that 'all moral philosophers err in this respect' (1930: 117), that they consider duties to the self only as an 'afterthought', secondary to duties to others. Duties to the self, Kant says, should have 'pride of place' (1930: 118) and the duty not to lie is 'more a violation of duty to oneself than of one's duty to others' (1930: 118). Kant (like Aristotle) rejects the idea that we can treat ourselves *unjustly* – since in such cases we must always be consenting parties (1930: 117). Yet consent does not always remove injustice – not in law, anyway. So why should it in ethics? Duelling is illegal and maybe ethically indefensible even if the parties involved are consenting.

Be that as it may, is there not something similarly puzzling in Kant's idea that we can have duties to *ourselves*? Kant remarks that 'No one has framed a proper concept of self-regarding duty' (1930: 117). Maybe, though, the concept cannot be made sense of. To be under a duty is to be bound – not free – in a certain respect. If I am under a duty to you – say to deliver some goods as promised – then I am bound by that duty unless *you* release me, or some other circumstance imposes a competing and overriding obligation on me. At any rate, I cannot simply choose to release myself from the obligation if it so pleases me – though you can, if it so pleases you. If I have a duty to myself the one bound and the one doing the binding is the same individual. So what is to stop me from releasing myself, if it so pleases me, from these obligations that I owe myself? But if I have that freedom, it seems I am not really bound at all.

Even if we are not persuaded that it makes sense to speak of duties to one's self, we may still think that Kant does right to go beyond the notion of trust, important though that is, in giving an account of the importance of truthfulness – of what makes truthfulness a virtue. Kant says: 'By a lie man throws away and, as it were, annihilates his dignity as a man' (1964: 93).[2] He claims that even lies which are told without malice: for example, lies 'arising from mere frivolity or even good nature' or 'to achieve a really good end', manifest a 'baseness' which must make the liars contemptible in their own eyes (1964: 93). Is Kant right to suppose that all lies have this effect on the tellers of lies – or even should?

There is such a thing as 'dupers' delight'. St Augustine (354–430) (in his essay 'On Lying' observes as much: 'A man may tell a lie unwillingly; but a liar loves to lie, and inhabits in his mind in the delight of lying' (1847: 402). Francis Bacon (1561–1626) also comments on how men love lies – enjoy lying whether or not they look to gain anything by them (1825: 3). Shakespeare's Iago is a case in point. Such characters do not seem to think less well of themselves. On the contrary, they take a pride in their craftiness. These people have no conscience – no shame. What, though, of those who do have a conscience? Are they bound to be ashamed (feel degraded) if they lie? Surely they will not if they think that the lies they tell are justified. Isn't Kant's claim only plausible if applied to those who lie *against conscience*? And then it seems that what is debasing is not the thought that one is lying but the thought that one is acting badly. For those who have a conscience that thought will disturb whatever the occasion for it – not just when what occasions it is a lie.

There does seem to be a particular connection between lying and a kind of contempt or failure of respect for people that does not attach generally to bad sorts of actions. Stealing may show lack of respect for property but is not a direct affront to the people from whom one steals in the same way. There is something peculiar to the confrontational nature of lying that makes it seem a very personal kind of insult – a slap in the face. But that suggests a contempt towards those one is seeking to deceive, not towards oneself. Maybe, though, liars have particular difficulty trusting others – and are liable to suspect that they are themselves victims, and so as contemptible as their own victims. Thus Graham Greene says of Scobie (in *The Heart of the Matter*): 'It seemed to Scobie one of the qualities of deceit that you lost the sense of trust. If I can lie and betray, so can others'. Eventually, Scobie comes to mistrust his own servant, Ali, who has served him loyally for fifteen years: 'I've lost the trick of trust' Scobie muses. There may be something in the idea that lying breeds a kind of contempt and cynicism, not just towards others but even towards oneself.

I have given Kant's assertion – that lies manifest a baseness that must make liars contemptible in their own eyes – a psychological cast. That is not how he intended it to be taken. He was not forecasting psychological problems that liars store up for themselves. Rather, he was pointing up the baseness, as he saw it, in the very deed: the self-abuse involved, that the liars misuse their own rational powers – using language not to convey truth, which is what it is for, but to convey falsehoods. This line of thought in Kant seems to me unpersuasive. Of course we need to be able to use language to convey truths; and, maybe, that is what it is for, though it is not its only use. But why must it be contrary to reason or morally remiss to use it some-times to convey a falsehood? Telephones, it might be said, are for communicating with other people. That is what they are for and why they exist. But if I find a way of telephoning myself and do so, is that a misuse or abuse of the telephone? Eccentric, maybe, but possibly not as dotty as it sounds. Maybe I am trying to eradicate my accent and hearing my voice over the telephone is a good way of testing how far I have succeeded.

Objection to the idea that truthfulness is a core virtue

If core virtues are indispensable, how can it be that untruthfulness is a tolerated, familiar feature of our daily lives? We began this chapter with the observation that dishonesty is a very ordinary vice. The idea of a vice being quite ordinary seems to undermine the notion that we cannot get on unless we avoid vices – core ones at any rate. Yet even though there are many manifestations of vices in our daily lives it does not follow that such behaviour is tolerated – let alone, that it should be. There are many instances of unkindness. We do not on that account suppose that unkindness does not matter – or that people generally do not think that it matters. What is indispensable in regard to vices is not that we succeed in avoiding them, but that we recognize them for what they are and uphold attitudes of intolerance towards them (that we do not become apathetic or indifferent).

It is also possible that we exaggerate the amount of untruthfulness we encounter day by day. We need to distinguish what truthfulness involves from other related but distinct traits. Truthfulness, I will argue, is not the same as candour or openness – even supposing the latter is a virtue. Moreover, I will argue, being truthful does not necessarily mean being a truth-seeker, a truth-lover or a truth-spreader. Hence evidence that people pass up opportunities to seek truth or share truths is not necessarily evidence of a failure of truthfulness.

Truthfulness is not to be confused with candour or openness

Candour, if it is a virtue, is distinct from truthfulness. But is it even *a* virtue? Is a willingness to share our thoughts, feelings, attitudes and intentions something to be nourished? Is such a tendency either amiable or useful? Let us call the opposite tendency, the tendency to hide one's thoughts, feelings or attitudes or intentions, reserve. Is reserve a vice?

Candour is often *not* amiable: Hjalmar (in Ibsen's *The Wild Duck*) says, 'in my house no one ever speaks to me about ugly things'; Mark Twain observes, 'Good breeding consists in concealing how much we think of ourselves, and how little we think of other persons'. It is most likely candour that Josh Billings has in mind when he remarks, 'As scarce as the truth is, the supply has always been in excess of the demand' (quoted by David Nyberg 1993: 137).

Is candour useful? Reserve would seem to be more obviously useful: for example, to protect information we hold in confidence and to preserve our privacy. Nyberg observes:

> Every important right needs a social system to protect it. The right to privacy is no exception... It is protected by laws, by ethical codes, skills of concealment and deception ... We need privacy to survive just as surely as we need communal civility. Neither would be possible, and more importantly, a satisfactory balance between the two would be beyond reach, without deception.
>
> (1993: 134–5)

For the moment let us postpone discussion of deception – whether it is necessary as Nyberg claims. At least we may agree with him that hiding one's true feelings or thoughts is often necessary. Perhaps, then, reserve is a virtue and candour a vice. It is candour, not reserve that is a threat to self-esteem and hope. Dr Relling (in *The Wild Duck*) observes: 'If you take away make believe from the average man, you take away happiness as well'.

And isn't candour also an impediment to friendship? Nyberg says, 'An atmosphere of pure truth telling is no more fit to support friendship than an atmosphere of pure oxygen is fit to support life' (1993: 143). He says, 'Given the nature of trust in friendship there is an important and serious role for deception to play in keeping a friendship going' (1993: 141). Where Nyberg speaks of 'pure truth-telling' I take him to mean candour: not hiding one's thoughts, feelings, attitudes or intentions from one's friend. Nyberg does not distinguish deception from hiding as I think we should. Let us consider whether if he'd said simply that hiding has an 'important and serious role' in friendship, we should agree.

Does real friendship preclude hiding one's true thoughts, etc.? Christine Korsgaard observes how you might, in order to win someone's friendship, withhold some information. But she seems to regard this as only a transitional phase. The need for reserve goes away as the friendship gets established. This comment suggests that reserve indicates lack of trust. But that is only one possible explanation why you might be reserved with friends. There are plenty of reasons for hiding your thoughts, etc. from friends that do not imply the least doubt of their trustworthiness. Korsgaard insists that 'if mutual trust is ever to be *achieved* [between us], the day must come when my calculations about the effect of my telling you things stops; that is what it *means* for *me* to trust *you*' (1996: 310).

But there can be mutual respect and affection between friends even though they exercise reserve towards each other, cautiously avoiding mention to each other of matters that they know would sadden, aggravate or annoy? Individuals who are dear to us and whom we respect can be profoundly loved and loveable despite our not seeing eye to eye with them on every subject. Friends can be aware of such differences and choose to keep off these sensitive areas for the sake of their friendship. Such caution need not demonstrate lack of trust. Even if hiding is compatible with friendship, that is not to say that it has a 'serious and important role'. Just imagine, though, what it would be like to share one's life with someone who exercised no reserve whatsoever when with you. Would this be a welcome proof of a person's trust? Would it not drive you mad?

At least, it is evident that there is no incompatibility between hiding a truth from each other and trusting each other. If I don't tell you a secret this is not necessarily because I do not trust you, it may simply be that I owe it to someone else not to tell.

If we are to make a credible case for candour being a virtue, we need to treat it not as opposed to reserve but as involving a mean between complete unreserve and complete reserve: as being open only about thoughts, etc. that *should (or may) be shared*. In other words, only if we incorporate judgement and reserve into our account of candour as a virtue, does it turn out to be a useful trait. We do not then have to interpret hiding as automatically evidence of lack of the virtue. We can accept that utter unreserve would be tiresome and improper. If utter unreserve is not the ideal at which we all should aim, we need to look critically at what is meant when people talk of 'complete' or 'utter' honesty as if *this* were obviously desirable. If they mean by this phrase utter unreserve, it is not. Obviously, those who are truthful also exercise reserve: otherwise we could not trust them to keep our confidences: 'who will open himself to a blab or babbler?' asks Francis Bacon in his essay 'Of Simulation and Dissimulation' (1825: 18).

Truthfulness we have found to be an aspect of justice: and something that we owe one another generally. Candour, if it is a virtue, would seem to be an aspect of prudence: hence, a different virtue. We are not under a general duty to be candid with one another. Of course, candour is sometimes needed and owed, on account of particular duties we are under: for example, members of a mountaineering expedition need to be candid with each other about their current physical fitness, and about what climbing experience they already have. Contemporary writers on medical ethics tend to conflate truthfulness with candour, honesty with openness. For example:

> Honesty becomes the general fiduciary commitment to protect and promote the interests of the patient if surgical ethics is to guide the clinical judgment and practice of surgeons in a comprehensive way. The surgeon must be the expert he or she represents himself or herself to be if he or she is to honor the patient's rights not to be deceived, to be fully informed of risks and benefits, and to be free from avoidable risks.
>
> (McCullough *et al.* 1998: 6)

In this passage it is assumed that truthfulness towards patients (honesty in communication) requires candour (giving them information). I will argue that the duty to inform patients is not part of what honesty or truthfulness requires – except if the information is promised.

Truthfulness does not imply truth loving, seeking or spreading

Philippa Foot observes that there belongs to

> Truthfulness not only avoidance of lying but also that other kind of attachment to truth which has to do with its preservation and pursuit. A man of virtue must be a lover of justice and a lover of truth.
>
> (1985: 207)

But this seems to pack two very different virtues together under the heading of 'truthfulness'. A love of truth comes under the virtue of wisdom or prudence, whereas as we have seen, an unwillingness to lie comes under justice.

But is love of truth a virtue (or part of a virtue)? Surely it is. Love of truth and understanding protect us against ignorance and irrational beliefs which are factors that prevent us from living well and doing well – factors which we can arm ourselves against, avoiding vices like gullibility and prejudice. But love of truth is supposed to do more than arm us against bad reasoning; it suggests an inquiring mind. Those who have the virtue are wisely inquisitive, not omnivorous gatherers of information. What kind of knowledge do they seek?

Sherlock Holmes despises the uncritically inquisitive mind. When Watson expresses astonishment that Holmes does not know that the earth travels around the sun, Holmes observes:

> You appear to be astonished …Now that I do know it I shall do my best to forget it …. You see, … I consider that a man's brain is like a little empty attic, and you have to stock it with such furniture as you choose. A fool takes in all sorts of lumber of every sort that he comes across, so that the knowledge which might be useful to him gets crowded out, or at least jumbled up with lots of other things, so that he has difficulty in laying his hands upon it. Now the skilful workman is very careful indeed as to what he takes into his brain-attic. He will have nothing but the tools which may help him in doing his work, but of these things he has a large assortment, and all in most perfect order. It is a mistake to think that the little room has elastic walls and can distend to any extent. Depend upon it there comes a time when for every addition of knowledge you forget something that you knew before. It is of the highest importance not to have useless facts elbowing out the useful ones.

Watson interjects, 'But the solar system!' to which Holmes retorts: 'What the deuce is it to me? You say that we go round the sun. If we went round the moon it would not make a pennyworth of difference to me or to my work.' (*A Study in Scarlet*)

In repudiating knowledge that is not useful Holmes appears to deny the possibility that some things are worth knowing for their own sake. Aristotle thinks otherwise. He defends the life of contemplation as the kind of life most worthy of humans – a life in which knowledge is sought and valued not *for* anything but simply because one wants to understand how things are. Imagine what life would be like if the world were perfect. There would be no illness, so no need for doctors or nurses; no criminals, so no need for policemen; no wars, so no need for soldiers. In such a world, though, how could people live worthwhile, fulfilling lives: how could we enjoy life? What would be worth doing? How, indeed, asks Aristotle, can the gods live happily: what can their happiness consist in?[3]

> We assume the gods to be above all other beings blessed and happy; but what sort of actions must we assign to them? Acts of justice? Will not the gods seem absurd if they make contracts and return deposits, and so on? Acts of a brave man, then, confronting dangers and running risks because it is noble to do so? Or liberal acts? To whom will they give? It will be strange if they are really to have money or anything of the kind. And what would their temperate acts be? Is not such praise tasteless, since they have no bad appetites? If we were to run through them all, the circumstances of action would be found to be trivial and unworthy of gods. Still everyone supposes that they *live* and therefore that they are active; we cannot suppose them to sleep like Endymion. Now if you take away from a living being action, and still more production, what is left but contemplation?
>
> (Ross 1954: *Nicomachean Ethics*: 10.8)

Alasdair MacIntyre, like Aristotle, believes that our lives are defective if we do not engage in enquiry, if we are not contemplative. MacIntyre supposes that this kind of enquiry needs to be something we do together. He claims that the moral life is, among other things, 'a life of communal enquiry' (1995: 333). Now if our failure to participate in this quest is a moral failing, participation must be open to us all: it has to be something that we are all able to do – hence, be at fault for neglecting to do. The quest also has to be something that we all need to join in. Just as courage as a moral virtue is something everyone needs and benefits from, not just soldiers, so commitment to truth-seeking must be something that everyone can commit to and benefit from, not just scholars.

I suggest that 'wisdom' captures better than 'truthfulness' what this quest might be about and why it is something we all need to go in for. Foot suggests that the virtue of wisdom has two parts: 'In the first place the wise man knows the means to certain ends; and secondly he knows how much particular ends are worth' (1978: 5). Elaborating on the first part, Foot suggests that those who are wise in this way are good at choosing the means to certain general ends – 'ends having to do with such matters as friendship, marriage, the bringing up of children, or the choices of ways of life' (1978: 5). Not everyone is wise in this way. Yet to be so one does not need to be especially clever or have access to special training: 'Some people are wise without being at all clever or well informed: they make good decisions and they know, as we say, "what's what"' (1978: 6). Foot says that the second part of wisdom is 'much harder to describe, because we meet here with ideas which are curiously elusive, such as the thought that some pursuits are more worthwhile than others, and some matters trivial and some important in human life' (1978: 6). She suggests that someone who lacks this kind of wisdom has 'false values' (1978: 7).

We need not delve further in trying to understand this virtue here. We already know enough, I suggest, to see that: 1) love of truth belongs to wisdom rather than truthfulness and 2) the wise are truth-loving, seeking and spreading only selectively. Thus the fact that people suppress and conceal truth does not necessarily indicate that they are being untruthful. It does not necessarily even indicate that they are not truth-loving in the manner of the wise. The kind of attachment to knowledge or understanding that the wise have is not menaced just because people keep secrets from each other. Suppose that MacIntyre is right in claiming that all of us should be somehow involved in the quest after wisdom. Our doing this does not require that we share everything we know with one another. Gaining wisdom, both aspects of it as sketched by Foot, is not especially helped by the sharing of information or hindered by not doing so. For all that we now know a lot more about the world than did our forbears, do we have any reason to suppose we are any the wiser as a result – wiser in the matters that make us think of wisdom as a virtue?

In short, were we to take every instance of concealing or suppressing truths as an instance of untruthfulness, it would appear to be absurd to proclaim untruthfulness to be a core vice: something we have all got to avoid. We cannot be blamed for what we cannot help. But it is a mistake to suppose that being truthful means being truth-loving, seeking and spreading. Another virtue, wisdom, does require of us some truth-loving, seeking and spreading; but even there, only in a selective way.

The universality of core vices and virtues

Core vices and virtues are grounded in basic facts of life about human nature and human circumstances. Cowardice, foolhardiness, irascibility, are impediments to living well and doing well, whoever one is and whatever one's circumstances. Similarly, I am claiming that untruthfulness is a core vice and truthfulness a core virtue. But can we generalize about human needs across societies in this way? Is any attempt to set forth what constitutes living well bound to be parochial? Foot observes:

> Granted that it is wrong to assume an identity of aim between people of different cultures; nevertheless there is a great deal that men have in common. All need affection, the cooperation of others, a place in a community, and help in trouble. It isn't true to suppose that human beings can flourish without these things – being isolated, despised, or embattled, or without courage or hope. We are not, therefore, simply expressing values that we happen to have if we think of some moral systems as good moral systems and others as bad. Communities as well as individuals can live wisely or unwisely.
>
> (1982: 164)

In any society, surely, there is the same need for people to limit how they are prepared to treat one another by adopting certain generally agreed rules – especially in regard to the use of force and fraud. Of course, there are various different and competing ideas about what constitutes good living both within and between different cultures. Perhaps there is less diversity of opinion, though, about what kinds of actions and practices wreck our prospects of living well or doing well.[4] If so, that would be another reason why we may find it easier to make headway if we focus our attention more on vices than on virtues.

Various different fleshings out of what the contents of rules of justice should be may be equally satisfactory for avoiding the evils that make untruthfulness a vice. Particular fleshings out may serve a community well for a while but come to need amending from time to time. One feature that must be present is that the rules of justice (what we owe one another), whatever they are, are generally agreed upon and taken seriously within a community. Alasdair MacIntyre doubts whether such agreement is (anymore) to be found in regard to truthfulness: 'The dominant culture in North America fails to provide any generally accepted and agreed-upon public rule about truth-telling and lying, by appeal to which we could in relevant instances call each other to account' (1995: 323).

If MacIntyre is right, how can we remedy the situation? Can we work out rules that would provide an adequate curb on our lying and deceiving tendencies? Whatever rules we propose need to be simple and straightforward – or else how are they to be learned and how is anyone to know if they are being respected or not? If the rules need to be upheld and violations must not be tolerated, we need to be able to recognize and agree what the rules permit and forbid.

4 What truthfulness requires

> One of the most embarrassing problems is how to avoid lying, especially when one would like people to believe something untrue.
>
> Pascal

What teaching do we need to adopt to uphold truthfulness? Do we need to teach that lying is always wrong? Or that sometimes, maybe often, lying is unavoidable and justified? Are there honest lies (lies that are not lapses of virtue) as well as dishonest lies? Are there occasions when lying is a duty? If a teaching that we must never tell lies is a bad teaching (because it asks us to do the impossible or because there are occasions when we ought to lie) what should we replace that teaching with? Should we modify the teaching by tacking on certain exceptions? Do we need a strict rule but one that is narrower in scope? Does truthfulness require the same strictures against intentionally deceptive words or tricks that do not involve lying as against those that do?

Jon Krakauer tells of how when the mountaineer, Rob Hall, was stranded near the peak of Everest and his friends in Base Camp far below were urging him to start climbing down, he kept asking after the whereabouts of his companion, Andy Harris. Cotter, a longtime friend of Hall, 'tried to steer the discussion away from Harris, who in all likelihood was dead, "because we didn't want Rob to have another reason for staying up there." At one point Ed Viesturs came on the radio from Camp Two and fibbed, "Don't worry about Andy; he's down here with us"'(1998: 231). Some hours later, Hall still had not moved from his position on the South Summit and his friends below continued to urge him to try to descend. He again asked after Andy's whereabouts, saying: 'Some of Andy's gear is still here. I thought he must have gone ahead in the nighttime. Listen, can you account for him or not?' Wilton attempted to dodge the question, but Rob persisted in his line of enquiry: 'OK I mean his ice ax is here and his jacket and things,' 'Rob,' Viesturs replied from Camp Two, 'If you can put the jacket on, just use it. Keep going down and worry only about yourself. Everybody else is taking care of other people. Just get yourself down' (1998: 232). What in such circumstances did truthfulness allow or require?

Compare another incident in which a man, close to death, also sought the truth. When Robert Koch and his German team were racing against a French team to discover the causative agent of cholera, Koch heard that the French team had succeeded. He went to the Frenchmen and asked permission to see what they had found and to his relief 'soon saw that they had mistaken platelets – particles which are the normal constituents of the blood – for the cholera bacillus'(Reid 1974: 91). Just a few weeks later one of the members of the French team, Thuillier, became infected and was dying. He sent for Koch who went to his bedside. 'Have we found the cholera bacillus?' he asked. Robert Reid records: 'Koch, to his eternal credit, lied. "Yes," he replied'. Thuillier died shortly thereafter (1974: 92). Should we agree with Reid? Was Koch justified in lying? Would it have been wrong of him to have told the truth?

Thomas Percival records the following biographical account:

> The husband of the celebrated Arria, Caecinna Paetus, was very dangerously ill. Her son was also sick at the same time, and died. He was a youth of uncommon accomplishments; and fondly beloved by his parents. Arria prepared and conducted his funeral in such a manner, that her husband remained entirely ignorant of the mournful event which occasioned that solemnity. Paetus often inquired with anxiety, about his son; to whom she cheerfully replied, that he had slept well, and was better. But if her tears, too long restrained, were bursting forth, she instantly retired, to give vent to her grief; and when again composed, returned dry eyed, and with a placid countenance, quitting as it were all the tender feelings of the mother, at the threshold of her husband's chamber.
>
> (Leake 1927: 196)

Some lies are mischievous, but these lies, doubtless, were kindly meant. Denying the truth in these circumstances, arguably, was doing no harm or was doing less harm than telling the truth would have done. Whether or not we think any or all of these lies were justified in the circumstances, we may at least suppose that many lies we tell are justified – perhaps, thinking that they are harmless white lies. Are not white lies common and unavoidable? Is it not absurd to insist that morality requires us to do without them?

Sir Isaiah Berlin, in his eighty sixth year, was interviewed about his views on death and dying. He said that he saw no reason to believe that there is a world after death: 'It is just a comforting idea for those who can't face the possibility of total extinction'. He went on to say:

> We didn't talk much about death at home. I think my father hoped that there was a future life. In fact, when he was dying, he asked me if I thought there was going to be life after death. I said that yes, I did. That was a lie. A lie, which I uttered because he obviously wanted it to be so and hoped we'd be able to meet again, and I didn't want to tell him what I saw as the bleak truth.

So I did not tell the truth, and I don't in the least regret it. Since I believed that nothing would follow one's death, why should I cause a dying father pain?

(*The Times*, 19 July 1996: interview with Anna Howard)

Is this, as Isaiah Berlin seems to think, an example of a 'white' lie?

In this and the next chapter we will take up these questions: whether it is possible to do without lying; whether it is arbitrary to single out lying from other kinds of intentional deception, adopting a particularly strict rule just against it; and, finally, what teaching truthfulness requires and permits.

But first, we need to clarify what we mean by lying. Those who claim that lying is unavoidable – is part and parcel of our everyday life – most likely define lying quite broadly to include not just blatant lies but also other intentionally deceptive words and deeds – even, maybe, including pretences or concealments (whether or not done *in order to* cause anyone to believe what is false).

What to count as 'lying'

Some people define 'lying' very loosely indeed. Arnold Ludwig, for example, in his book, *The Importance of Lying*, uses as his working definition: 'any type of behaviour which deviates from truth'(1965: 4). This, of course, leaves things extremely vague: it does not even distinguish between unknowingly deviating and deliberately doing so. Following on from this definition, it comes as no surprise to find that Ludwig maintains: 'Lying plays an important and necessary role in the life of man'(1965: 229) and that he does not consider lying to be even presumptively wrong.

Similarly, Paul Ekman, in *Telling Lies*, does not differentiate between lying and deceiving. His definition of a lie or deceit (he says that he is using these words interchangeably)(1985: 26) is: where 'one person intends to mislead another, doing so deliberately, without prior notification of this purpose, and without having been explicitly asked to do so by the target' (1985: 28). Ekman goes on to say, 'There are two primary ways to lie: to *conceal* and to *falsify*. In concealing, the liar withholds some information without actually saying anything untrue' (1985: 28). Ekman acknowledges that 'Not everyone considers concealment to be lying; some people reserve that word only for the bolder act of falsification' (1985: 28).

It is important to bear in mind the broad scope of Ekman's definition when he talks about the 'ubiquity of lying' (1985: 23) and when he disagrees with those who make out that lying is inherently evil (1985: 268). Thus, for example, commenting on the meeting at the White House on 14 October 1962 between Gromyko and Kennedy during the Cuban missile crisis Ekman says that *both* men lied: the former by giving false assurances, the latter by concealing the fact that he knew he was being lied to (1985: 268). Ekman observes that while others might demur at his calling Kennedy a liar, he does not take the view that all lies are reprehensible (1985: 23). Naturally, if we fall in with Ekman's broad definition of lying, we are likely to agree with him that some lies are innocent and even dutiful. He instances the importance of nurses learning to conceal their 'negative emotions' when they have to tend patients in gruesome conditions (1985: 55). But we surely do not normally think of concealing emotions *per se* as a type of lying nor necessarily even as intended to deceive.

The nurses, for example, may deliberately (and conscientiously) hide their 'negative emotions' not with the *aim* of causing their patients to think what is false (that the nurses are not horrified or frightened or whatever), but simply to prevent the patients from noticing that the nurses are horrified or .... The point is: deliberately hiding the truth need not involve trying to get others to believe what is false. A GP may adopt a disguise, dark spectacles, not wanting to be recognized by her patients while bustling about town to do the shopping and be home in time for tea. The intent behind the disguise is not to cause her patients to believe falsely: 'this woman is not my GP' but simply to pass them by unnoticed. Similarly, wearing a loose pullover to disguise how thin you have become may be simply an effort to shield people from realizing how frail you are. Your aim need not be to persuade them that you are robust. You may put on smiles in company to cover your inward sadness: though you do so consciously, you need not be doing it in order to make people think that you are merry. People who are bereaved are expected to put on a brave face. In short, often there is no intent to deceive behind our efforts to conceal a truth.

Alasdair MacIntyre, quoting from the report based on a large national survey conducted by James Patterson and Peter Kim claims that lying is endemic in America today: '91% of Americans lie regularly'(1995: 319). 'More than 2,000 Americans' took part, each answering 'over 1,800 questions' over the course of the day. As the respondents were guaranteed complete anonymity they had 'no reason to be hypocritical or to lie' (Patterson and Kim 1991: 4).

But when these people owned up to all these lies, just what were they counting as lies? There is no indication in the book Patterson and Kim published about their findings that those questioned were asked what *they* meant by lying (whether they were including every form of pretence, concealment or evasion). People *were* asked what they meant by a 'serious' lie. Their answers were consistent with their construing lies to include every form of deceptive behaviour. Patterson and Kim report, on the basis of their survey, that:

> The majority of us find it hard to get through the week without lying. One in five can't make it through a single day – and we're talking about conscious, premeditated lies. In fact, the way some people talk about trying to do without lies, you'd think that they were smokers trying to get through the day without a cigarette.

> (1991: 45)

But whether or not we should be shocked by this revelation depends on what we take the respondents to have been talking about when they said that they frequently lied. Maybe, they *were* only thinking of 'telling others what you believe is false in order to deceive them'. But how are we to know? At the end of their chapter titled 'American Liars' Patterson and Kim offer a truth test for readers to administer to themselves. It includes, alongside questions like: 'Have you ever lied about your age, your income, or your education?' and 'Have you ever told anyone, "I love you," without meaning it?' many other questions, to which an affirmative answer would *not* be an admission of a lie.

For example:

'You are losing your hair at a rapid rate. Would you consider wearing a wig or hair-piece?'

'Do you socialise with people you really don't like?'

'Do you do things that no-one else knows about in the privacy of your home?'

Notice that answering 'Yes' to the last question would not even be an admission of intent to deceive if that implies attempting to cause someone to believe what is false.

In the same test, other questions are asked where the 'correct' answer, the answer of those who are not liars, is supposed to be 'Yes'.

These include:

'You break an expensive vase in an antique store. Nobody sees you do it. Would you tell the owner?'

'You have an unplanned one-night stand with a stranger. Your spouse does not suspect. Would you confess?'

Now, of course, those who answer 'No' to these last two questions are admitting that they would act secretively and, moreover, that (at least in the first case) they would withhold information from people who were owed it. But in neither case would the withholder of information be *telling a lie*. The fact that Patterson and Kim lump together questions about lying with questions about concealment suggests that they are operating with a broad definition of lying which does not distinguish it even from secretive behaviour, let alone from other deceptive behaviour. For all we know, many of those they questioned were also assuming a very broad definition of lying, in which case their answers are not so startling or worrying as Patterson and Kim – and MacIntyre, seem to suppose.

Some authors are suspicious of those who define lying more narrowly, so as not to include all intentionally deceptive behaviour. They accuse those who reject the broader definition of 'conflating' two tasks: the conceptual task of definition and the moral task of justification. (Cliffe *et al.* 2000: 4). These authors do right to object to such conflations, to 'moralized' definitions, so-to-speak. But selecting a narrower in preference to a broader definition need not signal any such trickery. If one is out to persuade people that all lies are wrong, one does well to adopt a narrower definition of lying. Equally, if one is out to persuade people that some lies are not wrong, one does well to adopt a broader definition. Thus it is no surprise that Augustine and Kant, who both aim to show that lying is always wrong, operate with a narrow definition (and Sissela Bok who aims to show that lying is not always wrong, operates with a broader definition). It is not true, though, that Augustine and Kant conflate the two tasks. Both of them first explain what they mean by 'lying' and then proceed to offer arguments as to why doing that is always wrong. Their arguments are not mere restatings of their definitions.

There is no reason, then, to mistrust the attempts by those who defend a strict teaching against lying, to draw certain distinctions. They will distinguish lying from being secretive, from aiming to conceal things, from pretence and disguise. They will note that lying is a particular way of attempting to deceive, conceptually different from other ways – whether or not these differences are *morally* signif-icant (which has then to be separately argued for). They are simply recognizing that it would be absurd to renounce all lying if in so doing one were renouncing all forms of deception, pretence and subterfuge. Thus, for example, while Kant is famously unwilling to condone any lies, he does not object to secrecy as such: 'No man in his true senses ... is candid' (1979: 224).

Moreover, Kant distinguishes *deeds* calculated to deceive others from the bald assertions of falsehoods we make with the same intent. Only the latter he counts as lies. To pack your suitcase in front of someone with the intention of deceiving the person into thinking that you are about to go on a journey is not to lie. To *say* to them that you are about to go on a journey if you have no such intention is to tell a lie. You may be at fault in either case, but what you are *doing* in the first case is misdescribed as lying.

Nor does Kant regard what is *said* in order to deceive as necessarily a lie. In his definition of lying, it is to be distinguished even from other kinds of intentionally deceptive communications such as some evasions, equivocations or half-truths. Kant's attitude is illustrated by the following incident that he relates in the Preface to *The Conflict of the Faculties*.

In 1794 Kant was reprimanded by King Friedrich Wilhelm ll, for having 'misused' philosophy to 'distort and disparage many of the cardinal and basic teachings of the Holy Scriptures and of Christianity'(1979: 13) (with particular reference to Kant's book, *Religion within the Limits of Mere Reason*). The king warned Kant 'not to be guilty of anything of the sort in the future' (1979: 13). Kant declared in reply: 'as your Majesty's loyal subject, ... I shall in future completely desist from all public lectures or papers concerning religion, be it natural or revealed' (1979: 19). While Kant expected the censors to take this to mean that he would *never* publish anything of the sort, Kant gleefully points out that he did not actually say this. Kant says that he chose the phrase 'as your Majesty's loyal subject' 'most carefully, so I would not renounce my freedom to judge in this reli-gious suit forever, but only during His Majesty's lifetime' (1979: 19). (Kant knew when he gave his pledge that the King would not live long.) A false promise is a kind of lie. But Kant's promise, though intended to mislead, was not a lie.

The notion that we need a strict teaching against lying does not get off the ground unless we distinguish lying from other ways of hiding the truth. Other ways may be just as wrongful, just as untruthful, *in certain circumstances*. The point is that, even so, in very many familiar circumstances that we all find ourselves in regularly, pretending, concealing, even deceiving are not only very commonly unavoidable but also often are innocent, even sometimes commendable – not, in context, untruthful.

David Nyberg maintains that while deliberate deception is quite simply impossible for us to forswear, this need not be reason for gloom or despair since often our deceiving is innocent and not any way at odds with moral decency. On the unavoidability of deception he says:

> An atmosphere of pure truth-telling is no more fit to sustain relationships than the atmosphere of pure oxygen is fit to support biological life. Social life without deception to keep it going is a fantasy, and even if it were possible it would be undesirable.
>
> (1996: 187)

We may agree with Nyberg that we cannot and should not do without deception without necessarily agreeing that we cannot and should not do without telling lies.

Whereas it might seem that Nyberg is *opposing* Kant's rigorous stance against lying, in fact many of the examples that Nyberg gives to illustrate our regular and often perfectly innocent and respectable recourses to deception or secrecy, are instances with which Kant need have no quarrel. Kant too recognizes that concealment and secrecy are often necessary and justifiable and sometimes a duty: trustworthy people do not betray secrets; they conceal them – sometimes, with deliberately deceptive words or actions. Kant recognizes that disclosure is sometimes a duty and sometimes not. In so saying he does not contradict his view that lying is always wrong. Candour is to be distinguished from truthfulness. Truthfulness requires that we never lie, according to Kant. But it does not require that we are always candid.

This important distinction between the requirements of truthfulness and the requirements of candour is obscured where the discussion is couched in terms of 'truth telling'. The very expression, 'tell the truth,' is itself a source of confusion. It is sometimes used to mean 'Do not lie!' and sometimes used to mean 'Inform!' Consider the Caucasian proverb cited by Nyberg: 'A man who tells the truth should keep his horse saddled' (1993: 7). If we interpret 'tells the truth' here to mean simply 'tells no lies' the proverb is unpersuasive; whereas if we interpret 'tells the truth' here to mean 'hides no truth, discloses all he knows,' it is very plausible. Nyberg's own talk of 'pure truth telling' suggests that what he has in mind here as 'truth telling' is informing, rather than simply not lying. Nyberg observes:

> There is choice in truth-telling; we do have a range of truths to tell. Many questions do have more than one truthful answer. It may sound strange to say so, but I think the virtue of truth-telling is determined by just this kind of selectivity. We ought to try for the right truth in the right amount in order to produce the best effect for the people involved. In other words, it is probably better to tell the right truth rather than the whole truth or no truth at all.
>
> (1993: 158)

Clearly, Nyberg is talking not about whether or not we should lie, but about what we should and should not disclose (the proper management of information). He goes on:

> There is a certain amount of deception needed in selecting the right truth – if by deception we mean showing or emphasizing some things while hiding others, in an artful display intended to create a well-managed impression or idea in somebody's mind.
>
> (1993: 158)

There is nothing here with which Kant need quarrel. He too sees the need for judgement and discretion over what one discloses, how, when, where, and to whom.

Kant does not deny that people often quite justifiably use evasions, euphemisms, half-truths, concealment, pretences and various deceptive tricks in order to protect privacy, or to fend off mischief-makers, or to outwit the enemy, or to promote cheer and cordial relations between people, or simply to maintain domestic peace. Recall Nyberg's observation: 'We need privacy to survive just as surely as we need communal civility. Neither would be possible, and more importantly, a satisfactory balance between the two would be beyond reach, without deception'(1993: 135). He points out how secrecy and deception can play a valuable part in sustaining hope, self-respect and friendship: 'There are times when the truth can destroy self-image, self-respect, and the intimacy generated by loving gestures'(1993: 161):

> I think extolling the right to truth and denying the complementary right to be deceived is to misunderstand one of the important elements of moral decency, which is to tell the truth selectively and deceive with discretion so that others can find reasons for self-respect and be spared suffering wherever possible.
>
> (1993: 161)

'Given the nature of trust in friendship there is an important and serious role for deception to play in keeping a friendship going' (1993: 141).

There is nothing in any of this that Kant need dispute. It is only if the deceiver takes to lying that Kant objects.

Let us hereafter understand by a lie, the asserting of what one believes to be false in order to deceive someone.

Putting our definition of lying to the test

Before we proceed to discuss when if ever we may be justified in telling lies, let us consider whether the definition here proposed is at least a good conceptual fit: does it match up with what people tend to mean by 'lies'? Does our definition of lying help us to sort out some of the hard cases – where even people of good sense and good will have not always agreed what to count as a lie? Suppose, for example, that only if you state what is false can you prevent your hearers drawing a false conclusion? If you say what is false just in order to *prevent* erroneous belief, are you still lying?

Johann Sommerville describes how Sylvester (1460–1523; Italian Dominican) handled an example that was often used in debates about the implications of the duty not to lie.

> A traveller on arriving at the gates of a city, is asked by the guards whether he has come from some particular town which they believe to be infected by the plague. The traveller knows that there is in fact no plague in the town, or, alternatively, he knows that though there is plague there, he has not contracted it. If he confesses that he has come from the town, the guards will not admit him. It may be argued that he has no duty to tell them where he has come from, though he does have a duty to satisfy them that his admission will not jeopardise the health and safety of their city. In these circumstances it was held to be permissible for the traveller to reply not to the guards' question but to their 'remote intention', as Sylvester termed it. In other words, what the guards really wanted to know was whether the traveller was carrying the plague. If he was not, he could say 'no'. Given the circumstances, this reply was ambiguous, and, in this sense truthful.
>
> (Sommerville 1988: 169)

Was it?

Henry Sidgwick imagines another predicament where false speaking might be needed to prevent error:

> In speaking truth to a jury, I may possibly foresee that my words, operating along with other statements and indications, will unavoidably lead them to the wrong conclusion as to the guilt or innocence of the accused, as certainly as I foresee that they will produce a right impression as to the particular matter of fact to which I am testifying.
>
> (1962: 97)

Yet, if our remoter intentions can make false words innocent, the way is cleared for our fending off all sorts of irrelevant and awkward questions: as when my interviewers ask me my age as if that were relevant to my fitness for the job I seek. Can I, knowing that they only want to know the particular matter of fact in order to judge my fitness for the job, give them the false answer that prevents their making the mistake of turning me down as too old? At any rate, whether or not such stratagems (for example, those we have just described from Sylvester and Sidgwick) are sometimes justified, they do plainly involve lying as we have defined it here. What is actually said is false and intended to deceive.

Our definition also enable us to rule as to whether or not recourse to equivocations or the use of 'mental restriction' should count as lying. Jonsen and Toulmin examine how Christian casuists were led eventually to draw a sharp line between equivocation and mental restriction.

> The former takes advantage of the fact that linguistic usage permits a word or phrase to have several meanings: the speaker merely avoids making it clear which meaning he intends his utterance to have, hoping that his questioner will interpret it in some sense other than he intends. For example, someone might ask a physician, 'do you care for this person?' hoping to discover whether the person was the physician's patient. The physician, observing the confidentiality of the relationship might answer, 'no', meaning 'I don't care for him in the sense of being fond of him'.
>
> (1988: 201–2)

Another example:

> 'Off with their heads!' and the procession moved on. Three of the gardeners remained behind to execute the unfortunate gardeners, who ran to Alice for protection.
>
> 'You shan't be beheaded!' said Alice, and she put them into a large flower-pot that stood near. The three soldiers wandered about for a minute or two, looking for them, and then quietly marched off after the others.
>
> 'Are their heads off?' shouted the Queen.
>
> 'Their heads are gone, if it please your majesty!' the soldiers shouted in reply.
>
> *(Alice in Wonderland)*

These are examples of equivocation. They do not involve telling lies by our definition. What is said is intended to deceive but is not false *per se*. Kant's undertaking 'as your Majesty's loyal subject' relied on an equivocation. Robert Sanderson, Professor of Case Divinity at Oxford, relied on just such an equivocation to demonstrate how Royalists could in good conscience take the Engagement Oath (imposed by Parliament after the execution of Charles 1). Sanderson suggests how key words and phrases in the Oath were conveniently ambiguous (see Jonsen and Toulmin 1988: 212).

Evasion is another stratagem that may be used to conceal a truth, or to delay its disclosure. In Shakespeare's *Macbeth*, Ross seeks out Macduff to report the dreadful news that Macduff's wife and children have all been murdered. Ross does not want to blurt out this news too abruptly and tries to prepare Macduff, talking first in a general way about the grim plight of their 'poor country'. When Macduff asks for news of his own family, if they are safe, Ross parries: 'They were well at peace when I left them' a reply which immediately alarms Macduff: 'Be not a niggard of your speech...'.

Contrast the stratagem involving 'mental restriction', whereby what was said, though literally false, was claimed not to be a lie provided one added a mental reservation to oneself – as if, for example, to the unwelcome caller asking if your husband is at home or the sponger asking if you have any money, you reply 'No' (not for you) (Jonsen and Toulmin 1988: 202). It was this latter stratagem that especially gave casuistry a bad name, and not without reason. By our definition, mental restriction does not rescue what one says from being a lie: what one says is clearly false and is meant to deceive.

Our definition of lying allows us to distinguish (with results that seem not to be counter-intuitive) what counts as a lie from what does not, even in some hard cases. But is lying, as we have defined it, unavoidable? Don't people frequently tell little lies, white lies – or lies which they believe to be such? Is a teaching which denounces all these unrealistic and not to be taken seriously?

Annette Baier (1990: 270) maintains that there needs to be a certain 'solemnity of occasion' for one's false assertions to count as lies. Consider how often in casual conversation we edit our revelations as we talk to protect our own or other people's privacy, altering times or names or other features of what we tell in small but deliberate ways – and not only to protect privacy, but also to spare the hearers tedious and irrelevant details that would clutter conversation to no advantage. Such a practice sounds innocent enough – but does it aim to deceive – to get hearers to believe what is false, or merely to conceal? The boundary here between what is not a lie and what is a trivial lie may be hazy. If you were party to such a conversation and noticed that the speaker was editing (not just omitting things but substituting false things) would you think to yourself: 'That is a lie'? 'Lie' might sound over-solemn: perhaps, rather, one might call it a fib or fabrication – i.e. a trivial lie.

Rather than qualify our definition of lying in the way suggested by Baier, I suggest that we recognize that some lies are trivial and that the boundary between these and assertions which are no lies at all is not a sharp one. Straddling the boundary are the many social conventions that involve us in saying things on which no one relies – the polite words: 'So pleased to meet you!' 'So glad you could come!' or, on receipt of a present: 'Just what I've always wanted!' – Kant's example: the 'your obedient servant' at the end of a letter (1964: 95). No one is deceived by such expressions – though, of course, they don't have to be insincere.

Trivial lies

Can we and should we repudiate trivial lies? The importance of truthfulness we have found to derive from the importance of trust – which truthfulness preserves – and the importance of showing a kind of respect for one another. Trivial lies, it may be argued, should be tolerated: far from these posing a threat to trust or respect, are they not vital for sustaining fellowship? Are they not positively supportive of trust and respect? How can we manage to protect our legitimate needs and concerns – our privacy, security, civil relations and sense of fun – if we foreswear the little lies, the trivial lies?

Maybe, though, this only seems a daunting prospect if we forget our definition of a lie and lapse into thinking of *reserve* as somehow being a violation of the duty not to lie. Kant, stickler though he is about lying, cautions us against being unreserved (candour) even with dear friends: 'Even to our best friend we must not reveal ourselves, in our natural state as we know it ourselves. To do so would be loathsome' (1930: 206).

Francis Bacon (in his essay: 'Of Truth') asks:

> Doth any man doubt, that if there were taken out of men's minds vain opinions, flattering hopes, false evaluations, imaginings as one would, and the like, but it would leave the minds of a number of men poor shrunken things, full of melancholy and indisposition, and unpleasing to themselves?
>
> (1825: 4)

But if we decide not to attempt to deprive one another of all these props, we do not have to start telling lies – only to be cautious and selective in our informing. The duty not to lie, even if it is a strict duty, does not require us to go about challenging or correcting other people's false beliefs.

Thus before we fall in with the idea that trivial lies are important for sustaining fellowship, preserving our privacy and so forth, we need to recall our definition of lying and notice that much of what people may think of as 'trivial lies' are not lies at all: merely concealings. That granted, what about the residue: where we are definitely telling lies though only about trifles? Since by definition trivial lies are unimportant, do we need to ban them?

Trivial lies are unimportant *in themselves* – they deceive us on matters of no importance to or for us. Yet *toleration* of trivial lies (our own or other people's) may be dangerous. William Paley observes: 'I have seldom known anyone who deserted truth in trifles, that could be trusted in matters of importance' (in Kerr 1990: 183). Paley here echoes a familiar worry – one that St Augustine voiced (instancing the little lies told to others merely 'to sweeten conversation' in contexts where the hearers are unlikely to be fooled or to mind). St Augustine, in his essay 'On Lying', (1847 : 463) quotes from *Ecclesiastes*: 'He that despiseth small things shall fall little by little' (1847: 463).

How seriously need we take this worry that little (trivial) lies may lead to big ones? Is this so likely that we should not tolerate the trivial lie, or is it enough that we heed the warning and be on our guard against such a slide? I suggest that we do need to take this warning very seriously – for three reasons. In the first place, we understand by the term trivial lies, lies which those at the receiving end would not mind about (if they realized they were being lied to) – where being deceived does not matter to or for those who are deceived. But what matters to or for others is not always obvious. The usual reliable way of checking if we are right in our opinion about what matters to or for others (asking them) is debarred where we are minded to lie to them.

In the second place, there is a danger that people will suppose that lies are trivial provided they do no harm, or 'minimal' harm, or less harm than would otherwise occur. But once we extend what we count as trivial lies beyond those that are harmless, to include those that do minimal harm or less harm than would otherwise occur, we open the way to justifying serious lies. 'Minimal' is easily, but wrongly, assumed to mean little, or not substantial. But, of course, what is minimal may be far from little. The mimimum requirements to qualify for entry to a prestigious college may be quite stiff. Likewise, the course of action that does least harm may still do substantial harm. Indeed, the standard justification offered in defence of benign lying is that in the circumstances less harm results from the lie than would otherwise occur. In short, if we count among trivial lies lies that do minimal harm or less harm than otherwise would occur, we have no reason to object to many serious lies – lies which do matter to or for the deceived.

A third risk in our condoning trivial lies is that we may wrongly suppose that it is harmless to tell lies that are intended only to spare people distress where it is safe to suppose that those lied to will never know. The lies told to Thuiller and to Berlin's father are cases in point. The truth would have pained them but they would never find it out. Yet they were still harmed by being lied to. It is a common mistake to suppose that you are only harmed if you *suffer*: the notion that 'what you don't know can't hurt you'. But you may be harmed by being deprived of information that matters to you even if you never find this out. Being spared suffering matters, but it is not the only thing that matters and sometimes not what matters most.

The lies that were told to Rob Hall, Thuiller, Berlin's father and Paetus were not trivial. Each of these men was seriously interested in knowing the truth of the matter. Theirs was not idle curiosity. Whether or not we think that in the circumstances these lies were justified, we cannot claim that they were justified on the grounds that the lies told to them were trivial or that they were harmless. They were neither.

Serious lies

Can we and should we repudiate serious lies? Let us understand by 'serious lies' simply lies that are not trivial: lies where those who are deceived are fooled about things that do matter to or for them. Do we need a strict teaching against the telling of serious lies – or can trust and respect be adequately safe-guarded by a more flexible teaching? Is it enough to treat the duty not to lie as simply presumptive: lies would require a justification – a necessity? Such a necessity could be some other competing duty that in the circumstances overrides the prima facie duty not to lie.

This would be to place the duty not to lie on a par with the duty to keep one's promises. Nobody supposes that every promise must be kept whatever the circumstances. We would hardly dare make or seek promises if they were taken to be so tightly binding. Of course, some promises are more tightly binding than others. But with many promises we expect and want people to use their judgement about whether to do as they promised when the time comes to deliver. Circumstances change and often in ways that are not predictable. The fact that people sometimes fail to keep their promises does not necessarily dent our trust in them. The failure is something that can be openly acknowledged, explained and apologized for. But whereas with promises it is possible (if not always judicious) to be quite open about our decision not to keep them, the same openness is *not* possible with lies. If it is 'necessary' to lie, it is necessary to do so secretly. Hence the readiness to allow a necessity to justify a lie is likely to be more subversive of trust – because less open to scrutiny – than is the readiness to allow a necessity to justify the failure to keep a promise. The nurse who says to you: 'You can trust me, I won't lie to you – unless I have to' inspires *mis*trust. Not so, the nurse who says, 'Trust me, I will keep my promises if I can'.

Yet even if a teaching which treats the duty not to lie as merely prima facie is too weak to support trust and respect, need we choose as the alternative a strict rule that proscribes all lies – at any rate, all serious lies? Sissela Bok considers such an 'absolutist' stance to be counter-intuitive and contrary to common sense (1978: 42). As she observes, even the duty not to kill other people is regarded by most people as qualified – to allow us to defend ourselves against murderous attack, for example.

> If to use force in self-defence or in defence of those at risk of murder is right, why should a lie in self-defence be ruled out? Surely if force is allowed, a lie should be equally, perhaps at times more permissible?
>
> (1978: 41)

If one thinks here just about the harmful consequences – of killing one's assailants as opposed to lying to them, isn't it obvious that the killing is more harmful?

All the same, I suggest, there may be some sense in the notion that we need a stricter teaching against lying than against killing. Consider how we might as a society approve an exception to the duty not to kill being accorded to the police – might even approve their being allowed to 'shoot to kill' under certain carefully regulated circumstances. Our trust in the police need not be shaken even though we granted them this power. We would, of course, be vigilant to see that they did not misuse it. Should we in like spirit allow the police to lie to the public in certain circumstances? Would this not undermine the fragile trust we have in the police? How could we oversee their practice to make sure that they did not extend their lying practices to deal with other 'necessities' than those we had envisaged? The point is not that lying does more harm than killing but that a 'license to lie' would be so much harder to regulate than a 'license to kill'. Hence it might make sense after all to allow the police powers to shoot to kill but not allow them any qualifications on their duty not to lie.

Bok supposes that the absolutists on the matter of lying have been driven to their 'highly counterintuitive' view because of their religious beliefs – the thought that God forbids all lies. Yet, of course, the absolutists do defend their position with arguments that are evidently directed at everyone, not just fellow believers. Is Bok right to dismiss these arguments as inadequate? Let us recall briefly some of the arguments put forward by two famous absolutists, St Augustine and Kant.

St Augustine

St Augustine, in his essay 'Against Lying', defines a lie as a falsehood told with the intent to deceive. (1847: 454) Thus, he discounts jokes that involve false assertions:

they are not intended to deceive, as context and tone make clear. He also points out that to hide the truth is not the same thing as to utter a lie. (1847: 447) Even so, in his essay 'On Lying', he does not deny that lying is commonplace: 'Lies abound in living but should not be encouraged in teaching' (1847: 468). Though he defends the teaching that we should never lie, he admits that there are some hard cases – especially, he thinks, in respect of benevolent deception. Whether there can be a lie that is 'a kind of honest, well-meant, charitable lie' says Augustine, raises a question that is 'indeed, very full of dark corners, and hath many cavern-like windings' (1847: 383):

> If a sick man should ask a question which it is not expedient that he should know, and might be even more grievously afflicted even by thy returning him no answer, wilt thou venture either to tell the truth to the destruction of the man's life, or rather hold thy peace, than by a virtuous and merciful lie to be serviceable to his weak health?
>
> (1847: 388)

His other illustration of benevolent deception describes exactly the predicament faced by Arria (1847: 463). Augustine observes that although those who refuse to lie in such circumstances may be censured by some people, they are not to blame. But this seems rather to assume what is in question: that the rule against lying does *not* permit this exception. Otherwise, they might be to blame. Anyway, Augustine's reassurance about blame seems beside the point: it is hardly likely that Arria was minded to lie in order to avoid censure from others.

The more impressive argument against making an exception for benevolent lying offered by Augustine is to point up the slippery slope difficulties once we allow it. In other words we need to consider not just the particular predicament of someone like Arria. We need to consider the implications of a teaching that condoned benevolent deception: would it not seriously undermine trust. Can you trust the word of someone who says 'I will not lie to you unless I think it is better for you not to know the truth'?

Augustine also considers other kinds of exceptions to a strict rule against lying. He is less sympathetic to these: like lying to those who are themselves liars – lying heretics, for example. Might this be defensible where the purpose of one's own lie is to expose the lies of others? Augustine thinks not. One has here to consider the general implications of allowing such an exception. Augustine suggests that if one is prepared to do any evil kind of act if it might prevent a greater evil, one is rendered powerless in the face of evil – there is nothing one cannot be driven to do by an evil tyrant who threatens to do something even more evil unless one complies. Augustine also rejects the notion that an act which is in itself evil may still be justified if doing it is necessary to achieve a good end – like thieving to get the funds needed to build churches (his example).

Whether or not one agrees with Augustine that morality does not permit our doing a lesser evil to prevent a greater or choosing evil means to achieve worthy ends, one must still reckon with the dangers he claims ensue if one softens the rule against lying. In a particular case a lie might indeed do more good than harm. But we have to consider how we would justify the lie – the precedent it becomes for future choices – the implications for our general practice in regard to lying.

Augustine also remarks that anyone who goes about teaching that lying is sometimes permissible is not likely to be trusted as a teacher. That may be true if one simply announces that lying is sometimes justified, sometimes necessary, without offering any further explanation. But might one preserve trust by explaining more clearly and precisely under just what circumstances one is prepared to lie? Christine Korsgaard (1996) discusses the predicament described by Kant where you are confronted by a murderer seeking out your innocent friend, who has taken refuge in your house. She argues that making public our willingness to lie in just such circumstances need not undermine trust. Of course, murderers knowing that people are likely to be so minded will try to disguise their intentions. They will not necessarily give up asking questions – because they will suppose that we do not realize what they are about (1996: 135–7). Yet can we so firmly bracket off this one exception – our willingness to lie to murderers – to foil their purposes? If it is permissible to lie to murderers what about other evil-doers – rapists, child-abusers, drug-peddlers, muggers, thieves? Is it so clear that the line can be firmly held? Recall Augustine's worry that little by little we will be drawn into making more and more exceptions to the rule against lying.

Kant

Kant, like Augustine, rejects appeals to necessity to justify a lie:

> If necessity is urged as an excuse it might be urged to justify stealing, cheating and killing and the whole basis of morality goes by the board. Then, again, what is a case of necessity? Everyone will interpret it in his own way and, as there is no definite standard to judge by, the application of moral rules becomes uncertain.
>
> (1930: 228)

Yet Kant seems to waver over the matter of white lies (defined by him as lies forced upon us by necessity): 'The forcing of a statement from me under conditions which convince me that improper use would be made of it is the only case in which I can be justified in telling a white lie' (1930: 228).

> If my enemy takes me by the throat and asks where I keep my money, I need not tell him the truth, because he will abuse it; and my untruth is not a lie because the thief knows full well that I will not, if I can help it, tell him the truth and that he has no right to demand it of me.
>
> (1930: 227)

But, says Kant, 'Let us assume that I really say to the fellow ... that I will tell him the truth, and I do not' then I *am* lying and the lie is wrong. Even though the thief is not owed the truth, says Kant, the lie is 'an infringement of the rights of humanity' (1930: 227).

Kant's wavering here is not from a strict teaching against all lies, but over whether one should count as a lie what is said in circumstances where 1) it is unreasonable to suppose that the speaker is actually professing to inform and 2) where the enquirer has no right to the knowledge sought. Here one might draw on the notion of a 'white' lie – as permissible and not really a lie (cf. how artificial silk is not silk, a toy soldier is not a soldier). But if we were to permit white lies so defined, would we not open the way to a far too flexible teaching about lying? There are two aspects to the above situation upon which Kant dwells: the 'necessity' that the thief puts him in – 'taking me by the throat' – and the fact that the thief has no right to the information sought. As Kant himself maintains, mere necessity *by itself* is not a defence for lying – or, if it is, we must accept that the duty not to lie is merely a prima facie duty – often overridden. What, though, of the idea that one is not obliged to tell the truth to enquirers who have no right to the information they seek? Is that a plausible exception to make to the rule against lying?

Is lying only wrong where information is owed?

Annette Baier maintains that there is nothing wrong with lying *per se*: only with doing so where that is 'tantamount to a form of perjury' (1990: 270). Lying presupposes appropriate circumstances: that one is, so to speak, 'put on the mat' (1990: 270). But working out just when deceptive speech amounts to lying and just when lying is wrong is, on Baier's account, (sometimes) no simple matter. That is why she says that honesty is a 'hard' virtue: hard not just because we can be seriously constrained by what it requires of us, but because working out what it does require of us sometimes turns out to be quite complicated. 'Learning what counts as a lie — like learning what counts as a debt or broken promise' (1990: 271) demands study: 'Complex rules are involved, and fairly subtle contextual clues have to be picked up' (1990: 271).

Baier's own account of what makes lying wrong when it is wrong seems to subsume the duty not to lie under the duty to inform. Because the latter duty is not one we are generally under, she argues, we are under no blanket general duty to refrain from lying. Lying is wrong only where we are bound to speak the truth. 'Veracity,' says Baier, 'is knowing when one is bound to speak one's mind and then speaking it as best one can' (1990: 270). On this account, wrongful lying involves telling people what is false when the circumstances give them the right to expect to hear only what is true:

> The obligation not to lie, as I have construed it, is conditional on a clear understanding that the truth is then to be spoken. A [wrongful] lie is false pretences, an untruth where truth was offered, perhaps even promised. But we are under no permanent duty to deliver the truth about our state of mind to others… .
>
> (1990: 272)

Thus, though, anyone may try to 'put you on the mat' not everyone has the authority to do so.

But is the duty not to lie merely derivative from the duty to inform? Suppose that you have no right, no claim right, to the information which you innocently ask of me, does that mean that I can do you no wrong if I choose to respond to your enquiry with a lie? I arrive at the party without my spouse and you innocently enquire why he isn't with me. The truth is that we have just had a row, but I say instead that he is tied up at work – a flat lie. Now my lack of candour in response to the question is not *as such* a failure of duty; I am within my rights keeping the row private. But that is not to say that there is no wrong in my telling a lie. After all, there are other ways of protecting my privacy – an evasion, pretending not to hear, a half-truth ('He's not in a party-going mood tonight – he's had a bad day'). According to Baier, one only has 'a right to get straight answers to questions one has a right in certain circumstances to pose' (1990: 280). Now suppose that you have at least a weak right to ask – it is not wrong of you to ask, not prying, not impertinent. You may still not have a strong (claim) right to a straight answer (you may be within your rights asking and I may be within my rights not answering). But even if I happen to be within my rights not answering, not giving you a straight answer, that surely does not by itself make it all right for me to lie to you.

Consider, again, the lies told to Rob Hall and Thuiller: did they have a right to expect the truth in those particular circumstances? Were they within their rights to ask? Were they owed the truth? Even if they were not owed it, did they still have a right not to be lied to? If Koch had been honest would he have had to remain silent or answer evasively? If Hall and Thuiller did have a right not to be lied to, was it an absolute right or one which was justifiably overridden by some other duty or need?

When Kant at a later date returns to the question whether the duty not to lie is exceptionless, he dismisses the idea that the duty is conditional on the enquirer's right to know:

> Truth in utterances that cannot be avoided is the formal duty of a man to everyone, however great the disadvantage that may arise from it to him or any other; and although by making a false statement I do no wrong to him who unjustly compels me to speak, yet I do wrong to men in general in the most essential point of duty, so that it may be called a lie ..., that is, so far as in me lies I cause that declarations find no credit, and hence that all rights founded on contract should lose their force; and this is a wrong which is done to mankind.
>
> (1923: 362)

Here Kant is appealing to the same consideration that weighs with Augustine: how can any exception to the strict rule against lying be allowed and our trust in one another's word still be sustained? Thus, he says:

> Truthfulness is a duty that must be regarded as the basis of all duties founded on contract, the laws of which would be rendered uncertain and useless if even the least exception to them were admitted.
>
> (1923: 363)

The most convincing argument offered by both Kant and Augustine on why we need the strict teaching 'Never lie!' is quite simply the difficulty of writing in exceptions around which a firm line can be drawn. If a firm line cannot be drawn then trust will not be preserved, and the strict duty will collapse into a merely presumptive duty.

MacIntyre's norm: uphold truthfulness and truthful relationships

Alasdair MacIntyre objects to any modification of the strict rule against lying which takes the form 'Never lie except...'. As he urges, what is needed is some rule which both explains the norm *and* its exceptions. That way the slippery slope dangers are avoided (for if exceptions are just tacked on, there is no principled barrier to adding further exceptions under pressure). Moreover, as MacIntyre observes:

> The principle that permits or requires a lie must not be some independent principle, potentially in conflict with the principle forbidding lying, since, for reasons that Kant also makes clear, our moral principles must be a consistent set, consistent to this degree that they do not, in any situation that has occurred or will occur or may occur, prescribe incompatible actions, so that one or the other has to be modified in an *ad hoc* way.
>
> (1995: 350)

Accordingly, MacIntyre seeks to base both norm and exceptions on the duty to uphold truthfulness and truthful relationships:

> Uphold truthfulness in all your actions by being unqualifiedly truthful in all your relationships and by lying to aggressors only in order to protect those truthful relationships against aggressors, and even then only when lying is the least harm that can afford an effective defense against aggression.
>
> (1995: 357)

MacIntyre says that this duty requires that one is 'unqualifiedly truthful', which suggests that acting on this duty involves more than merely not telling lies or attempting to deceive: it suggests that the duty requires being informative and open as well. But while being informative and open may also be a duty, isn't it at any rate quite a different sort of duty from the duty not to lie? The duty not to lie, is a side-constraint type duty whereas the duty to be unqualifiedly truthful (informative) suggests an ideal that, arguably, it is one's duty to aim at. Duties that direct us to pursue ideals are aspirational: they do not dictate what we must or must not do on specific occasions. The duty not to lie is of a different kind: it belongs to the framework duties of justice within which we pursue our other duties and aims (like the regulatory rules of a game), including the aim or duty to *promote* truthfulness.

MacIntyre's rule allows one to lie to the murderer at the door, but does it do so for the right reason? He recounts the predicament of a Dutch housewife who during the Nazi occupation was sheltering a Jewish child whose parents had been arrested and sent to a death camp. 'Confronted by a Nazi official who asked her whether all the children living in her home were her own she lied' (1995: 352). Of course, MacIntyre wants to accommodate this lie. But in what sense would the woman be protecting a 'truthful relationship' – relationship with whom? With the child? The child might be an infant – would it even make sense then to talk of her relationship with it as 'truthful'? Perhaps, the thought is that only by lying is she able to be true to her word: she took the child in and in so doing assumed responsibility to protect it from harm. But doubtless Kant would insist that she would not be obliged even so to use any means whatever to protect it: he would not condone her recourse to a lie.

Kant aside, surely the simple truth is, the woman is justified in lying because doing so is necessary to protect someone whose most basic right – against murderous assault – is not acknowledged by the official. Yet if we say that the duty to protect life can override the duty not to lie, how are we to know when it does and when it doesn't, or what other duties, needs or concerns also can override the duty not to lie? How can we avoid the *ad hocery* to which MacIntyre rightly objects?

Korsgaard and the duty not to lie under ideal and non-ideal conditions

Christine Korsgaard seeks a way of softening Kant's 'rigourism' on the matter of lying,[1] while still being true to the spirit of Kant's ethical theory. She observes:

> One of the great difficulties with Kant's moral philosophy is that it seems to imply that our moral obligations leave us powerless in the face of evil.[2] Kant's theory sets a high ideal of conduct and tells us to live up to that ideal regardless of what other persons are doing. The results may be very bad.
>
> (1996: 133)

She illustrates her point with the famous example of Kant's stance regarding the murderer at your door.

Neither Kant nor the Utilitarians deal adequately with the murderer at your door scenario, according to Korsgaard. Kant is too unbending – never willing to compromise in the face of evil; the Utilitarians are too bending:

> The utilitarian wants to make everyone as happy as possible relative to the circumstances, and pursues this goal regardless of how unfriendly the circumstances are to human happiness.
>
> (1996: 149)

What is Korsgaard's solution? She argues that in non-ideal circumstances (when confronted with evil) you may be justified in departing from standards that are appropriate in ideal circumstances if you do so only in order to restore the ideal and provided that anyone else situated as you are would be equally justified in doing so. This 'double-level theory' (inspired by John Rawls' distinction between ideal and non-ideal theory in *A Theory of Justice*, 1971) would allow you to resist being made the 'tool of evil-doers' (the murderers at your door) by fending off their questions, with lies if need be. In non-ideal circumstances, Korsgaard suggests, the ideal, according to which everyone's autonomy is respected and no-one is ever used as the mere tool to further other people's purposes, becomes 'the goal' rather than 'what you live up to' (1996: 148).

> The formula of humanity [according to which we must treat people never as mere means and which, according to Korsgaard, therefore rules out lying] is inapplicable because it is not designed for use when dealing with evil. But it can still guide our conduct. It defines the goal toward which we are working… It gives us guidance about which of the measures we may take is the least objectionable.
>
> (1996: 151)

This solution to the 'murderer at your door' type problem seeks to meet Kant on his own ground. Kant's objection to lying to the murderer does not depend on some supposed right even of murderers to be told the truth, but on the evil you do yourself by telling a lie and the disrespect you show for another's autonomy. On Korsgaard's account these evils, the self-abuse element and the contempt for another's autonomy, is not lost sight of by the liar who only speaks falsely as a last resort and with a view to restoring the conditions under which treating people with basic respect (not lying to them or coercing them) is again possible.

Korsgaard's way of dealing with the murderer at the door does not involve tacking on an exception to the rule against lying. Rather it suggests that the kind of rule truthfulness requires alters if we are living under non-ideal conditions: the duty not to lie ceases to be a side-constraint type (perfect) duty and becomes a goal type (imperfect) duty. As soon as 'conditions permit', the duty reverts to being of the side-constraint type. Korsgaard's strategy provides a fundamental norm from which both types of duties derive. It avoids the *ad hocery* that MacIntyre deplores. The fundamental norm is to treat people with respect. Treating people with respect means not using them as 'tools', not bypassing their assent with the use of force or fraud. Any action which 'depends for its nature and efficacy on the other's ignorance or powerlessness fails the test' – fails to treat the other with the respect owed (1996: 139). If you are coerced or deceived into acting you are being used as if you were not able to make your own judgement: 'lying treats someone's reason as a tool' (1996: 141).[3] If you are caught up in evil circumstances, rather than allow yourself (or others?) to be the tool of evil doers, you may need to act in a non-ideal way in order to restore the ideal circumstances under which it is possible for people to refrain from lying without becoming the tool of evil-doers: 'In evil circumstances, but only then, the kingdom of ends can be a goal to seek rather than an ideal to live up to' (1996: 153).

Consider, though, the implications of Korsgaard's double-level theory, according to which the kind of duty we are under not to lie changes from side-constraint type to goal type when we face evil circumstances. This suggests that necessity legitimates if (though only if) our object is to get rid of evil circumstances. It sounds alarmingly like the sinister Brechtian teaching that lies and violence are necessary, hence morally defensible, to end lies and violence.

Just when are the conditions under which we live, or the circumstances that we find ourselves in, to be counted as sufficiently evil to justify our shifting from treating the duty not to lie as a side-constraint to treating it as a goal? The murderers who are bent on doing evil might be mad rather than bad. Are those circumstances no less non-ideal? The murderers might even be conscripts coerced into rounding up types deemed 'enemies' by the regime in power: *they* are being used as tools. Are we then justified in using them as tools, lying to them? Korsgaard only applies her theory to the murderer at your door scenario. But what are the implications for other evil circumstances in which we might find ourselves? Don't we typically only consider lying where we are under some necessity, where the conditions in which we find ourselves are non-ideal? I would not need to lie about my age to get an interview, were the interviewers not prejudiced. In an ideal world, interviewers would not be ageist. Suppose that my employers refuse to pay me the wage that I was promised (and I now realize they never intended to), may I steal back from them what is rightfully my own? Admittedly, in neither of these cases does it seem that my aim in lying or stealing is to bring back ideal conditions under which lying and stealing would not be necessary to avoid being used unjustly. Korsgaard stipulates that only if one's aim is to restore ideal conditions is it defensible to resort to lying under non-ideal conditions. Let us label this: the restoration motive.

I suggest that Korsgaard's double-level theory yields a rule which is either too lax or too rigorous. If the rule omits the restoration motive it is too lax. It pretty well allows us to lie our way out of difficulties which in a better world we would not face. If it includes that motive it is too rigorous. Is it plausible that lying to the murderer at the door will help to restore ideal conditions? Think of the Dutch housewife in MacIntyre example: is it credible that her lying will have helped one tiny bit to undermine the Nazi regime? Might that have been her motive? Should it have been?

The late Rabbi Grun told of how when he, in his early teens, arrived at one of the Nazi death camps, he was asked his age, and lied: consequently he was sent with the older men to the work camp while the women, children and the elderly were led straight off to the gas chambers. It is hard to imagine anyone finding themselves in circumstances more evil than that. But to make out that his lying was defensible, must we suppose that the child Grun lied *in order to* restore ideal conditions? Was it not enough that he wanted to save his skin? Is one only justified in lying to evil-doers if there is some prospect of ending their power therewith?

Moreover, if people are living under non-ideal conditions – under a tyranny, say, in which their basic rights are routinely not respected, in which lying, stealing and cheating are the only ways ordinary decent people have for meeting their basic living needs, is the aim of restoring ideal conditions a possible intention for them to have? They may wish for such conditions, pray for them, but bringing them about may be quite beyond their power. Are they then obliged to treat the duty not to lie as a strict side-constraint even in their dealings with their corrupt rulers? In short, doesn't the requirement that only if one lies with the restoration motive is one's lying defensible, leave us with a teaching against lying which is harsh – and unreasonably and improperly so?

Hobbesian realism in place of Rawlsian idealism

What moral rules, what standards, should we live by? Korsgaard's approach to this matter, like John Rawls', is 'top-down': the first step is to design rules that would suit an ideal world – a world in which there is no injustice – and only then to go on to consider how these rules need to be modified or adapted for the real world we inhabit, in which we are sometimes faced with injustice. In Rawls' Theory of Justice (1971) his focus of attention is upon the first project: to establish what is just in an ideal world – and Rawls says that he is not going to attempt to discuss the second project (what is just in a non-ideal world?) – except to discuss 'one fragment' (the problems of civil disobedience and conscientious refusal); and even then, mainly on the assumption that the real world is nearly ideal (1971: 351).

I propose that we adopt instead a 'bottom-up' approach – a more Hobbesian approach. Thomas Hobbes works out what justice means for us (what it is and why it matters) not by reflecting on the rules that would suit angels in heaven and then suggesting modifications to fit our imperfect selves and circumstances, but rather by reflecting on how a shared understanding of justice and commitment to it is needed to raise us up from the natural state of chaos and anarchy which would be our lot were we not willing and able to recognize and uphold general duties: duties, for example, curbing violence and fraud. In other words, Hobbes invites us to look down at what we would descend into without our notions of obligation, duty and justice: it is against that dismal backdrop that he sets forth the rules we need to live by. (Geoffrey Warnock's *The Object of Morality* (1971) is another instance of what I am calling the bottom-up approach.)

The Hobbesian approach can explain why we need to support trust and respect in our dealings with one another – hence, to have a strict teaching against lying – but it also explains why this teaching binds us only if it is reasonable to expect a reciprocity: that we are members of a community in which the most basic rights are respected and safeguarded. Absent such background conditions and our own compliance with duty, our own constraint in the matter of violence or fraud, ceases to make sense – except that we would have reason to do what we could to restore such conditions (to seek peace). In short, Hobbes argues that our obligations to refrain from lying, or stealing or deeds of violence all presuppose that we are protected, our rights against others are upheld:

> No man is supposed at the making of a Common-wealth, to have abandoned the defence of his life, or limbes, where the law cannot arrive time enough for his assistance.

(1909: 230)

Hobbes is not suggesting an exception to the strict rules against lying, stealing and so on. Rather his point is that the rules that define our general duties (some of which may be strict and others of which may be more discretionary in character) all presuppose we live under certain conditions – conditions under which it is rational to be bound, limited, in the means we may adopt in pursuit of our various aims. If we consider the alternative – discarding the self-imposed restraints – and the consequential chaos we would face if we did so, we can see that we are rational in continuing to be bound even though our rights are only imperfectly secured and we regularly suffer injustice. Only where we find that our vital interests are no longer safeguarded by the law or its officers is it rational, and defensible, for us to do whatever is necessary to save ourselves: 'When a man is destitute for food, or other things necessary for his life … it is no crime to steal' (1909: 232, cf.170).

Hobbes's account of moral obligation suggests how we can preserve the strictness of the duty not to lie and at the same time explain why the boy Grun was not acting wrongly *at all* when he lied to the Nazi officer. It is not that his duty to save himself outweighed his duty not to lie. It is not that necessity justified his choosing 'the lesser evil'. It is not that his duty to be truthful was no longer a side-constraint but merely something to which he aspired. Quite simply, he had no obligation, living under such conditions: he was within his rights: 'For the right men have by Nature to protect themselves, when none else can protect them, can by no Covenant be relinquished' (1909: 170). The inalienable right that Hobbes ascribes to us to defend ourselves must surely extend to our defence of one another. We seek peace and covenant with one another in order not just to achieve our own personal security but that of our families and comrades. Hence, we can justify the lie told by the Dutch housewife to protect her charge (MacIntyre's example).

What about other cases where a lie is told to save a life – Kant's example of lying to the murderer at your door, the case of Arria lying to her husband for fear the news about his son would kill him or Ed Viesturs lying to Rob Hall for fear that the truth would distract Hall from trying to save himself? Are all of these defensible lies? If so, is the strict teaching advocated by the likes of Augustine and Kant not, after all, one we should endorse?

In the light of our reflections on truthfulness what, then, should we teach about lying and about other ways of hiding the truth? The teaching will need to reflect our understanding of the importance of truthfulness and of how lying in particular endangers it. I have argued that provided we avoid defining lying to include all ways of attempting to hide truths, the undertaking never to lie is not an impossible one. But does truthfulness really require an unqualified repudiation of lying? So far we have studied the reasons why Augustine and Kant thought only a strict, non-discretionary teaching would serve. But before we endorse such a stand we had better think further about its implications – how such a strict teaching would apply to the hard cases and whether it is not wildly out of kilter with our intuitions.

5   The teaching we need to preserve truthfulness

Mr. Hale to Goody Proctor:
It is a mistaken law that leads you to sacrifice. Life, woman, life, is God's most precious gift; no principle, however glorious, may justify the taking of it. I beg you, woman, prevail upon your husband to confess. Let him give his lie. Quail not before God's judgement in this, for it may well be that God damns a liar less than he that throws away his life for pride.
Elizabeth:
I think this be the Devil's argument.

Arthur Miller's The Crucible

Quite obviously the rules or teachings we need depend on what purpose they are meant to serve. I take it that the purpose of moral teachings is to help make it possible for us to live tolerable lives, lives that are not wretched in ways that we can take steps to avoid. Thus, following in the tradition of philosophers such as Aristotle, Hobbes and Hume, we should take as our starting point familiar truths about human needs and circumstances (about what Warnock [1971], who also follows in this tradition, calls 'the human predicament'). Our aim in this study is to work out what teachings we need in regard to truthfulness. That we need any teachings at all on this matter is something that I have sought to establish by appealing to a couple of familiar truths: 1) that our lives would not go well at all if we could not trust one another and 2) that trust depends on truthfulness. I have also suggested that untruthfulness undermines respect as well as trust. Respect for others and for ourselves is also something we need if we are to fare well in life. The question of respect (what it is and why it matters) is something I have only gestured at. Even if that element is discounted, though, the connection between trust and truthfulness is surely quite enough on its own to explain the importance of truthfulness (why it is a virtue) and hence the need for a teaching that clarifies how we need to act to avoid untruthfulness.

So far, so good. What I have just said seems neither new nor contentious. But the account I have begun to give (in the last chapter) of what truthfulness requires does already part company with contemporary mainstream thinking on these matters. I have suggested that we can and, it seems, should, repudiate both trivial and serious lies: in other words, all lies. Mainstream thinking treats the duty not to lie as on a par with the duty to keep promises. Both are prima facie duties. Both permit one to exercise discretion in deciding whether in these or those particular circumstances one is actually bound not to lie or to keep a promise. We have considered why Augustine and Kant insist that a stricter teaching is necessary in regard to lying. They both treat the duty not to lie as non-discretionary.

Of course, a rule can be non-discretionary and yet have some exceptions built into it. The rule, 'Never move a pawn diagonally except when taking a piece with it' is as strict and non-discretionary as the rule: 'Never move a castle diagonally'. But if we introduce some exceptions into the rule against lying we face the *ad hocery* problem pointed up by MacIntyre – unless we can underpin the rule and the built in exceptions with some rationale that explains why there are just these exceptions and no more. Otherwise, there is no protection against other exceptions getting tacked on. Especially, because lies have to be deployed with stealth, a teaching which leaves us uncertain about what exceptions we and others are entitled to permit ourselves, seems doomed to self-destruct. We have considered some of the ways in which the rule against lying might be softened – for example: to permit trivial lies, or to permit lies that might save life, or to minimize harm. The problem with allowing exception to the rule on any of these or other grounds seems to be how to do so without unravelling our general intolerance of lying: how to avoid the *ad hocery*. It would appear that only a strict and exceptionless rule will serve.

This view, as I say, is not mainstream. Since its implications may be harsh, it is as well to pause and spell these out. Am I being overhasty in claiming that the rule against lying must apply without exception? Let us review the reasons for adopting such a stance and consider the implications for some of the hard cases we have touched on.

Trivial lies

Even so-called trivial lies, I have argued, should not be tolerated. (But, of course, we discount some untruths which are not rightly categorized as lying: untruths told in contexts where there is no intent to deceive.) Three objections to tolerating trivial lies have been made:

1 It is too difficult to judge whether the lie one wishes to tell is trivial – whether being denied the truth does not matter to or for the person to be duped;
2 There is too easy a slide from condoning lies which do no harm to lies which do minimal harm or do less harm than would otherwise occur;
3 Many suppose (wrongly) that a lie to spare distress which will not be discovered is harmless.

These objections might be treated as reason to advise caution in the use of trivial lies, rather than to ban them altogether. It may be argued that we should weigh against the risks pointed up in these objections, the benefits, the convenience in daily life, of permitting ourselves trivial lies. But this idea that we can soften the teaching we need to condone trivial lies underestimates the risks of doing so. Such a softening would not be safe – especially not so in respect of medical and nursing practice where sustaining trust is so very important. No doubt, many of the impulses to tell lies to or for patients are kindly meant, or anyway, not self-serving. But as I hope to show there are usually alternative ways of hiding truths from patients or for them that do not involve telling lies.

Serious lies

What should we say about serious (non-trivial) lies? The uncompromising position of Augustine and Kant in regard to serious lies is generally held to be excessively 'rigorous'? Does it require us to act in ways that offend against our intuitions and common sense? If it obliges us to 'tell the truth' to murderers at the door, Sisela Bok, for one, as we have noted, thinks it offends against both. If the teaching, 'Never tell (serious) lies!' yields absurdly strict results, we will need to look again at the assumptions on which it rests.

So far we have only found a way to justify the telling of lies by (and for) people who are being denied their basic rights – who are treated as non-persons (as the Jews were by the Nazis). Lying is defensible in such cases, but in so saying we do not need to modify the strict exceptionless rule against lying. Rather, we acknowledge that the rules of justice, including the rule against lying, apply only to those who are protected by them: they presuppose a reciprocity of obligations. What about the other hard cases we have mentioned? Can we apply the Hobbesian defence for the lie told by Grun to justify any of these lies – and, if not, should we still stand by the strict teaching?

The other hard cases we mentioned fall into the following categories: lying to spare someone distress (the lies told to Thuiller and to Berlin's father); lying to save life (the lies told to Rob Hall and to Caecinna Paetus) and lying to protect an innocent life against an aggressor (the murderer at one's door). Let us consider lies of these three kinds: should exception be made for any of them?

Lying to spare people distress

There is no question of saving life here – only of withholding information that would distress deeply the enquirer. Some people may say that the lies told to Thuiller and to Berlin's father were harmless. Did these men need to know the truth? Would it have benefited them in any way to hear it? If it would only make them miserable, why tell them? While I would agree that such considerations might justify an evasive answer, I do not agree that they would justify lying. These lies were not harmless because the information sought, however distressing, mattered to the enquirers – or probably mattered. If it did not, an evasive answer might well have persuaded the enquirers to leave off asking.

Admittedly, even granted that these lies did harm it may be true that the harm was a lesser harm than the truth would have been. This might be reason for regarding the lies to be considered in themselves as defensible. But the teaching we need to live by in regard to lies cannot tolerate exceptions being made for these grounds: to spare people distress or to prevent (greater) harm. To allow exceptions to the rule against lying on these grounds would render the rule entirely flabby and inadequate. The fact that considered in themselves the acts may have been preventing harm is beside the point. It is not a fact that should lead us to modify the rule against lying.

Lying to save a life

What about the examples of Hall and Paetus? It was feared that these men would die if they were told the truth. They were in desperate straits. But they were victims of misfortune, not injustice. Is that relevant? The Hobbesian defence for Grun's lie is not that he rightly puts his own survival before truthfulness but that truthfulness cannot be obligatory on him given that he is being denied his basic rights. Thus though Paetus and Hall might also only be saved by a lie, one cannot justify lying to them by an extension of the argument used to justify Grun's lie. The reason that Paetus and Hall are imperilled has nothing to do with a failure of the state or its officials to respect or safeguard their basic rights.

But isn't a lie, even a serious lie, a small price to pay to save a life? If we consider the particular act and the reason for doing it, it seems wholly reasonable and defensible. Still, reasons for actions are always precedents for like actions in like circumstances. How can we justify exceptions being made to rescue these men with a lie without thereby committing ourselves to a teaching that permits exceptions elsewhere – where a life is in peril – or something else equally, possibly more, important?

Lying to assailants

The Hobbesian defence for lying might seem to cover this kind of case at least. But the matter deserves careful study. Even making an exception to allow lying to the murderer at one's door sets a precedent. If that lie is justified, why not the lie told to Rob Hall – and so on? Bok argues that we need not see this one exception as subversive to the strict rule: the occasion is so isolated – how rarely will anyone be confronted with such a case! She concludes: 'There would be very little risk, therefore, of such a lie contributing in any way to a spreading deceptive practice' (1978: 109). Yet she herself notes how our attitude to the liar might vary depending on the degree of violence threatened by the aggressor, the degree of innocence of the one pursued, and the liar's relationship to the one pursued. The particular case of persecutors hunting down one's innocent friend may seem a very clear case where protective lying would be defensible. Even so, consider the implications for other cases that are similar but not quite the same.

Suppose the aggressor is your sister's ex-husband. He is angry, maybe drunk, but clearly dangerous. If you are justified in lying to protect her life then, are you equally justified to protect her if it is evident that he is not intent on murder but on giving her a beating? If lying then too is justified, what if he has come simply to shout verbal abuse – he does not try to enter your house just stands outside shouting – but you could get rid of him by telling him she is not there? Now the justification for the lie has dwindled maybe to your wish not to have your sleep disturbed – and that of your neighbours. Where can a firm and non-arbitrary line be drawn between the justifiable defensive or protective lie and the unjustifiable?

Bok argues that a policy of 'lying to persecutors seeking innocent victims' is one we could publicly advocate without undermining people's respect for veracity. She says that:

> Someone who advocated the opposite policy of total honesty to persecutors would be a dangerous individual in times where life-and-death crises arise more frequently; one who could be trusted with no confidential information at all.
>
> (1978: 109–10)

But notice that those who reject the former policy need not espouse the latter. (Notice too how describing the rigourists' stance as 'Always tell the truth!', rather than as 'Never lie!', encourages just this confusion.) To refuse to lie to murderers is not the same as to insist on giving them the information they seek. As we have already noted, neither Augustine nor Kant advocate 'total honesty' if that is supposed to include revealing confidences.

Is lying defensible wherever the use of force is?

Bok also claims that 'Wherever it is right to resist an assault or a threat by force, it must be allowable to do so by guile' (1978: 144; cf. 41, 109, 213). 'Guile' implies intent to deceive, perhaps with a lie, perhaps not. Since I am concerned here only to uphold a strict teaching against lying, let us narrow Bok's claim to the claim that where one has a right to resist by force one has a right to resist with a lie. Bok does not *argue* for this view: perhaps it seems too obvious to need defending. I suggest that the thought behind it is that lying and using force are unprincipled, objectionable and wrongful in the same way: that they – are 'manipulative', they violate another's autonomy. Now if in certain circumstances the duty to respect autonomy is overridden by some other duty, then the principled objection to using force or lying does not apply: how in the circumstances to fulfil the overriding duty, whether by force or with a lie, can be decided simply on pragmatic grounds.

Suppose, for example, that I have had some drinks and am now minded to drive home in my car. You realise that I am in no fit state to drive. You try to dissuade me but I will not listen to reason. While normally you have no right to stop me driving, under the circumstances where I am a danger to myself and others you are within your rights stopping me. Bok would say, if you are justified in forcibly intervening you are justified in thwarting my purpose with a lie. Perhaps I am looking for my car keys and ask if you know where I have put them and you, knowing very well, say 'No!' In such circumstances, lying might seem a sensible, better way of thwarting my will – less hurtful to all concerned than would be a recourse to the use of brute force.

If the only objection to lying were how it violates people's autonomy this argument would be persuasive. But we have seen that the duty not to lie is not dependent on other people's entitlement to hear the truth. You would not be wronging *me* by lying to me to stop me driving. You would not be violating my autonomy. Still it does not follow that your lying would be morally permissible in this case. Again, we need to think about the effect on trust if this were to be our teaching: 'Only lie to people who have no right to know what they want to know!' We have already discussed this way of restricting the duty not to lie and have found it wanting.

Bok is keenly alert to the problem of working out a teaching that is adequate to sustain our respect for veracity. Her solution to the 'problem of expanding deceptive practices' is not to advocate an exceptionless rule, but to urge rather that we subject our practices and policies to what she calls (after Rawls) a 'publicity test'. Thus she maintains that respect for veracity would not be threatened if we made public our readiness to lie to persecutors hunting down victims. Yet she also notices how even this exception may be expanded:

> In principle, then, both deception and violence find a narrow justification in self-defense against enemies. In practice, however, neither can be contained within these narrow boundaries; they end up growing, perpetuating themselves, multiplying and feeding on one another, to produce the very opposite of increased safety. Constant effort must, therefore, be made to contain them and to limit their scope.
>
> (1978: 145)

Excuses and justifications

Even if there is no way to justify some exceptions to a strict rule that does not undermine the rule, should we still defend the lies told to the murderer at one's door and the lie told to Rob Hall and to Caecinna Paetus. Faced with such a situation who would fret about the precedent being set? Shouldn't our sympathies go all the way with those who told these lies? Can we consistently sympathize with these liars yet stick by the strict teaching which forbids their telling? We need here to distinguish the wrongness of the act from the blameworthiness of the actor. What is done may not be justified, may be wrong, yet the doer *wholly* excused from blame.

It might sound odd to suppose that someone who (knowingly) does what is wrong can be blameless – especially if we say *in advance* that if you were in such and such a situation and lied you would be doing wrong but you would not be at all to blame. Take for example the rule against perjury. Perjury is a criminal offence – no exceptions; but if someone perjures himself and it turns out he was acting under duress – his life was being threatened by gangsters – the law may excuse him, acquit him. Even so the law does not say that what he *did* was not wrong. And we can see why the law is unwilling to write an exception into the strict prohibition on perjury: if duress became a justification for perjury, it would rather invite people to apply duress on witnesses! As the saying has it: 'Hard cases make bad law'.

Just as we do not blame a bank-teller for handing over money at gunpoint – we do not think in the circumstances that the bank-teller shows any failure of virtue – so we may consider that Arria was not to be blamed for lying to Paetus, nor Ed Viesturs for lying to Rob Hall. Their lies may be wholly excused, though we do not for that reason see fit to modify our strict teaching.

Lying in self (or others') defence

Perhaps, though, I have exaggerated the difficulties of drawing a firm line once any exceptions are built into the strict rule. After all, the law makes an exception to the strict duty we are under as private citizens not to kill: self-defence is a justification, not merely an excuse. If the law is able to draw a firm line around this defence, why can't we expect to do so likewise in respect of the duty not to lie? Should we not at least allow lying to be justified where it is necessary to defend life and limb? Isn't Bok right to insist that such a policy if publicized would not undermine trust within our society? Hobbes insists that 'No man is obliged (when the protection of the Law faileth) not to protect himself, by the best means he can' (1909: 232). Not to defend oneself would be irrational. How can morality oblige us to act irrationally?

If, though, we introduce just this exception to the strict duty: that we are justified in lying in self (or others') defence, it is crucially important that the reason behind this exception is understood, and that the scope of this extension is well-defined. Thus, it needs to be made clear that the reason behind making this exception is not that we are entitled to lie to defend ourselves against any and every kind of unjust treatment. Nor does it entitle us to lie to fend off enquirers just because they have no right to know. Nor does it rely on the idea that wherever use of force would be justified so too is lying.

The two kinds of situations that I have now allowed – where lying is justified – both concern occasions where the liar is bereft of the usual background conditions of reciprocity and protection which account for the bindingness of general moral obligations. The general duty we are under not to use force or fraud presupposes that we live in a community in which such duties are generally recognized and upheld. That was no longer the case for Grun. He had no general duty given his situation to refrain from lying. If you should open your door to an assailant, you might also be cut off from the protection of the law and its officers, and hence entitled to defend yourself and others. This right would not extend to justifying your lying in other situations where you are being treated unjustly by a fellow citizen, since it is only where there is a direct threat to life and limb that you are cut off from effective protection of the state. In short, the general obligations we owe one another, including the duty not to lie, presuppose a background of reciprocity and state protection. Absent that background, as it may be absent in times of civil war, under a tyranny, or even, rarely, if you are suddenly confronted by a direct and violent threat, and the general obligations no longer apply.

We do not need, then, to modify the strict teaching, 'Never lie!', even though we grant that some lies are justified – like Grun's lie and the lie to the murderer at the door. We should not think of these lies as justified *exceptions* to the rule. Rather, we should recognize that our moral teachings about the general duties we owe one another – what truthfulness requires of us – are put forward on the understanding that those at whom they are directed enjoy certain basic rights and protection against injustice. The teachings are not supposed to apply only to those who live in an ideal world. But they do presuppose certain background conditions – the reasonable expectation of protection against assault.

Deception

I have been defending a strict teaching against lying. Intentionally concealing truths from people (by other means than lying), I have argued, is not necessarily an indication of untruthfulness. Indeed, it is sometimes one's duty to keep truths concealed – even from those we trust. Of course, intentional concealment (even, pretence) need not, and often does not, involve intentional deception. Intentional deception implies the aim to get someone to believe what is false. As we have already remarked, often one's aim in concealing is merely to prevent others from discovering a truth. (Recall our examples: you put on a loose pullover to disguise how thin you have become. You need not here aim to cause friends to think 'How frail she has become!' merely to prevent their noticing this. You wear dark glasses so that you can get about town without everyone recognizing you and stopping you to chat. You do not here aim to cause anyone to think 'That person is *not* my GP'.)

What, though, should we teach about words and deeds that are intended to deceive but that do not involve lying? Is the trust that truthfulness preserves as threatened by our deceptive tricks and words that do not involve actual lying as by lying? I suggest that intentional deception is *not* a bad kind of act – unlike lying. As with any kind of action that is sometimes all right and sometimes not, deceiving is always going to be bad if done from a bad motive. Spitting is not a bad kind of action. Spitting when brushing your teeth is entirely innocent. But spitting to insult is another matter. On the other hand, a good motive does not necessarily make an action which is neither good nor bad in itself a good action. Concealing, for example, is in itself neither good nor bad. Suppose you conceal my wallet from me in order to steal its contents to give to a good cause. What you do is wrong not because it involves concealing but because it involves stealing. It is wrong in spite of the good motive.

A very familiar type of intentional deception that is generally considered to be all right, is the deception that is part and parcel of many games – including those we compel our children to learn to play at school. In tennis we try to trick our opponent into scurrying to the wrong corners. In many games wrong-footing our opponents with deceptive moves is part of the art of the game – what we are taught to admire. Admittedly, there are some games in which lying, too, is a permitted strategy. Even so, it is noteworthy that we do not teach these games in schools nor give prizes to those who are outstandingly good at them.

It might seem that our tolerance of deception in games is no good reason for supposing that we do not think intentional deception to be presumptively wrong *outside* of the game-playing context. After all, people know when they are taking part in these kinds of game and that what is allowed in that special context need not be allowed elsewhere. But notice, deception is not simply put up with in these games – it is the essence of them. In teaching our children these games and hero-worshipping those who excel at them, we show that we admire, and want them to emulate, skilful deception.

Fine distinctions

To some moralists any conceptual differences there are between lying, deceiving by other means, concealing and pretending are from a moral standpoint, petti-fogging. They suppose that someone who was wholly truthful would not act in any of these ways. They observe, however, that no-one is wholly truthful, 'totally honest'. We all pretend and conceal regularly. That, it is said, already demonstrates the inevitability and the necessity of being untruthful. What we cannot help but do, cannot be wrong. Moreover, pretending and concealing even when it is avoidable is sometimes admirable and virtuous. Truthfulness should, therefore, only be advocated in a qualified way. In a better world, it is often supposed, we would not need to pretend, conceal or deceive, but in the world as it is, we sometimes, maybe often, have to do these things.

This way of thinking seems to me riddled with error. Concealing and pretending are indeed part of the fabric of life, but they need not involve any deceit. Hence we should not so quickly assume that it is impossible to live without continually being deceitful. Robert Solomon observes: 'One cannot imagine getting through an average budget meeting or a cocktail party speaking the truth, the whole truth, and nothing but the truth'(1993: 33). That is, of course, true, but it does not follow that one cannot get through either without telling any lies, or even without inten-tionally deceiving anyone. It only seems necessary and unavoidable to deceive or lie if we do not make distinctions between different ways of obscuring or hiding truths. As I have defined deceiving and lying, both involve intending to make someone believe something that is false. This specific intention is not pervasive and unavoidable in all our social dealings. Moreover, we need to take note that talking with people has other perfectly proper and innocent purposes besides the exchanging of information. If we conducted ourselves at cocktail parties as if this were the sole, or main point of conversation, we would soon run out of invitations.

We have noted how common it is for people to lump together the various ways in which truth is deliberately concealed, as if however it is done it demonstrates a lack of truthfulness. We conceal truths from one another all the time, often reasonably, but since virtues are by definition traits that we can acquire and need to acquire, a trait that stops us concealing truths from each other could not be a virtue. We would neither be better nor be better off if we became completely transparent in our thoughts, attitudes and intentions to one another. Hence truthfulness does not require such transparency of us, nor even that we aim at it as a worthy ideal. Truthfulness requires virtually always that we do not lie. Sometimes it requires more of us: that we do not deceive, maybe also that we do not conceal or pretend –

and sometimes we have a duty to reveal – maybe, routinely so, in certain medical and nursing contexts.

There are many occasions when people deceive or conceal by word or deed in circumstances that are subversive of trust and are indefensible. The point is that it is not under this description, that what one is doing is deceiving or concealing, that it is subversive of trust. Still the same action which is deceiving may be a betrayal of one's word – because, for example, one has promised not to deceive about the matter in hand. Going for a walk *by yourself* is not under *that* description unjust – if you promised not to go without me, that is another matter!

Though deception which does not involve lying is not a bad kind of action *per se*, that is not to say that those who take trouble to deceive without actually lying earn some credit on that account. Where it is wrong to deceive, going out of one's way to avoid doing so with a lie may not in anyway mitigate the wrong. Where, though, the deceiving is not wrong in itself, going out of one's way to avoid lying suggests honesty of character – as in the case of Fred Vincy in George Eliot's *Middlemarch*. When tetchy old Featherstone tells Fred Vincy not to bring any more books to Mary Garth, Featherstone's young much put-upon house-keeper, because, says Featherstone, he 'cannot abide to see her reading to herself', he says to Fred: 'You mind and not bring her any more books, do you hear?' to which Fred replies, 'Yes, sir, I hear'. Eliot observes: 'Fred had received this order before, and had secretly disobeyed it. He intended to disobey it again'. We can admire Fred's careful choice of words – it is an indication of his honesty that he makes a point of avoiding making a false promise. But we only admire such careful attempts to avoid lying in concealing one's intentions where the concealment is not itself base.

A credible teaching?

To uphold truthfulness, I am claiming, we need to adopt a strict rule against lying: trivial as well as serious. We should say, that is, that everyone is under a duty not to lie – a duty that is not merely prima facie - a duty that allows no exceptions. Yet this general duty is one that we are bound by only if certain background conditions obtain. We have general duties towards one another on the understanding that we are members of a community and that there is a reciprocity of obligation (each of us refrains from uses of force and fraud on the understanding that this is a shared commitment within the community). Moreover, we are bound by these general duties on the assumption that the community provides us with protection against injustice – so that we do not need to settle scores on our own behalf, by having recourse to force or fraud.

There is, though, no such general duty, not even a prima facie duty, requiring us not to conceal, pretend or deceive (in ways that do not involve lying). Concealing, pretending and deceiving where lying is not involved are not *in themselves* subversive of trust.

On this account someone who is truthful repudiates lying – except in Grun type situations or when faced with the murderer at the door. But this same person can be expected to favour concealing, pretending and deceiving on many occasions without a second thought or twinge of conscience. Such an account is out of line with what is usually written about truthfulness (especially with the literature on the topic in medical ethics). It will be condemned as too strict on lying and far too lax on other ways of deceiving, and on pretending and concealing. Maybe there are special reasons for modifying this teaching for doctors, nurses and other health professionals. We will pursue that question in the chapters to come. But is it a teaching that can be commended as part of ordinary morality: for example, what we should teach our children?

Consider, first, whether children should be told 'Never lie!'. Is that an unreasonable, over-demanding thing to tell them? If what they are actually told is 'Always tell the truth!' it might be: because they might take that to mean that they must never deceive or conceal and that is indeed absurdly and unreasonably restrictive. They will straightaway notice that their parents conceal truths from them and from others and often with a clear conscience. So how can the advice never to conceal be serious?

To be sure, the teaching 'Never lie!' is not altogether self-explanatory. Children need help learning what is a lie and what is not. They will need to understand that certain expressions are mere conventional forms of politeness. They will also need to learn the difference between promises that are not kept but were sincerely made and those that are not kept and were never intended to be kept: the latter kind of promising, is a kind of lie.

What about teaching children that concealing and deceiving which does not involve lying (like being evasive, telling half-truths, using deceptive tricks) are not even presumptively bad? This might sound a quite shockingly lax thing to tell children. It positively invites them to be devious and crafty! I would suggest that this only sounds perverse if one assumes that deviousness and craftiness are characteristically used from bad motives. Is that a reasonable assumption? Do not parents routinely use deviousness and craftiness to get their young children to eat up their food, pick up their clothes, and go (back) to bed? Imagine what a trial bringing up children would become if one took seriously the notion that truths should not be concealed from them – that any concealing or any deviousness towards them violates a prima facie duty. Or would parents who did suppose themselves under such a prima facie duty not see it necessary to behave any differently from those who did not: wouldn't they always be able to justify overriding the duty not to conceal by appealing to their duty of care? Perhaps, though, those parents who considered themselves under a prima facie duty not to conceal or deceive would expect the necessity of doing so to be something temporary – that would only be necessary while their children were little.

The reality, I suggest, is that we never outgrow the need to use deception and concealment in our dealings with one another, including, perhaps, most especially, with those who are nearest and dearest. Nor should we assume that characteristically we use these strategies with bad motives or that if we were more virtuous we would have less recourse to them. Concealment and deception are not just a source of delight in sport, they also have a significant role in theatre and the arts, and in humour. Far from parents doing their children a service by teaching them that concealment and deception are bad kinds of action, that teaching, were it heeded, would debar the children from many innocent and worthwhile pursuits – even maybe from making and keeping friends. Learning how to conceal and deceive and how to detect others doing the same is an important part of juvenile education.

How, though, can children learn to trust their parents or parents their children if deceiving and concealing are not discouraged? My claim is that these stratagems are not in themselves subversive of trust – unlike lying. Children still need to be taught to be truthful – not to lie – since truthfulness is a virtue. Of course, they also need to learn other virtues – kindness, fairness, courage and so on. Otherwise, they will be using concealment and deception in morally indefensible ways – in selfish, cheating or cowardly ways. In such a case it will not be the concealment or deception *per se* that is objectionable but the use to which these stratagems are put.

Even if concealment, pretence and deception (not involving lying) are not subversive of trust, are they not incompatible with the respect we owe one another? Is there something essentially demeaning about the use of these strategies? Does using these strategies on someone demonstrate a kind of contempt for them? Why should it? Do parents show contempt for their infants when they play games of peek-a-boo with them? If they make a game of necessary routines, to persuade a reluctant child, are they showing less respect than if they were simply to inform the child of what it would be prudent or civil for the child to do?

No doubt the most contentious part of the teaching that I am advocating is the claim that intentional deception is not even presumptively bad. Concealing is one thing; intentional deception, quite another. Surely, there is something at least presumptively bad about trying to get someone to believe what is false. Charles Fried thinks so. He maintains that it is wrong to 'falsify truth' whether one is out to deceive oneself or someone else:

> This is because a free and rational person wishes to have a certain relation to reality as nearly perfect as possible. He wishes to build his conception of himself and the world and his conception of the good on the basis of truth.
>
> (Fried 1978: 66)

Is it so obvious though that the more informed we are the more free and rational we are able to be? If we could have a genetic print-out to tell us what diseases we are likely to succumb to, would that make us more free and rational? Does it not depend very much what we are informed of as to whether the knowledge increases or decreases our freedom and ability to act rationally? We have already noted that the wise are not omnivorous in their truth-seeking.

Perhaps, though, it is somewhat simple-minded to suppose that a teaching 'Never lie!' can stand quite alone. Does it not need shoring up with a discouragement against at least verbal manoeuvres that are intentionally deceptive? In the Hitchcock film *The Trouble with Harry* one of the characters proposes a certain evasive reply as something that can be said 'without cutting the hem off truth's garment'. Truthfulness, maybe, needs a hem around the duty not to lie, especially since what should count as a lie is not something that is firmly understood or agreed. Hence, we should at least be on our guard about intentionally deceptive communications – they are not as innocuous in themselves as is going for a walk. On the other hand, we do not have a general prima facie duty to avoid them. Casual deceiving may be counselled against. We need not force all moral reasons or considerations into the category of duties. A counsel does not oblige but it does give guidance.

Implications of this teaching for medical ethics

We have studied what truthfulness is, why it matters and what it involves, and the implications for what teaching we should adopt in life generally – what, for example, we should teach our children. Let us now return to our particular interest, which is to work out what teaching in regard to truthfulness is appropriate for health professionals. Is the teaching that I have argued we need to adopt in life generally precisely the teaching that doctors and nurses should adopt? If not, how should it be modified and why?

The teaching I am advocating is conspicuously not the teaching one finds in texts on medical ethics. The mainstream view in the medical ethics literature is softer on lying and harder on concealing, pretending and deceiving. The duty not to lie is often held to be more strictly binding than the duty not to deceive (in other ways) – but all the same, it is held to be a prima facie duty. Doctors and nurses, it is said, have to lie, ought to lie, sometimes.[1] On the other hand, it is virtually always made out that there is a strong presumption against other deceiving words and deeds (not involving lying) and even against concealing and pretending that involves no deception. Health professionals are said to have a duty to inform. Of course, where one *is* under such a duty, one has no business concealing information, let alone intentionally deceiving.

6 Doctors and nurses as 'caring pragmatists'

> I deny the lawfulness of telling a lie to a sick man for fear of alarming him. You have no business in consequences ....You are to tell the truth ....of all lying I have the greatest abhorrence of this because I believe it has frequently been practiced on myself.
>
> Samuel Johnson

Thurstan Brewin urges that doctors and nurses need to be caring pragmatists and not to fall for the ethicists' 'high-sounding ethical principles' (1993: 162). The pragmatist, says Brewin, gives 'wise advice and sound decisions in particular circumstances'. Brewin suspects that ethical rules 'lead to mental laziness' and that 'abstract ethical principles that are too 'firm' may 'inhibit the careful weighing of all the pros and cons, so necessary before coming to a wise pragmatic decision' (1993: 162). Doesn't the rule 'Tell the truth!' have precisely this damaging effect? He deplores 'rigid' adherence to 'total truth-telling' regardless of the particular needs of patients, the advice of relatives and the judgement of doctors and nurses. He blames this rigidity on the baneful intrusion of 'academic ethics' into medical education – by which he means medical ethics taught by non-medics. This intrusion is not just unhelpful, it is positively harmful. He illustrates this specifically with reference to the typically uncompromising stance on truth-telling that he says is adopted in academic ethics (1993: 162). This, he protests, 'May make young doctors and nurses feel guilty when, for example, instinct, common sense, and compassion all tell them not to go too far with truth-telling ...' (1993: 162).

While I have a deal of sympathy with Brewin's grouse about this teaching on the matter of truthfulness, I (being myself an 'academic ethicist') do not think so well of his solution – of banishing the ethicists. Rather, I think, his complaint points up the need for a more thorough, probing, study of truthfulness, what it involves and the implications for medical and nursing practice: the very purpose of our present enquiry! If the teaching that (some) academic ethicists advocate yields absurd guidance (as becomes apparent to those who see what happens when their colleagues try to 'apply' it), there must be something amiss with the teaching or with how it is being interpreted.

As we have already noted, the very expression 'Tell the truth!' invites oversimplification and muddle. Howard Brody observes that: 'Most real-life cases [concerning what to tell patients] are not simple choices between two radical alternatives which are labeled "Tell the truth!" and "Tell a lie!"' (Brody 1983: 82). Whether or not Brody is right depends on how one interprets the expression: 'Tell the truth!' If one means by it 'Do not lie!' then the two alternatives are exhaustive: either you are lying or you are not. But if one means by it 'Fully inform!' then there are, indeed, many alternatives to *that* which do not involve lying – and which need not involve any dishonesty, any failure of truthfulness. The alternative to being 'totally truthful' meaning by this, hiding nothing, is not necessarily being more or less untruthful. Because of the ambiguity inherent in 'Tell the truth!' I suggest that we should try to avoid using this phrase.

Discussions of truthfulness in the medical ethics literature, though, focus very much on 'truth-telling'. 'How truthful should doctors or nurses be?' is typically taken to be a question primarily about how much information should be disclosed to patients (or relatives). The focus of attention is thus on information management – which is, indeed, an important issue. One consequence of this approach is that the particular issue as to whether or when lying is defensible is likely to get side-lined. After all, if doctors and nurses do have a general duty to inform, doing anything short of that is disreputable: be it lying, deceiving, concealing or simply, not disclosing. Hence, fine distinction drawing between lying and other ways of deceiving will already sound irrelevant and suspect. Where their duty is to inform – be open – the duty not to lie is simply one of a set of derivative duties from that general duty. Why then would they be interested in drawing fine distinctions between lying, deceiving and concealing except with a view to evading their responsibilities?

It might sound as if the standards of truthfulness upheld in the medical ethics literature these days are high – far above the bottom line rule that would proscribe lying only. But the next step that is taken in explaining what truthfulness requires of doctors and nurses is to emphasize that the duty to inform – like many (if not all) other duties is only a prima facie duty: sometimes other duties override this one and the doctor or nurse may then be morally obliged to conceal information, possibly with a deceptive trick, possibly with a lie. The net result: less deceiving and concealing, but more lying. By this, I mean: those who accept this line on truthfulness – that they are under a prima facie duty to inform (and that is *why* it may be wrong to lie or deceive or conceal) – will, on the one hand, be circumspect about deceiving and concealing, not just about lying, but will, on the other hand, routinely find it 'necessary' to do all three. If all three are ranked alongside one another as prima facie objectionable for the same reason (violating the duty to inform), then a rigid teaching, against lying only, becomes a nonsense. If the duty not to lie, like the duties not to deceive or conceal, is simply derivative from the duty to inform, and the duty not to lie is a strict, exceptionless duty, then the duties not to deceive or conceal must be so too and the duty to inform must itself be 'absolute'. But, of course, nobody thinks this!

Since being 'totally truthful' (concealing nothing, disclosing all) is so obviously an absurd thing to advocate, the notion that one should take a strict line about lying is dismissed as ludicrously off beam. The idea of being uncompromising about truthfulness is discredited. Brewin observes:

> Let us be honest: hardly anyone – relative, partner, nurse, or doctor – sticks rigidly to total truth-telling. There is often something held back, just as there is in ordinary life. Those who make a point of telling their neighbours everything they 'have a right to know' about what is going on around them will not usually be congratulated on their impeccable ethics.
>
> (1993: 162)

In similar vein, John Lantos observes:

> A certain amount of lying, or at least of hypocrisy, seems to be part of every child's moral education, a part of what it means to be a civilized human being, and certainly a part of what it means to be a doctor.
>
> (1997: 84)

Brewin and Lantos are here supposing that being 'totally' truthful implies volunteering unvarnished truths to all and sundry. They are confusing truthfulness with candour. These are distinct concepts. We have seen that if candour is a virtue, it is, at least, a *different* virtue. So many discussions of what truthfulness involves get off on the wrong foot by scrambling together truthfulness and candour. Maureen Mancuso *et al.*, for example, talking about whether people in public life have a right to privacy in matters personal (like, whether the prime minister or president smoked pot when a student) say: 'The principle of privacy requires that some things remain off limits; the principle of honesty demands forthright and unwavering candour. At a certain point these principles inevitably clash' (1998: 163). But honesty does not demand candour. Abe Lincoln was admired for his honesty – he was called 'honest Abe' – *and* for his wiliness.

'Truth-telling' has become a prominent issue in medical ethics because of the move to rid medical and nursing practice of paternalism. While such paternalism continues to prevail in some countries, in many 'Western' countries, there has been what John Lantos describes as a 'sea-change' in medical and nursing practice.(1997: 86) He sees the demand on doctors nowadays 'to tell the truth' as something which has been largely imposed from outside the profession, by changes in the law. Of course, the changes in law have been buttressed by moral arguments concerning autonomy and, relatedly, the right to know.

Lantos also points up some of the changes *within* medicine that have led to the 'sea-change' in regard to the sharing of information with patients. He mentions four (Lantos 1997: 86–9)

1 That doctors nowadays may know a patient is sick (or soon will be) before the patient has an inkling;
2 That treatments can be toxic and risky: it is only fair that patients are forewarned;

3 That a range of options of varying effectiveness and with different side-effects may be available where which would be most appropriate for a particular patient may depend on that person's circumstances and personal preferences;

4 That clinical research is deemed to be a high priority and many patients are recruited to trials.

The upshot of all these changes within medicine and the pressures from without has been a general movement towards more and more disclosure. Presumably, in so far as these factors are explanatory, we can expect to see medical and nursing practice undergoing the same changes elsewhere where these features develop. Antonella Surbone points to indications that this is happening in Italy (1992).

From patients' viewpoint, though, this trend may be a mixed blessing: there is a trade-off between informing the patient and benefiting the patient. Thurstan Brewin remarks that 'telling all possible side-effects protects doctors against litigation but does not always serve the patient best' (1996: 66). Lantos says:

> As doctors, we usually inform patients of some but not all of the risks of an antibiotic before we prescribe it, or some but not all of the things that a blood test might reveal before we order it. We may exaggerate the expected benefits of treatment if we want people to consent to it or exaggerate the harms if we do not.
>
> (1997: 84)

This, of course, is medical paternalism – just what the law has sought to curb. Lantos acknowledges that doctors have 'embraced' the concept of informed consent. From a risk management standpoint, disclosure is now essential – to avoid being sued. But from an ethical standpoint, does disclosure mean sharing the burden of knowledge and responsibility or off-loading it? Lantos:

> If we tell patients about bad outcomes and they consent, then they are responsible, not us. Rather than a way of sharing power, truth telling and the process of seeking consent has become a way of evading accountability.
>
> (1997: 89–90)

Be that as it may, the prevailing view to be found in present-day medical ethics literature on truthfulness suggests a very different teaching from the one that I have argued should be adopted in life generally. It suggests that health professionals have prima facie duties not to lie or deceive or conceal, and that these duties are all derivative from the duty to inform. The duty to inform is itself derivative: from the basic duties to provide care and to respect patients' autonomy. Patients are said to need to know, to fare better if kept in the picture and able to participate meaningfully in decisions about their treatment. Patients are also said to have a right to know, to make their own choices about their own lives. Of course, while the need and the right may often pull in the same direction, sometimes they do not. Sometimes, patients exercising their 'right' will refuse what they need (unless the information they are given is somewhat 'doctored'). Hence, health professionals will regard the duty to provide care and to respect autonomy as both prima facie and potentially in conflict. Thus, while on this view concealing, deceiving and lying are all three presumptively wrong, the presumption may be overruled in particular situations.

Now the teaching we need in life generally, I have argued, is very different. We need to adopt a strict rule against lying. As for deceiving without telling lies or other secretive acts, we do not need to adopt a rule proscribing these, though there is some sense in counselling against casual deceiving. Even if that is the teaching we should adopt in life generally, what we should teach our children and aim to adopt ourselves, is it a suitable teaching for health professionals? Or do their duties require some modifications: more flexibility on lying, less on deceiving and concealing? Trust and respect are surely every bit as important in medical and nursing practice as elsewhere in life. All the same, maybe what being truthful involves in the context of patient care is somewhat different.

Let us now consider what the effect would be for patients if doctors and nurses were to follow the teaching on truthfulness that I have been advocating. In this chapter we will study what it would be like if doctors and nurses were to apply the teaching I advocate in regard to lying – that is to say, if they treated the rule against lying as strict and exceptionless. In the next chapter we will study what it would be like if doctors and nurses were to adopt the teaching that I advocate in regard to deception (that does not involve lying) and concealing or pretending – that is to say, if they did not consider themselves even prima facie bound not to deceive, conceal or pretend.

Do caring pragmatists sometimes 'have to' lie?

Before we consider some of the situations in which it may seem that lying to or for patients might be justified, let us recall what we, here, are taking 'lying' to mean. A strict rule against lying, we have noted, is only credible as a moral teaching, if we are clear and careful about what we count as a lie. We are defining lying as *telling* people what you believe to be false in order to deceive them. Thus we discount untruths that are conspicuously spoken in jest and not meant to mislead others. We also discount some conventional expressions – conversational courtesies that no one takes at face value or is expected to: for example, 'So glad to see you!' Thus, if the GP called out to a patient in the middle of the night reassures the apologetic patient saying 'No problem!', this is not a lie – however untrue. The definition of lying with which we are operating here also distinguishes lying from other ways of hiding the truth – even if one is doing so in order to deceive. So in order to answer the question whether caring pragmatists sometimes 'have to' lie, we are not here including situations in which they might 'have to' conceal some information from patients (or for them) or situations in which they might 'have to' use some deceptive trick on them (or for them). At the moment we are only concerned with telling lies to or for patients: is this ever 'necessary'?

Needless to say, if lying, even as defined here, abounds in the world at large, we should not be surprised to find many instances of doctors, nurses (and patients) lying. Evidence is to hand. The Audit Commission, the Government spending watchdog, reported recently that fraud among GPs, pharmacists, dentists and opticians had more than doubled in one year: GPs inventing patients to inflate their lists, dentists putting in claims for work they have not done, and the like. The Commission claimed that the NHS is being defrauded of £80 million a year by GPs claiming for bogus patients (Paul Nuki and David Leppard in the *Sunday Times*, 7 November 1999). Bryan Christie reports that: 'A survey of medical students found that 36% said they'd be prepared to cheat in exams, falsify patient information, plagiarise other people's work, or forge signatures' (Christie 1999). We will ignore, though, the telling of lies that are obviously indefensible. We are not here concerned with blatant skulduggery, the hands in the till type of dishonesty, but with the possibility that lying might be, or anyway seem to be, necessary to the conscientious practitioner – lying in the line of duty (Cicero [106–43 BC]):

> We do not need to discuss cut-throats, poisoners, forgers of wills, thieves, and embezzlers of public moneys, who should be repressed not by lectures and discussions of philosophers, but by chains and prison walls; but let us study here the conduct of those who have the reputation of being honest men.
>
> (Griffin and Atkins 1991: 127).

Trivial lies

Truthfulness, I have argued, does not permit trivial lies – even though, by definition, a lie that is trivial deceives on a matter that is of no importance to or for the person lied to. The point is that though the trivial lie, considered in itself, does not matter, the toleration of trivial lies, one's own and other people's, we have found, undermines trust. We have noted the following factors that account for this risk:

1 The difficulty of telling whether the truth denied really does not matter to or for anyone;
2 The ease of sliding from lies which are reckoned to do no harm to lies which are reckoned to do less harm or 'minimal' harm;
3 The common mistake of supposing that a lie which prevents suffering does not matter.

Consider an example Thurstan Brewin gives of a 'white lie' he told and which he defends.

> A man was dying of cancer and his bedridden 85-year old mother 'phoned. I told her that he might have only a few days to live. She asked to have a word with him and I took a phone to the bed and he just refused to speak to her. I begged him to say a few words, but all he would say – in a voice filled with hatred, anger and bitterness – was 'I've nothing to say to her'. I returned to the phone and had no hesitation in telling his mother that he was not well enough to talk to her – a white lie that most people, I think, would feel was right in the circumstances.
>
> (1996: 144)

Is this an example of a trivial lie? Is it a defensible lie? It seems to me that it was neither. Not trivial, as we have defined that notion: the truth of the matter surely was of concern to the mother. Was it anyway defensible: to spare the mother unnecessary distress? I suggest that it was not defensible. There would have been other ways to spare the mother, equally deceptive, maybe, but not involving telling a lie. It is one thing to try to spare someone distress by concealing information or by trying to fob them off with a half-truth; quite another to do so with a lie. To be sure the intended effect on the mother would be the same: she would be deceived. But we have seen that tolerance of lying, even trivial lying, is subversive of trust, in a way that deceiving and concealing need not be.

Even if we think that this was a defensible lie, considered in itself: what precedent does it set? The trainee at the doctor's elbow needs to *understand* why this lie is permissible when lies usually are not. Is it that the strict duty not to lie applies *vis-a-vis* patients, but not their relatives? Is it that the strict duty not to lie applies in the context of consent seeking – but elsewhere a more flexible attitude to lying to patients or relatives is to be recommended? Is it simply that all things considered telling the lie does less harm than the alternatives? (Notice, though, that revealing all is probably *not* the only alternative to lying to the mother.) To be sure, there may not have been a trainee at the doctor's elbow: no one will ever know then about this lie; not the mother, not the son, not colleagues. Yet the doctor himself knows. For what other lies is this lie a precedent for him?

Another example of a 'white' lie (trivial lie?) was discussed at a conference held in 1978 at the University of Michigan Medical School. (Ganos *et al.* 1983: 77–97). The case for discussion concerned a medical student sent to greet a new patient coming in to hospital for an emergency Caesarean operation: to examine her, start an IV and prepare her for surgery. When the student meets the woman and her husband, the latter says, 'Thank goodness you are here, doctor!' The student is about to correct this mistake but thinks better of it and introduces himself as 'Dr. Boyer' – is this a trivial lie or not? The speakers and the participants (98 per cent of them) agreed that the lie should not have been told. But they did not consider that the student was obliged to volunteer information either – for example, about how inexperienced he was. Of course, the student could have allowed the couple to remain deceived without actually telling a lie. He could have introduced himself as 'John Boyer', omitting any title. Would that still have been dishonest? If the couple continued to call him 'doctor' would it have been untruthful of him not to correct them?

In this case, whether the student lied or deceived or allowed the couple to be deceived, the motive and consequence would have been the same. Even so, it makes sense to avoid the lie, *because of the value of going by the rule and of being seen to do so*. Going by a rule that prohibited both lying and deceiving by other means may be too strict. Not so, a rule prohibiting lying. While in this or that particular case the outcome will be no different if one lies, or deceives by other means, that is not to say that being rule-bound makes no difference.

Some lies might seem trivial in that although the information concealed matters, it is being concealed only as a very temporary expedient – like lying to parents when summoning them to the hospital when you would rather not tell them over the telephone that their child has suddenly died, but if they put you on the spot by asking a direct question, are you justified in lying? Surely the lie is not trivial, but is it defensible? Again, one needs to think not just of the particular situation, but of the implications if you allow yourself such a lie. Notice that the parents in this case would find out that you had lied. They would understand and might not, maybe should not, at all resent it, but when they asked other questions about the circumstances of their child's death, such as why it happened or whether their child suffered any pain when he died, they would not know whether to believe you. However firmly you reassured them, they would know that you might this time be telling the truth but equally you might not be.

Another case: a working mother asks her GP for a sick note for herself. She is well but her child is ill. The mother is afraid she will lose her job if she takes time off to be at home with her child. The GP might see it to be very much in the child's best interests that the mother should be able to stay at home and that she should not get sacked. The lie on her behalf might seem quite trivial – only enabling her to have a few days off work – to which she would be entitled if she were ill herself rather than the child. Another mother might deal with this predicament by lying to the doctor – asking for a sick note for herself – on the grounds of stress, perhaps. But this mother does not lie. She does not claim to be ill. Is the GP justified in telling a lie on her behalf? He might know well that the harm her employer would suffer would be negligible.

Here again, we need to think about the precedent. What does the mother learn about the doctor's willingness to lie on this occasion? In this instance, his lie is of course precisely what she is wanting. He is being helpful – understanding her predicament – but at a later time it might be enormously important to her to know that her doctor will not lie to her – even out of kindness. How does the GP explain (to the medical student at his elbow or to himself) his policy on lying to or for patients?

Serious lies

Howard Spiro presents the following scenario. A patient who is acutely ill with a ruptured liver asks you as he is being wheeled into the operating theatre: 'Doc, am I going to make it?' Spiro observes that these days doctors

> Will give a weasel answer, 'Well, maybe, we're going to try'. Nobody is willing any more to grab the patient's hand and give the reassurance, '*Sure* you're going to make it'. They give two reasons. One is, 'I want to tell the truth, I've been raised to tell the truth, I don't believe he's going to make it, I shouldn't tell him that he's going to make it if I don't think he is'. And the other one is, of course, the malpractice issue ... .
>
> (Spiro 1997: 241)

Is the comforting firm reassurance – grasping the patient's hand and saying '*Sure*, you will?' a defensible lie? Is it even a lie? The situation in which the conversation takes place is relevant. This is *after* the discussion which led to the patient giving consent, the discussion during which the patient was informed so far as the traumatic circumstances permitted (including the patient's ability and willingness to be informed). In this subsequent context arguably the patient is not now asking a question as an afterthought but seeking support and comfort and the doctor who responds is not answering a question (with a lie) but lending support with soothing words:

> Reassuring a patient in acute pain who must undergo an emergency operation that everything will be all right hardly falls into the same category as telling a patient with a gastric cancer that he has a little ulcer.
>
> (Spiro 1986: 124)

But anyone who takes seriously the importance of avoiding telling lies will look for alternative ways to reassure in such circumstances. The weasel words are not the only alternative to outright lying. That said, we can still admit, as does Kant, that people who are put on the spot may not have their wits 'always ready' (1964: 95). It is one thing not to blame the doctor who lies in these circumstances, quite another to hold him up as an example for others to follow.

Are there, though, certain exceptions – categories of defensible serious lies? Does the caring pragmatist sometimes 'have to' lie to child-patients, or to patients who are themselves liars, or to patients who are confused, deluded or truculent? Does the caring pragmatist sometimes 'have to' lie for patients?

Lying to children

A friend tells me that when she was 12 years old she was sent to an orthodontist. Before she would open her mouth to let him inspect her teeth, she said, 'I've got a loose tooth. Will you promise me that you won't pull it out?' He promised. She opened her mouth. He whipped it out. A trivial incident? It still rankles with my friend many years on. She says, 'I should have sued him!' and I don't know that she is joking. It might seem that a lie that is obviously going to be immediately exposed is a special case. It aims at inducing a false belief but only momentarily – like telling a child 'This won't hurt!' where the aim is to calm the child so that, though it will hurt, it will hurt and distress less than if the child is resisting. But whether the kindly further intent justifies the lie, it is still a lie. The means chosen to calm the child (the lie told) is also intended. Is such a lie defensible? It provides a quick and convenient fix in the short term, but what precedent does it set for the child, the parent, and the doctor? On the other hand, is saying to an adult patient: 'This won't hurt much' a different case entirely? The adult patient is worldly wise and may be able to recognise such words as spoken in code – words recognised to be aimed at soothing rather than at informing (Lesser 1991: 158).

While lying to children in answer to their questions about what is wrong with them, about the purpose of procedures they are being subjected to, or about the probable outcome is generally frowned on by doctors and nurses these days, lies which are not directly related to treatments may seem more defensible. Suppose for example that a mother asks the nurse to tell a lie to the child as to why the mother is not visiting: real reason – she is drunk – or finds visiting and seeing the state of her child too upsetting. In such circumstances would the nurse be justified in lying to the child – to spare the child distress? Here again, if one considers the situation in isolation, the lie might seem the kind solution. But one cannot consider the situation in isolation. The exception to the rule is made for a reason: to spare the child distress. Where else will this exception be applicable? Can you trust nurses if their policy on lying is openly acknowledged to be: 'We will not lie to you unless it is to spare you distress!'?

Lying to liars

Some patients flagrantly and maliciously lie to doctors and nurses – patients, for example, who are afflicted with the Munchausen by Proxy Syndrome. Do their therapists have any obligation to refrain from lying to them? Surely the fact that some people are liars no more entitles you to lie to them than the fact that some people are thieves entitles you to steal from them. We have noted that the duty not to lie to people does not derive from their personal right. Rather, as I have argued, the duty is one we need to recognize and uphold in our dealings with one another generally in order to preserve trust and respect within a community. In any case, a crucial necessity in treating individual patients effectively, including women with Munchausen by Proxy Syndrome, is to win their trust (Day 1998). Lying to them would hardly be helpful.

Lying to patients who are confused, deluded or truculent

Ryan *et al.* (1995) suggest the following vignette to illustrate how lying to a psychotic patient who is deluded might be justified although the lie would neither be trivial nor 'critical' – by which they mean, life-saving. The vignette describes the predicament you as a psychiatrist might face if asked by a dermatological team to see a female patient whom the team suspects is suffering from a rare condition: delusional infestation. She believes that she has some as yet unidentified bug under her skin. Suppose that the team warns you that this patient will refuse to see you if you let on that you are a psychiatrist. Only if you conceal this information from the patient will you be able to help her. Ryan *et al.* say that people who suffer from this delusion are otherwise 'completely normal' and that if treated with antipsychotic medication they make a full recovery.

Clearly, telling a lie to such a patient would not be trivial. On the other hand, the patient's life is not at risk. All the same, as Ryan *et al.* observe, patients who suffer in this way are seriously affected: 'The patient may be tortured by her conviction and endlessly seek relief from her supposed condition' (1995: 74). But even if the patient asks you directly, as Ryan *et al.* envisage, 'Are you a shrink?' it is possible for you to answer with a half-truth rather than a lie. Indeed that is what Ryan *et al.* suggest: that you might say, for example, that you are a 'specialist in emotional problems'. They argue that lying and deceiving and concealing information from patients are morally on a par, and for this reason they favour calling all these strategies 'lies'. They suggest that in the circumstances you would be justified in concealing both that you are a psychiatrist and that the medication you are prescribing is 'antipsychotic': two lies, in their view.

In defence of these 'lies' they argue that 1) the deception in this unusual situation is likely to do more good than harm to the patient (it will free her from her troublesome condition; it will not cause her to lose trust since she is already untrusting – and anyway she can be expected not to resent what was done when she has recovered and it is explained) and 2) the deception will not violate her autonomy but restore it (her autonomy is impaired by the illness-caused false belief and the 'lie' is the only means to remove this impairment). Ryan *et al.* contrast these defensible 'lies' with the indefensible – like concealing from terminally ill cancer patients that they have cancer and are dying. In this case patients are more harmed than helped by the concealment. Moreover, they are denied the opportunity to make important decisions about the rest of their lives: their autonomy is violated.

Let us for the moment confine our attention to the question of whether in such a situation you as the psychiatrist might be justified in not merely concealing the crucial bits of information but in doing so with a lie (as I have defined 'lie'). Interestingly, although Ryan *et al.* maintain that lying is morally on a par with deceiving and concealing – all three are objectionable in a clinical context for the same reasons (that they usually do more harm than good and usually violate autonomy), they still urge that lying (proper) should be a last resort. Why? Because when the patient comes to be debriefed she is more likely to forgive being tricked with a half-truth than she is to forgive what 'are commonly regarded as lies' (1995: 76).

But doesn't that just go to show that lying is not on a par after all with deceiving (without lying) or concealing? If it is true that people's trust (reasonably or unreasonably) is more undermined if they discover that doctors or nurses have lied to them than if they discover that doctors or nurses have concealed information from them, does that not indicate that lying is more harmful, more subversive?

The teaching that I am advocating would allow you to conceal information and even to use deceptive tricks – telling half-truths and the like. It would not allow you to lie – not even as a last resort. Why not? Let us grant that as Ryan *et al.* suppose, deceiving the patient will in this unusual kind of case do more good than harm and will restore her autonomy. What about the precedent you would be setting? What would be the implications for other situations in which the only way you could help a patient, and restore/improve the patient's autonomy would be with a lie? Ryan *et al.* note that there may be implications for other conditions, treating dementia and treating children. Quite so! They seek to limit the circumstances in which deception would be defensible to those where a person's false belief is caused by an illness. But what difference does it make how one's false belief is caused? Whatever the cause, the justification they give for withholding information is that by so doing you aim to restore or improve health and autonomy.

Ryan *et al.* suggest that 'lying' in this particular kind of case would not have a damaging impact on patients' trust. They assume that the particular patient would be entirely understanding when debriefed – at least, that she would be if she had been told a half-truth, and should be even if she'd been told a direct lie. Well, maybe the patient would be wholly forgiving or approving even if she'd been lied to: she might be profoundly grateful. All the same, she would now know that doctors are prepared to lie if that is the only way they can prevail on a patient to accept a treatment that in their view will benefit the patient and restore autonomy. Will this not affect her trust in the word of her doctors on future occasions?

As for other patients, Ryan *et al.* say that the condition is so rare that people are not likely to hear about psychiatrists' policy in such cases. Anyway, those who suffer from the condition and so might be 'victims' of the policy, do not believe they have the condition so they would not be made more mistrustful even if they knew of it. All the same, patients who do know of the condition might well think that their doctors (wrongly) suspect that this is what they are suffering from. Anyway, if it were public knowledge that psychiatrists will conceal, deceive, even lie, to a patient if they believe that the patient's autonomy is impaired by an illness and that the deceptive strategy will do them more good than harm, wouldn't this have a bearing on one's ability to trust a psychiatrist in regard to many other problems besides psychotic delusions? Not only would it affect one's trust in psychiatrists, it would affect one's trust in doctors generally: it is the dermatology team that initially proposes deceiving, even lying to, this troubled patient.

Ryan *et al.* sketch another scenario in which they consider it to be defensible to deceive a patient (with a lie, if need be):

> You have just decided that a suicidal patient with a major depression will require involuntary admission. He is a very large man and he has the delusional belief that he is unworthy of treatment. He has already indicated that he would rather flee than come into hospital, so you have organised for the hospital security-guards to escort him to a secure unit. While you wait for them he asks you what the delay is about. You think that if you tell him that you have sent for reinforcements he will try to leave immediately. Though you do not think he will be able to escape, you do feel that without the security-guards both he and staff members may be injured in the ensuing struggle. In the circumstances we do not think it would be unethical to tell him, if pushed, that you are waiting for a blood result.
>
> (1995: 76)

This scenario is one where we can invoke the only defence I have allowed for lying – where life and limb are at immediate risk. Here the background conditions under which we are obliged not to lie to one another are temporarily absent (or so, at least, it may be reasonable to suppose – you may not know that the patient will put up a fight, only have good reason to fear so). Ryan *et al.* rightly qualify their defence of this lie with the phrase 'if pushed'. Usually one would not be pushed to lie. Usually there would be other alternatives besides either explaining that you are waiting for reinforcements or telling a lie: a half-truth or evasion might serve.

Suppose that the scenario were such that the patient, unless tricked with a lie, would do *himself* an injury though he posed no threat to you or your colleagues. Would you still be justified in lying to him if that were the only way to prevent him from doing himself a serious, possibly fatal, injury? The above defence for lying appeals to the basic right of self defence – which we have extended to defence of others under attack. But now we are considering someone who, while in a confused, depressed or deluded state, is about to attack himself. Since we are entitled to use lies if need be to defend others whose lives are threatened by assault, may we not do so whether the assailant is someone other than the intended victim or one and the same person? Here the person whose life is threatened is the hapless victim of his own confused or disturbed state of mind.

Truthfulness, we have said, is needed to sustain trust and respect. Are trust and respect undermined if we allow lying to patients only in those circumstances where they are threatening to injure or kill themselves or others? If we allow lying to the deluded or depressed patient who threatens to take his own life, what about the deluded or depressed patient who refuses a life-saving operation or medication or the anorexic who is refusing to eat? And might a neonatal intensive care team be justified in lying to parents about the prospects for their children on the grounds that parents of such babies are too distraught to be able to act as proxies when decisions need to be made involving 'heroic' interventions (Silverman 1998: 86, 193)? In short, would the precedent set by permitting lies to prevent confused patients from killing themselves open the way to a general acceptance of lying to patients where otherwise, on account of confused or deluded belief or depression, they would refuse consent to a life-saving or life-prolonging treatment?

The challenge here is to find a way of isolating the justification for lying in the one case (to prevent the confused from injuring themselves) from the other cases described above where confused patients (or confused proxies) make choices that imperil survival (refusing rescue). If we explain the defence for lying to save the confused patient from himself on the grounds that the patient, because of his confusion, is acting in a way that puts his own life in immediate danger, then that reason does seem to provide a precedent that allows lying, not just to confused patients who are bent on inflicting self-harm, but also to those who are refusing life-saving help. The mistake here is to see the justification for lying to the patient bent on self-harm as that the liar's aim is to save life or prevent injury. To be sure, the harm of the particular lie may be trifling in comparison to the harm (death) prevented, but we have to think not just of the particular case but of the rule by which we justify this lie.

We have already seen that a teaching that allows us to lie if that is necessary to save life is not a safe teaching – not a teaching that we could openly adopt if we are trying to preserve trust and respect. That this is so, seems obviously correct in regard to medical and nursing practice. If medical and nursing schools openly taught their students: 'Only lie to patients where that is necessary to save their lives!' how could we trust doctors' and nurses' advice? If they recommended a treatment to you as vitally necessary, you would have reason to suspect that if there were off-putting side-effects or risks, they might not want to tell you. Nor would it be any use to press them with direct questions: they might see fit to lie to you.

Suppose we modify the teaching by which we explain the exception to the otherwise strict rule against lying to patients thus: only lie to a patient if 1) the patient is not competent (for example, is confused, depressed, or deluded) *and* 2) the patient's life is at risk. Could we trust doctors and nurses if this were openly acknowledged to be their policy? Could patients with a history of mental illness trust the word of their doctors or nurses? Isn't trust no less essential, and no less dependent on truthfulness, in establishing a therapeutic relationship with patients who suffer from mental illness than with other patients? And anyway would not the same rule get widened to cover other patients who were being unreasonable in refusing to consent to the treatment they needed? People may be confused or deluded although not mentally ill – like, for example, the distraught parents of desperately ill babies.

The reason behind the lying I have defended (lying to confused patients who threaten to do harm to themselves or others) does not appeal to the 'necessity' of saving life or preventing injury but to the rationale that explains our general obligations not to lie to one another. That rationale, I have argued, presupposes certain background conditions – the reciprocity and the availability of protection against personal violence. Remove those conditions and it is no longer rational for us to forego defensive lying. Hence, the reason that permits lying to protect a person from aggression is not a reason that permits lying where other factors put someone's life at risk.

Patients who refuse a life-saving or life-prolonging treatment are not necessarily trying to kill themselves. There are many other reasons for refusing such an intervention than the wish to harm oneself. Terminally ill patients who want to go home to die rather than to stay in hospital, although they realize that away from hospital they will die sooner, do not quit hospital in order to *expedite* their death. That is a consequence which they can foresee, but need not be aiming at. Jehovah's Witness patients who decline rescue with blood transfusions are not trying to kill themselves by resisting this intervention (any more than we should assume of the person who offers his place in the crowded lifeboat to someone else that he is trying to kill himself). Hence, although I have extended the defence for lying to protect a patient against self-assault, this defence does not apply whenever patients refuse a life-protecting medical intervention.

Lying for patients

Consider the case, discussed in Beauchamp and Childress, of a five year old girl who has progressive renal failure and who is not faring well on chronic renal dialysis. Various family members are tissue-typed with a view to a possible transplant. Only the father turns out to be a good match but he changes his mind about donating. He wants the doctor to conceal this change of heart with a lie: 'to tell everyone else in the family that he is not histocompatible'(1994: 49). 'He maintains that truth-telling would have the effect of "wrecking the family"' (1994: 49). The doctor in the case, 'is uncomfortable with the request, but after discussion he agrees to tell the man's wife that "for medical reasons the father should not donate a kidney"' (1994: 49). Beauchamp and Childress later remark that 'Kantians' would not approve of this concealment (1994: 56), but we have seen that Kant, at any rate, is careful to distinguish lying from deceiving and concealing. It is not so obvious, I think, that Kant would disapprove of the doctor's strategy – if it is reasonable to interpret what is said as concealing with deceptive but not lying words (what counts as 'medical' reasons may be conveniently vague). Is the doctor's handling of the situation so different from Kant's own when he was called upon to give an undertaking that he would not publish on certain topics?

Later, Beauchamp and Childress illustrate their own view that sometimes lying for (and to) patients is justified with a scenario very like the above except that the person being protected is a teenager: 'Lying is sometimes justified to shield a vulnerable teenager who does not want to donate a kidney to a sibling' (1994: 101). Why should the age of the person to be protected be relevant? The under-lying assumption would seem to be that a teenager-sibling is more vulnerable than a father. Be that as it may, how would this exception to the general firm rule against lying be explained? Can we trust doctors whose avowed policy in regard to lying is that they will only lie if it is necessary to protect a patient who is especially vulnerable? Does this policy not subvert trust in those who openly adopt it?

A doctor might be tempted to lie for a patient in order to enable the patient to get insurance cover for a treatment or in order to get round regulations that would debar the patient from access to a desired treatment. Suppose, for example, that you are a consultant running a private assisted conception clinic and a woman in her late fifties turns up: she wants to have a child and seeks your help to reverse her menopause, etc. If the regulations under which you are licensed to practice do not allow you to assist women of this age, and if you consider this particular regulation to be unreasonable and unfair, you might be tempted to lie about this woman's age. Would such a lie be defensible? Suppose that you do not lie but you notice that the patient seeking your help has lied to you about her age. Are you obliged to turn her away? Might you be justified in pretending not to notice? Even though you are not telling the lie, you cannot simply pretend not to notice without being dishonest. You are licensed to practice on the understanding that you intend to comply with the regulations. In this case you would be flouting them. You do not intend to keep the promise that is an ongoing one. False promises are a kind of lie.

Is it all the same a defensible lie? Let us suppose that you are quite right to deplore this particular regulation: that it reflects mere prejudice; it is unfair. Of course, you run a risk if you clandestinely break the rules, but conscientious prac-titioners may be prepared to take some risks for the sake of their patients. If they are caught out, perhaps the surrounding publicity will in the long run help to bring about a more enlightened licensing policy. I have argued, though, that the strict rule against lying is one we need to live by in this world, not merely in an ideal world where all regulations imposed by officialdom are reasonable and fair. Surely the same applies for doctors and nurses. If you are prepared to make a pledge to obey rules although you intend to ignore them when they are unrea-sonable, your pledge is dishonest. You could not publicize such a policy without showing your pledges to be worthless.

Caring pragmatists should not lie

So far we have only reflected on the effect on medical and nursing practice if the rule 'Never lie to or for patients!' were to be adopted. I have argued that caring pragmatists need to adopt the strict rule – because it is the only one that is adequate to sustain patients' trust. This argument is persuasive only if understood to apply just to *lying*. I am claiming simply that caring pragmatists could adopt this rule in regard to it. I am not suggesting that caring pragmatists could or should be similarly strict in regard to other ways of deceiving or concealing. Moreover, it must be borne in mind that caring pragmatists are rarely cornered in situations where the only alternatives are either to lie or to disclose: usually there are alternatives – like declining to answer a question where doing so would betray a confidence; like evading a question – so as to allow time for a relative to arrive and be present when bad news is imparted; like answering with a half-truth which conceals what a patient or other enquirer need not know and had better not know or not know just yet. When and whether any of these dodges are any better than an outright lie is something we will look into next. Meanwhile we should at least note there often are these alternatives. Thus it is quite misleading to present an either/or: as if you have no other choice than either to lie or to reveal all.

Finally, we should not pretend that the strict teaching is costless to adopt – that it will not sometimes require doctors and nurses to say things which will cause deep distress, and which may prompt patients to make unwise and tragic choices. If physiotherapists refuse to lie to their patients, they may fail to persuade them to make the efforts that are needed if they are to recover some mobility. Physiotherapists who are prepared to lie (encouraging totally unrealistic hopes) may have better results – at least in the short term. Their patients, when they realize they have been lied to, may also understand and not resent the lies. All the same, trust will be undermined – not just in the physiotherapists but in health professionals generally.

Consider the lie often perpetrated, from the kindest of motives of course, to relatives asking if the patient died peacefully or in pain. Why burden those who are already grief-stricken with the bleak truth? Are there ways of fending off that question which are not lying but which are intentionally concealing – even deceiving? If the enquirers persist, would you then regretfully have to admit that the end was not altogether peaceful? Perhaps a notice should be posted on the hospital walls: 'Do not ask if the patient died peacefully as a truthful answer often hurts!' If there is a taboo on answering this particular question truthfully, then medical and nursing staff will themselves know that there is no point their asking when it happens to be a relative of theirs who has died. Maybe that seems a price worth paying: better than sometimes having to burden the grieving with additional distress. But is this exception to a strict rule against lying so easily isolated and kept as the one exception? If what is supposed to justify it is the aim of sparing relatives distress, might not that reason extend to many other situations, both in what is said to relatives and in what is said to patients?

7 Deceptions and concealments in medical and nursing practice

> Besides (to say truth) nakedness is uncomely, as well in mind as body; and it addeth no small reverence to men's manners and actions, if they be not altogether open.
>
> Francis Bacon

Doctors and nurses, I have argued, should not permit themselves a moral license, a 'therapeutic privilege', to lie. The same duty that holds for people in their lives generally, a strict and exceptionless duty not to lie, applies no less to health professionals than to everyone else. We need to adopt this rigorous stance in regard to lying, because nothing else is adequate to sustain trust between people. The duty of truthfulness demands at least this of us: that we repudiate lying. Since trust is no less important in the context of medical and nursing practice, there is no justification for doctors or nurses relaxing this strict rule in regard to lying.

What about other ways of deceiving which do not involve lying: are they equally subversive of trust? Should we adopt the same strict teaching against intentional deception of patients or on behalf of patients, whether or not the method used to deceive involves lying? Hereafter, for brevity's sake, I will refer to deception which does not involve lying simply as 'deception'. I have argued that there is no general duty that obliges us even prima facie not to deceive one another (though there is good reason to counsel against casual deception). All the same it may be that doctors and nurses do have a prima facie duty not to do so – at least *vis-a-vis* their own patients. Even if there is no basic, general duty on us all not to deceive one another, doctors, nurses and other health professionals have special duties *vis-a-vis* their patients. Is a duty not to deceive one that derives from one or more of these special duties?

Don't health professionals have a duty to inform their patients – a duty that derives both from the duty of care owed to patients and the duty to respect patients' autonomy? A duty to inform would seem to rule out deceiving (and, of course, concealing). Is there not then at least a presumption against health professionals deceiving their patients? Of course, this duty to inform is one that is sometimes overridden by other more compelling obligations or rights – as when informing happens to necessitate betraying a confidence. Also, the duty to inform applies only in relation to certain matters – concerning the patient's own health needs and prospects. There is not even a prima facie duty on nurses to inform their patients about the health needs of other patients, however curious patients are to know.

The legal duty to inform is, of course, bound up with the getting of consent. The moral duty to inform may apply more widely. The necessity of getting a patient's consent may not arise for a patient who is dying, for example. The patient may still want and need information and have a moral right to be given it even where consent is not an issue. In the 1950s and 1960s, it was everywhere common practice for doctors and nurses to avoid telling cancer patients that they were dying and to connive with relatives in keeping the dying in ignorance as long as possible. That practice has since fallen into disrepute – in 'Western' countries, anyway. Much evidence suggested that the attempt to deceive was usually unsuccessful and that it left the patients who were dying feeling (and being) isolated and abandoned (quite the opposite from what was intended).

Thomas Hackett cites as a typical victim of the failure to inform the following case:

> A woman with a terminal breast cancer asked her doctor why her headaches persisted. When the doctor said it was probably nerves, she asked why she was nervous. He returned the question. She replied, 'I am nervous because all the tests have stopped, nobody wants my blood, and I get all the pills I want. The priest comes to see me twice a week, which he never did before, and my mother-in-law is nicer to me even though I am meaner to her. Wouldn't this make you nervous?' There was a pause. Then the doctor said, 'You mean you think you are dying?' She said, 'I do'. He replied, 'You are'. Then she smiled and said, 'Well, I broke the sound barrier; someone finally told me the truth'.
>
> (1976: 372–3)

A willingness to be open with dying patients has become one of the hallmarks of palliative medicine and nursing. Not every dying patient wants frank discussion. But as Dame Cicely Saunders observes: 'Once open communication is seen as a possibility the patient will lead in this area' (1994: 779). Many of the fears that beset the dying can only be allayed through frank discussion – fears for example that the dying will be prolonged through over-treatment or will be made wretched through under-treatment.

Those who work in the fields of palliative medicine and nursing emphasize the importance to patients (and their relatives) not just of giving information but of doctors and nurses showing willingness to discuss: 'Time taken to ease tensions with open discussion is rarely ill spent' (Saunders 1994: 781). Antonella Surbone, who has practiced in the US and in Italy and who wants Italians to learn from the American way, but to find a 'better Italian way', is particularly concerned to avoid the 'farce of deception' that has often surrounded the dying:

> Since I believe that the suffering person knows the truth, I think the only way to respect both Italian principles and the patient's autonomy and dignity is to let the patient know that there are no barriers to communication and to the truth.
>
> (1992: 1662)

Mei-che Pang's study reveals that there are nurses in China who believe that patients may be better off being told they are dying – but that this is something for doctors and nurses to advise families on, not something for doctors and nurses to tackle directly with their patients (1999: 252). Eduardo Osuna *et al.* conducted a survey to test the views of Spanish doctors. They report that while doctors 'prefer to channel information through the family who, since they know the patient better, can adapt or withhold any information' it is even so the patient who should be the 'arbiter' of how much information is given (1998: 108).

In short, there seems to be widespread support for a principle of openness with dying patients: a growing recognition that well-meaning protective attempts to deceive dying patients who seek information are generally ineffective and counter productive. Non-western supporters of the principle derive it simply from the duty of care: the needs of the dying. If they talk of a 'right' here it is a right that derives from a need. Patients' needs arising from their illness have always been regarded as the focal point of the duties of doctors and nurses. Thus, the trend towards more openness with the dying does not necessarily indicate any 'westernizing' departure from the traditional Hippocratic teachings; to do good, or, at least, to do no harm. Rather, new insights into the needs of the dying have led to a modification of practices, encouraging openness rather than secrecy. The openness is deemed to do more good.

Though at least showing willing to share information seems appropriate in the care of the dying, it may not be so in every other field of practice. How much patients are benefited or harmed by information-sharing could well differ from one clinical context to another. Patients may not need to have information withheld if they are beyond cure, but what of those who can be cured but only if they undergo difficult or frightening ordeals? Simply from a caring standpoint, are there some kinds of situations where patients (or their relatives) are helped if information is withheld or concealed? Let us consider some of the kinds of situations where this might be claimed – and whether in the circumstances the concealment, or in some cases, deception, compromises truthfulness.

Unwillingness to disclose unconfirmed hunches

Doctors may withhold information about their hunches and expectations until the results of tests confirm them. If patients quiz them about the possibilities, they might see fit to be deliberately evasive. Provided they do not lie, their evasiveness at this stage is not dishonest. If pressed with direct questions, doctors can refuse to speculate. They are not obliged to share all that is in their mind and it might not seem to be in a patient's interests to know that. The patient can ask and the doctor can decline to answer. Maybe the doctor ought to answer if the patient presses for more information, but if the doctor refuses, this is not a failure of truthfulness. Even if doctors pledge (somewhat rashly) to share all the information they have about a patient with the patient, hunches are not information. A doctor awaiting test results does not yet have information. This is not an instance of defensible deception, because there is here no deceiving, no attempt to make the patient believe what is false; only an intent to conceal. It is an instance, then, of (defensible) concealment. The concealment might be indefensible – if, say, it is obviously causing the patient undue anxiety – but it is not a failure of truthfulness.

Covert video surveillance to detect child abuse

In 1997 David Southall *et al.* published the results of their study of child abuse in two hospitals, one in London and one in North Staffordshire. By installing hidden cameras in the children's ward by the beds of children with a history of unexplained illness they were able to capture on film parents (usually mothers) assaulting their children (for example, attempting to suffocate, to break an arm or forcing disinfectant into a child's mouth). Subsequently some of these parents admitted to having suffocated siblings who'd been diagnosed as victims of 'sudden infant death syndrome' (Southall *et al.* 1997). This is an instance of doctors using a deceptive trick for, but not on, the patient, but on others who are suspected of posing a life-threatening danger to the patient.

Is this practice dishonest? Surely it is not. To be sure, it involves intentional deception, not just concealment. It is not just that parents are not informed that they are being observed by hidden cameras. It is important that the parents are lulled into supposing that they are being left alone, that they are not observed. Deception is a legitimate tactic for preventing and uncovering crime. Our trust in the police is not dented because we know that they use concealing and deceptive strategies, like driving about in unmarked cars. Our trust in doctors is not dented because we know that they sometimes need to deceive relatives in order to safeguard their patients. Admittedly, this spying is especially intrusive of privacy: spying on a parent in the privacy of a bedroom – 'a paradigm symbol of privacy in our society' (Gillon 1995: 132). But the right to privacy is in such cases overridden by the rights of the child-patients to protection and possible rescue. Although it must go very much against the grain for doctors and nurses to be treating the parents of seriously ill children as possible enemies rather than as allies, the nature of Munchausen's syndrome by proxy requires drastic measures to be taken for the protection of children at risk. One of the startling revelations from the Southall study is that the parents who do these things appear to be innocent – they are good actors: 'Covert surveillance has revealed that many such parents appeared caring and kind in the presence of professionals, yet within seconds of being alone with the child, they became cruel and sadistic' (Southall *et al.* 1997: 753). Given the difficulties of detecting such abuse when the victims are often babies and the abuse may leave no visible marks, such deceptive tricks and invasions of privacy are readily defensible.

Truthfulness and the mentally ill or impaired

Hooker objected to lying to the mentally ill, but is trickery sometimes defensible? Consider the usefulness of using 'locked doors' on wards of patients who are not safe let loose – who need confining to protect them or others – but who can at least enjoy some freedom of movement provided they are not able to work out how to open doors. They could, of course, be confined by more overt means. But surely the less overt is defensible – and does not require anyone to lie to them, only to refuse to tell them certain things they might want to know.

Consider the case with which we began our enquiry (in Chapter One) – the truculent patient who was persuaded to stay in hospital after being secretly sedated with a doctored cup of tea. Was this a betrayal of trust? It was a deceptive trick. But it was necessary to make him stay – for his own and others' protection – and the alternative of using force to make him stay would surely have been no more respectful of his autonomy and a less safe way of securing him the care he needed. Why should his trust in doctors and nurses when he is debriefed be undermined? At least he can still trust their word. He may not always trust their actions. Next time he is offered a cup of tea he may ask awkward questions. But at least he can ask questions – and expect answers worth listening to.

Recall the scenario outlined by Ryan *et al.* (1995) in which a psychiatrist is asked to examine a woman who is suspected to be having a delusion of infestation and who is unwilling to see a psychiatrist. I have argued that a psychiatrist would not be justified in lying to the patient in order to help her, but would be justified in trying to conceal his psychiatric status with some evasion or half-truth. Nor would the psychiatrist need to reveal to the patient that the medicine prescribed was anti-psychotic. If though the patient were to ask point blank: 'Is this medicine anti-psychotic?' the psychiatrist should not lie. Although the intention behind lying or deceiving might be the same: to rid the patient of a very troublesome obsession – and although the expected and intended consequence for the patient might be the same: that the patient upon recovery is told how she has been helped and is duly grateful (or should be), there is still a morally critical difference in what the psychiatrist would have done.

In the one case the psychiatrist shows a willingness to lie; in the other case not. Thus, the patient discovers something in the one case and not in the other: that her doctor was prepared to lie to her. And she is not the only person who finds this out. The doctor also knows this. Quite possibly others know it too: the dermatological team, for example, who referred the patient to the psychiatrist. Whether or not any of these people think that lying was in the circumstances justified, I suggest that their trust in the word of doctors is affected. If the doctor lied, one knows *that* doctor's word is not to be trusted. One thing that doctor can no longer say is 'Trust my word!' That is surely a critical moral difference – for the doctor as well as for the patient.

Placebos as therapy[1]

Let us understand by a placebo, any pill, injection or procedure which is believed by the doctor or nurse who administers it to be beneficial, but only because of its symbolic features and not because of what it is in itself. Sugar capsules, for example, are pharmacologically inert – but doctors, knowing this, may still find that patients will be helped if given them with assurances that the capsules will alleviate symptoms – pain, at any rate.

People sometimes use the term 'placebic' to cover anything that doctors or nurses do that helps to reassure patients and boost their confidence with knock on effect on untoward symptoms. In this loose sense, even making an appointment to see one's doctor – or being put onto a waiting list, may be placebic. But we will restrict the term to only those forms of reassurance that involve *disguise*. A doctor may agree to perform a gastrointestinal endoscopy just to reassure a patient, even though the doctor is convinced that the results will be normal, but if the procedure is actually carried out, it is not the administration of a placebo – unlike if a doctor pretends to perform an endoscopy and in fact does something else (Spiro 1986: 40–1). Likewise, we should distinguish between the sham operation to check for the presence of a tumour in a patient's abdomen to placate an anxious patient and a real operation carried out for the same purpose. The former would be placebic, the latter, not. Procedures carried out merely to reassure the patient need involve no trickery or disguise. The doctor who agrees to perform an endoscopy simply to reassure the patient can explain to the patient that this is the sole reason for proceeding.

Thus, I am defining placebic treatments as treatments that use disguise and rely on pretence to reassure. It is because the patient suffering pain believes that the pill prescribed is analgesic that the patient is in fact benefited by taking it. The patient, in other words, is tricked into a false impression. To tell the patient that the pill prescribed is merely a sugar pill would be self-defeating. The trick depends on deception of the person it is practiced upon. Hence, of course, placebos are of no use as therapy for the relief of pain in dogs, cats or human infants.

The commonest agent of placebo is the pill or capsule. Placebos may be pure or impure. The pure placebo is a substance believed by the prescriber to be totally pharmacologically inert. The impure placebo is a substance which is pharmacologically active but which is administered in doses too low to be (pharmacologically) effective or which is used for a different condition – for example, administering antibiotic to a patient in the absence of bacterial infection or vitamins in the absence of vitamin deficiency. Doctors may prefer to use impure placebos. The impure placebo can have side effects which enhance its impressiveness – the impressiveness of the bitter tonic:

> If the pill has a side effect such as the dry mouth produced by anticholinergic drugs, the placebo effect may be enhanced, the patient surmising that if the drug is strong enough to dry his mouth, it must be doing good somewhere else.
>
> (Spiro 1986: 40)

Moreover, doctors may feel safer about giving a drug that is not inert – less risk of a malpractice suit. On the other hand, the impure placebo may do actual harm. Spiro mentions the harm that arises for example, from antibiotics being prescribed for the common cold (1986: 135–6).

So far as truthfulness is concerned, does it signify whether the pills prescribed are pure or impure placebos? Either way, it would seem that the patient is being deliberately misled. Howard Brody notes how at a conference in 1946 concern was voiced that the use of impure placebos was more likely to beguile doctors into self-deception (1977: 102). As he says, few doctors in those days worried about patients being deceived. In the 1940s there was a 'cavalier attitude' towards the deception of patients. Subsequently, he observes, the therapeutic use of placebos fell under a cloud for two reasons: 1) with the advent of the new wonder drugs doctors came to see themselves as proper scientists able to cure diseases; 2) with the 'discovery' of patient autonomy came a new concern that patients had a right to be informed participants in decisions.

Advances in medical science encouraged doctors to see themselves primarily as scientists curing diseases – able both to offer effective remedies for disease and to understand why they were effective – how they worked. The use of remedies that appeared to be effective but were not proven or explicable seemed unscientific – to belong to the quackery traditions of healers. Of course, patients continued to bring health complaints to doctors which science did not explain. Acute pain, traceable to tissue damage, could be addressed. Chronic pain was altogether more enigmatic: 'Acute pain is a challenge usually accepted by physicians, but chronic pain is a burden and a reproach' observes Spiro (1997: 38). Yet, if placebos are effective in relieving chronic pain, does it matter that the scientific explanation is lacking? Does it matter to the patient seeking a remedy from suffering? Obviously the effectiveness of placebos may be readily exaggerated. How many of those who recover while imbibing placebos would have recovered anyway, without any treatment?

Howard Brody (1997) argues that the same benefits that placebos achieve can be realized simply by demonstrating in other ways the doctors' sympathy, concern and support. He distinguishes the placebo from the placebo effect. The placebo is the deceptive pill or procedure that is a tangible demonstration of the physician's willingness to help. The placebo effect is the relief from pain or other symptoms that seems to occur as a result of that demonstration via the boost it gives to the patient's hope and confidence. But there can be alternative non-deceptive ways of giving tangible demonstration – like listening to the patient and taking the time to explain and discuss and perhaps educate the patient into useful strategies of self-help. Not enough attention, he says, has been given to these 'honest' alternatives (Brody 1997: 78). The physician is not obliged either to give a pill or do nothing. Talking, listening and explaining are not nothing (Brody 1980: 110).

If, though, there are occasions where non-deceptive alternatives are not effective, for example where the aim is to wean a patient off an addictive drug, doctors and nurses should not reject the use of placebos out of hand merely because they involve intentional deception. Brody does not claim that placebos can never be justified – only that the burden of proof lies with those who prescribe them. He surmises that doctors have too readily assumed that effective alternatives would have to be 'other drugs, surgery, and similar interventionist modalities' whereas providing emotional support, talking with the patient and providing education can be equally effective – in the long term maybe more so, than the quick fix placebo prescription (1980: 110).

Clearly, to give a patient sugar pills saying that they are analgesics is outright lying, but suppose the doctor prescribing a placebo says only what is true. Howard Spiro maintains that he has used placebos in what he considers to be an 'honest' way:

> Trying to relieve a patient with symptoms out of proportion to objective findings – particularly one complaining of pain the source of which I do not immediately recognize and which I suspect that I will never be able to categorize, or someone with weakness or lassitude which does not fit into the category of depression – I have often suggested 1,000 micrograms of vitamin B-12 to be injected three times a week for a month. Customarily, I have told patients something like this: 'I'm going to have you get some B-12 injections. They have helped many other patients, but I cannot explain to you why they work and I cannot promise you they will work. I can simply say that many patients tell me they feel better and stronger after such a course of therapy'.
>
> (1986: 1)

Respect for patients' autonomy

Spiro's 'honest way' relies on the use of impure placebos: patients are told only what is true. They are still, though, being intentionally misled, and no less so than they would be were the placebo pure. Is such trickery defensible? Does it not show a failure to respect patients' autonomy? However satisfactory the outcome for the patients so treated, does the method involve a violation of their rights? Spiro rather suggests that doctors, who actually treat patients and know first hand what their priorities are when they are ill, tend to put beneficence before autonomy whereas philosophers reverse these values. Doctors in their day to day experience encounter patients who 'talk not of long-term goals but of feeling better and who seem ready to trade freedom for relief' (1986: 126). 'Physicians usually agree on professional beneficence because they find that their patients do not want to think quite so much about these matters as philosophers claim' (1986: 126) Spiro suggests that the fundamental duty or commitment of physicians should be loyalty to the promise implicit in medical practice: to serve the patient's best interests. When patients are ill and suffering their first priority is not to exercise their autonomy but to get relief from the untoward symptoms.

The first priority of medicine may be just as Spiro says, but of course that does not entitle doctors to use any means whatever – irrespective of patients' rights. Just what respect for patients' autonomy is supposed to involve, and why it is owed, is itself far from clear. Beauchamp and Childress say that 'To respect an autonomous agent is, at a minimum, to acknowledge a person's right to hold views, to make choices, and to take actions based on personal values and beliefs' (1994: 125). What does this imply for doctors' duties? Does it mean that they must acknowledge that each of their patients has a right to some views, some choices, etc? If that is all that is implied, surely everyone acknowledges that! If, on the other hand, what it means is that doctors must acknowledge that each of their patients has a right to every view, every choice, etc., the claim is clearly absurd. In short, this account of what respect for autonomy 'at a minimum' requires seems either to demand so little as to be banal or to demand so much as to be absurd. Needless to say, the extravagant claim may be made in one breath and modified to banality in the next: with the admission that respect is owed only to legitimate choices – i.e. to choices one has a right to make. Hence, the assertion of the duty to respect autonomy may amount to no more than an assertion that patients' right should be respected.

Since Spiro talks of patients not 'exercising' their autonomy, he apparently takes autonomy to be a right – which doctors have a duty to respect. According to Spiro, patients who are suffering from untoward symptoms often choose not to exercise the right. Where patients waive the right, doctors are not failing to respect it if, as Spiro advocates, they make relief of the untoward symptoms the first priority.

Yet administering placebos seems hardly consistent with the promise to patients that they will be treated as equal partners in decisions about their treatment. Spiro's solution is to discard that unrealistic promise:

> While physicians have been learning to try to make the patient an equal partner in decisions about the patient's health, the equality so much talked about really does not exist in many physician-patient encounters, and we should not pretend that it does or should.
>
> (1986: 112)

Howard Brody, on the other hand, claims that either doctors relate to their patients as autonomous choosers capable of making responsible decisions for themselves or they relate to their patients as non-persons. It is, he maintains, just the capacity for autonomous choice that dignifies people and makes them worthy of respect. Even if that is so, the strategy that Spiro defends does not involve any failure to recognise patients' *capacity*. Doctors could only judge a patient to be waiving a right to exercise autonomy if they supposed the patient had the capacity to do so. The choice to waive the right is itself an instance of autonomous choice.

Let us note, though, the ominous significance of Brody's account of where and why respect is owed to patients. Brody says it is owed only to those who have the capacity for making responsible choices. If that is so, what guidance are doctors and nurses to be given for how they should treat patients who are clearly deficient in this capacity – for example, newborn babies, the demented, the comatose? Unabashed by the implications of tying the treatment of patients with respect, to patients' capacity for autonomous choice, Brody proceeds to remark that if 'certain humans, perhaps fetuses or the irreversibly comatose' turn out not to have this capacity – not therefore to be persons, 'their deaths might be permissible if other overriding moral values were thereby served'(1980: 134). He refers the reader to Tooley – who defends infanticide (Tooley 1972). Brody's own further remarks on what constitutes adequate cognitive awareness for one to count as a person implies that more than mere foetuses and the irreversibly comatose are 'as different from us, morally speaking, as a dog or a horse'(1980: 134).

Nowadays, it is easy to see what an inestimably valuable clinical resource living human beings who are deemed to be non-persons would be: for medical education, for organ harvesting, for human research – without any botheration over informed consent!

This idea that people are owed respect simply on account of their rational powers, their capacity for exercising autonomy, has sinister implications for health care. If the avowed aim of the mental health services, for example, is to protect and promote autonomy, what are they supposed to do with those in their care for whom this aim is impossible – for people, for example, with advanced dementia? Beauchamp and Childress say that the respect that is owed to people 'involves treating persons to enable them to act autonomously' (1994: 125). Are we to suppose, then, that those who are irretrievably nonautonomous are *not* owed respect?

Beauchamp and Childress assume that doctors and nurses will treat such people in accordance with the principle of beneficence. They say:

> Those who vigorously defend rights of autonomy in biomedical ethics, as do the present authors, have never denied that some forms of [paternalist] intervention are justified if persons are either wholly or substantially nonautonomous and cannot be rendered autonomous for specific decisions.
>
> (1994: 127–8)

Followers of the Beauchamp and Childress four principles approach might be minded here to bring another of the remaining principles into play once the principle of autonomy is out of play. If the irretrievably nonautonomous are not owed respect, why not humanely put them down and redistribute any harvestable organs to proper respectworthy people? Would this redistribution qualify both as maximizing beneficence and as distributively just?

Spiro, as we have noted, derides the idea that patients can or should be treated as equal partners in decision-making, but he has in mind the specific predicament of patients who suffer from chronic pain. He might be, anyway, and perhaps should be, much more sympathetic to the aim of treating patients as equal partners in other contexts. The old saying of Hoffman's, 'He who cannot dissimulate, cannot cure', may still apply in some areas of medical practice, but no longer applies generally. Moreover, curing is only one of the services that doctors aim to provide. Patients also seek medical advice to avoid becoming ill. Sharing accurate information, treating *them* as equal partners in the aim of avoiding illness, is surely both possible and reasonable.

Defensible deceptions and concealments

We have noted a number of circumstances in which doctors or nurses might decide to deceive patients or conceal information from them. Of course, if the deceiving or concealing is done from a bad motive it is always indefensible: for example routinely giving patients who turn up to the surgery with colds prescriptions for antibiotics merely to save oneself time and bother. But where the motive for deceiving or concealing is good, we should not assume that it is defensible – even if the outcome for the patient is good i.e. the patient gets better. Thus, for example, the fact that placebos work, relieving untoward symptoms, and are prescribed with that good intent, may not by itself vindicate their use. We have also to consider whether the trickery involved violates patients' rights – rights to information or rights of choice. Spiro claims that patients who suffer from chronic pain waive their rights to information – at least, they indicate that they want above all else to get rid of the pain. That is surely plausible, but it has to be admitted that doctors who suppose patients would prefer trading their right to information for the benefit of cure cannot ask them directly if this is what they prefer.

Yet though doctors cannot be open when they are using deception or concealment, they can still be open about their deceiving and concealing practices and policies. Bok instances how the public knowledge that the police use unmarked cars does not destroy the usefulness of this practice nor undermine our trust in the police (1978: 98). Doctors (and nurses) too, could be open with patients about their *general* deceptive and secretive practices and policies. It could be made known, for example, that placebos are sometimes prescribed – and that patients can sometimes be helped by these. Patients knowing of this possibility could always choose to ask directly on this or that particular encounter if they wanted to know if they were being offered a placebo there and then. Then, since, as I have argued, doctors must not lie, the patients would have to be told: they then could not be helped in this way. But that would be their choice. Some patients might prefer not to know. They might have suspicions, but see the sense in not seeking to confirm them. There need be no embarrassment about publicizing the practice of placebo prescribing: provided, of course, there is evidence that it works. Acknowledging the practice publicly would not give patients reason to mistrust their doctors – provided, of course, that doctors were also openly committed to not lying. Doctors who make more extravagant promises; never to intentionally deceive or conceal, though, do undermine trust, because the promise is so unrealistic – unless hedged about with conditions, perhaps that they will only deceive or conceal where doing so is deemed to be in a patient's best interests. But then the promise is belittled to insignificance.

Similarly, doctors and nurses could publicize generally their policies in regard to treatment and care of patients who are mentally ill or impaired: where and why they will sometimes use deceptive or concealing tricks. Again, some patients, aware of this possibility, might ask direct questions that defeat such tactics being pursued with them – like the patient who asks directly, 'Are you a shrink?' and who will not be fobbed off with an answer that is evasive. If doctors refuse to lie, they will sometimes be unable to deliver the treatment a patient needs, but the professional objective of tending patients' health needs is always subject to duties of basic respect owed – which include the duty not to lie.

Provided that doctors are firmly committed not to lie, patients can ask of their own doctors what their general policies are in regard to withholding information or using deceptive tricks. Those doctors who are more guarded about sharing information are not on that account less truthful. Some patients may prefer the more guarded approach, others not.

The duty to inform

Clearly, where doctors and nurses are under a duty to inform they ought not to be either concealing or deceiving. We have noted that the duty to inform might derive from either or both of two basic duties owed to patients: the duty of care and the duty to respect autonomy.

Under the heading of care, how much information is owed, whether openness is beneficial or not, depends, I suggest, on the context and case. While it seems plain foolish, indeed, dishonest, to promise that one will never deceive or conceal, that is not to say that the aim to be open and transparent is not a reasonable, suitable, and honest aim in some, maybe most, medical and nursing contexts – such as with palliative care. One can sincerely profess an aim while making it clear that the aim has to be balanced against other aims and subject to some side-constraints. The case for openness and transparency as the 'philosophy' that should prevail in palliative care is no longer disputed in 'Western' countries. But we should not assume that because openness has proven to be immensely better than secrecy for patients in one context, it must be so in all.

Patients who, after a stroke or a serious accident, face months of rehabilitation, may fare better if they are not told straight away exactly how bleak their long-term prospects are. They might be better off not knowing just how limited, though still enormously significant, are the gains to be achieved if they comply with the exercises they are set. Patients may prove to be more compliant and make better progress if they are shielded from some information, if physiotherapists are deliberately circumspect, even evasive. Provided the patients are not lied to, they can still trust the word of their physiotherapists.

Yet even if it is true that simply from the caring perspective, patients may, in some contexts, in rehabilitation, as opposed to those in palliative care, do better if kept somewhat in the dark, what about the other perspective: the duty to respect patients' autonomy – their right to know? If information is kept from patients, does this not mean that they are being treated without their consent? And isn't the requirement to pursue the caring health objectives as much subject to the side-constraint that patients consent as I have argued it is subject to their not being lied to?

The principle of adequately informed consent

Paul Ramsey refers to informed consent as 'the cardinal canon of loyalty' between patient and doctor or nurse (1970: 5). The consent-requirement is nothing new. Wherever medicine is practiced in good faith there is, always has been, the presumption that patients consent to be treated. That presumption has often relied on implied consent – the simple fact that patients co-operate, do as they are told.

But this assumption is often legitimate – for example, in many routine visits to dentist, GP or clinic. The very same presumption governs many routine transactions outside the medical context. What is new is the emphasis many people nowadays place upon the need for consent to be 'informed'. Of course, you have to have at least some broad understanding of what is up, to be consenting to a treatment, but how informed do you need to be for your consent to be real? Ramsey, while rightly emphasizing the central importance of consent, allows for some flexibility about the amount of information that is owed to patients. He speaks of 'adequately informed consent'. What is 'adequate' will depend on context and patient. Women attending antenatal clinics are asked to bring samples of their urine on each visit. They may be given a leaflet that explains why this is needed. But when the nurses collect samples, they will not quiz the women to see if they have read and understood the leaflets. The women are given the opportunity to be informed; they are not obliged to use it. Their co-operation signifies consent.

As Ramsey observes, no one nowadays would 'propose to eliminate the consent-requirement directly, but this can be done more subtly, or by indirection' (1970: 11). Patients, moreover, are at special risk just because there is always a temptation where the ends in view are praiseworthy to overlook the means: 'Stripped of the requirement of a reasonably free and adequately informed consent, experimentation and medicine itself would speedily become inhumane' (1970: 11). Thus, we need to be most cautious about practices and policies that aim to secure patients' consent by deliberately concealing information, as with our example of the patient who was known not to want to be seen by a psychiatrist. I submit that such procedures need not abuse the 'canon of loyalty' – the consent of these patients, though presumed, can be defended as 'adequately' informed – at least, if doctors make public when they are prepared to adopt deceptive or concealing practices and do not *promise* their patients openness in all circumstances. The 'canon of loyalty' does not require doctors to give the same amount or kind of information to all comers or on all occasions. What is 'adequate' information may, for example, sometimes turn on a person's cultural background – though, of course, doctors and nurses need to avoid stereotyping their patients according to their cultural origins.

There is, though, additional reason to be wary about deceptive or concealing practices when consent is sought to involve patients in trials as research subjects. Here the end in view is not, or not only, benefit to the patient, but benefit to medical science. It is one thing to calculate what is 'better' for an individual person to know or not know when consent is sought, where what is traded off is the various needs and concerns of one and the same person; quite another, to calculate what is better to tell or not tell to an individual person when consent is sought, where the trade off is between the needs or interests of different persons. In the latter case it is not so much that the calculation is more difficult, it is rather that it is highly problematic whether the calculation even makes sense. It may be better for the patient to be told, better for medical science that the patient not be told. But is there some *other* point of view from which to adjudicate between the possibly conflicting interests here: to judge what is simply 'better'? Isn't 'better' always better for A or for B or for C ...?

Rather than ask what is 'better', we need to ask what is just. Here, it seems plausible to insist that a trade off is not just unless at least those who are recruited as research subjects give their consent. But how much information need they be given for their consent to be real? Is openness owed to patients who are invited to participate in trials? What if a particular trial by its nature necessitates some concealing or even deceiving? Are there honest ways of enlisting participants in such trials – for example, inviting them in advance to waive the right to know certain things? Can consent in some circumstances be presumed – or is that to invite abuse of patients' trust?

8   Dishonesty in medical research

> He is – like most men – as honest as he can afford to be. But he cannot afford to be
> scientifically honest. Ordinary commonplace honesty is a cheap thing. The honesty
> that prevents you stealing my umbrella does not cost you much. But scientific
> honesty is a monstrously expensive thing.
>
> George Bernard Shaw

Should we suppose that truth-seekers are truthful? Jacob Bronowski seems to have
thought so. He says that for scientists 'nothing matters as much as the single-
minded pursuit of truth' (1977: 199) and that the 'professional veracity of
scientists allows no compromises. It tells each man that he must report what he
believes to be true, exactly and without suppression or editing…' (1977: 200). But
as Gerald Dworkin observes, this assumption that truth-seekers will be truthful is
quite unsafe: the idea that science is 'objective, self-correcting, concerned only
with the truth, immune from the biases and motivations that seem inherent in all
other forms of human activity' (1983: 66) and, hence, that scientists are honest and
rational, idealizes science and scientists. Dworkin illustrates this lofty misper-
ception of the scientist quoting from the eminent sociologist of science, Robert
Merton: who says that there is a 'virtual absence of fraud in the annals of science'
(Merton 1968: 613). Dworkin notes that while Merton said this in an address that
was given back in 1937, later, in 1968, Merton was still accounting for the absence
of fraud in science as due to 'distinctive characteristics of science itself … the veri-
fiability of results … the exacting scrutiny of fellow experts' (Merton 1968: 613).
Two assumptions underlie this idealization of science and scientists: both
unsound.

One of the assumptions fastens on the thought that the definitive aim or duty of
the scientist is to advance knowledge, to seek out the truth. It is assumed that such
an aim cannot be helped by dishonest practices – for example, by falsifying results
or fabricating data. Since scientists aim at the truth, don't they have an obvious
motive *not* to falsify; wouldn't it be self-defeating? The other unreliable
assumption made by the idealizers is that even if some scientists are minded to
falsify, they must realize that their dishonesty would soon be discovered since their
findings would not be replicated. The scientific method, it is supposed, prevents

lying, because the requirement that results be replicated constitutes a built in lie-detector (Mixon 1987: 47).

The first assumption is simplistic. Scientists engage in their truth-seeking investigations for a number of reasons – one of which may be curiosity – wanting to know, to understand and be able to explain. But they have other and further aims and other duties that may sometimes compete, and that always shape the way they do their work. Thus they (and their employers) do not just want to discover truths, but to do so *first*. Those whose lot it is merely to replicate the findings of others, the also-rans, miss out on the power and glory. Dworkin comments:

> It should come as no surprise that if originality, doing something for the first time, is rewarded with status and position, then there will be relatively few replications of experimental studies, and the opportunity for fraud will be present. Journal editors are reluctant to publish replication even when it casts doubt on previously published studies.
>
> (1983: 73)

David Goodstein observes:

> The Noble Scientist is supposed to be more virtuous and upright than ordinary mortals, impervious to the base human drives, such as personal ambition, and of course, incapable of misbehaving even in the smallest way.
>
> (1995: 31)

But the 'Myth of the Noble Scientist' is fading – and was, most likely, always a myth.

Most scientists are probably neither Holabirds nor Gottliebs: they aspire, like Martin Arrowsmith, to make significant discoveries in their work but also to enjoy some of the fruits of their hard work in more worldly and sociable pursuits.[1] We need not cynically suppose that because scientists hope to gain recognition and rewards for their work they do not genuinely also care to advance knowledge. Part of the allure of working in the biomedical sciences is surely that one may both make discoveries that will improve the life of others *and* reap a personal reward. No doubt consciousness of *how* one has come by the fruits of one's labour can add to or diminish the zest of one's enjoyment of them (not that dishonesty necessarily 'diminishes' – as Mark Twain observed, reflecting on the enjoyment of actual fruits: 'I know the taste of water melon which has been honestly come by, and I know the taste of the water melon which has been acquired by art. Both taste good, but the experienced know which tastes best').

In any case, the first assumption – the thought that since scientists are truth-seekers they cannot have reason to falsify – indicates at most a reason for not falsifying evidence or data. It does not provide reason against plagiarizing or misappropriating someone else's ideas. A scientist may steal someone else's data in order to find out what is true. And, of course, it is perfectly possible to want to know the truth *and* to want to put one's rivals off the scent – J.D. Watson, in *The*

Double Helix (1980), confesses he and his co-worker, Crick, deliberately misled Linus Pauling. Wanting to know is one thing; wanting others to know is quite another. (Plato never seems to get round to explaining why those who emerge from the cave of darkness into the light of truth can be expected to return to the cave to enlighten others.) Furthermore, deception may sometimes be a useful, even necessary way of getting at the truth, as where, for example, one is seeking evidence of patients' compliance or, indeed, of colleagues' dishonest practices. If one already has reason to suspect that the people under investigation are not willingly going to reveal what one seeks to discover, only covert, and possibly only deceptive, methods will serve. Thus, it is just not true that truth-seekers will naturally eschew deception – it depends, among other things, on the nature of the truth being sought.

As for the notion that scientists have to be honest in their work because if they are not, they are bound to be found out and disgraced; we know that this is not true. From time to time scandals of scientific frauds which have been perpetrated for years without discovery come to light. Coincidentally, in the very week that I write these lines, Kurt Eichenwald and Gina Kolata report on a case in point (*New York Times*, 17 May 1999). A Dr Fiddes of Whittier, California, has been found guilty of fraudulent research practices – fabricating evidence, falsifying data, rigging medical tests and inventing patients. He started out as a family doctor and then on discovering the lucrative business of drug trials he began enlisting his patients, and in due course opened up his own drug research business. Eventually, an employee who resigned from her job blew the whistle, reporting him to the FDA. A memo was filed. No action was taken. A year later more staff had resigned, one of whom again blew the whistle. When Dr Fiddes was finally cornered and obliged to cooperate as part of his plea agreement, he claimed that many other doctors were doing the same, that fraud was rampant in the research industry. Fiddes also claimed that he would never have been caught had it not been for disgruntled employees.

If he is right, doctors who carry on in his fashion are unlucky if they get caught: weighing the likely gains against the slight risks, it is a rational gamble. Fiddes succeeded in eluding both government and company monitors. It is easy to see how inadequate their scrutiny is against the determined fraudster. Monitors review paperwork from tests, but the paperwork may all be in order although the records have been deliberately falsified. Company monitors check records but are not allowed to carry out spot checks with patients. Government monitors can do so but rarely do unless they already have evidence of fraud.

Other instances of flagrant dishonesty in medical research have been discovered – and often the culprits are researchers with an established reputation, not just post doc students who might have some excuse, being new to the game, if they suppose that corner cutting is tolerated. There was the eminent immunologist, Dr Robert Good, who collaborated with Dr William Summerlin. For their research (at the Memorial Sloan Kettering Center in New York) they needed to have some rats with healthy black patches grafted onto their skin. When nature failed to provide, they just painted the patches on – but were caught in the act. That was back in 1974.[2] Since then a number of cases have come to light in the United States involving reputable scientists and universities: for example:

In 1983 John Darsee, a researcher at Harvard Medical School, was found by the National Institute of Health to have faked some data in his studies on heart disease. In 1984 the National Institute of Mental Health concluded that Stephen Breunig at the University of Pittsburgh, had fabricated data in a paper about drug therapy for hyperactive children. In both cases earlier internal investigations had cleared the scientists of blame.

(Hilts 1997: 44)

Hilts also mentions the recent and, in his view, 'most remarkable case of misconduct in the annals of American science' which has come to be known as 'the Baltimore case' 'named after the scientist who refused to investigate allegations of faked notebooks, Dr. David Baltimore, rather than after Dr. Thereza Imanishi-Kari, the scientist charged with the fraud' (Hilts 1997: 44). Baltimore was a Nobel Prize winner, former head of the Whitehead Institute and president of Rockefeller University – and has since been forced to resign.

Nathaniel J. Pallone and James J. Hennessy list a number of cases of 'real or apparent' misconduct reports in the press since 1990 involving biomedical science – for example:

Systematic deception over a period of thirteen years surfaces when it is learned that a Canadian physician cooperating with researchers at a major US medical school had reported fictitious results, on the basis of which the principal investigators had advised the medical community world-wide that a 'less radical' surgical procedure than mastectomy had proven effective treating cancer of the breast. Although the principal investigators had learned of the deceit years earlier, they had not retracted their claims in favor of the 'less radical' procedure.

(Pallone and Hennessy 1995: 4)

David Goodstein (1995: 30) conjectures as to why scientists in the *biomedical* sciences might be especially prone to dishonesty and comes up with three possible explanations:

1   They are under more intense career pressure;
2   They are more prone to believe that they already know the answers and need not go to the trouble of getting the data;
3   They think they are somewhat protected (more so than in the physical sciences) because experiments are not expected to be exactly reproducible.
    To these I would add a fourth explanation:
4   They see their 'corner-cutting' as justifiable in view of the pressing need to find cures for the incurable and less toxic drugs than those currently in use.

It is also possible, of course, that biomedical scientists are no more dishonest than other types of scientists but are more likely to be rumbled – especially if they are working in labs alongside others. GPs entering their patients in drug trials are not so likely to be caught out in fraudulent practices – unless they are careless, as seems to have been the case with a UK practitioner, Dr James Bochsler, who fraudulently entered patients in two trials, forging signatures on consent forms. He is reported in the BMJ to have been paid over £23,000. The discrepancies came to light only on an auditor's third visit when it seems that Bochsler had forgotten about the appointment and was taken by surprise (Dyer 1998: 1475).

As Pallone and Hennessy observe, these instances of flagrant dishonesty give the lie to the notion that 'the very canons of science themselves preclude misbehavior' (1995: 10). Marcel LaFollette writes:

> For every assertion that scientists are 99.99999 percent honest, or that only a tiny fraction of articles in the Medline data base have ever been formally retracted and hence fraud is rare and attention to it irrelevant, there have been social surveys that point to a quite different conclusion.
>
> (1995: 39–40)

For our purposes in this enquiry, let us put to one side consideration of practices by scientists which are uncontroversially dishonest – like the antics of a physician researcher, Elias Alsatbi who fabricated his curriculum vitae, copied a colleague's grant for his own use, published other people's data under his own name, and co-authored his pilfered data with fictitious collaborators; (Elliott and Stern 1997: 2)[3] or of Dr Malcolm Pearce, a senior gynaecologist who dishonestly claimed (in 1995) to have carried out the first ever relocation of an ectopic pregnancy (Jones 1999). Of course, no-one condones such practices – though such research misconduct is said to be endemic in the UK and US (Jones 1999: 660). But there are various other kinds of deceptive and concealing practices in biomedical research which are not so obviously unconscionable and which may be unashamedly adopted and defended by conscientious researchers. Should a line be drawn, for example, between 'harmless fudging' and 'real fraud' – the former to be tolerated, the latter not?

Harmless fudging

David Goodstein maintains that there is an important distinction to be made between 'harmless fudging' or 'minor hypocrisies' in science, and real fraud. He suggests that there are certain euphemistic expressions which are now so common that no one is misled by them:

> For example, 'owing to difficulties in sample handling' really means something like 'we dropped it on the floor'. 'It has long been known that ...' means 'I haven't bothered to look up the original reference.' 'Typical results are shown' means 'these are the best data I have ever managed to get'.
>
> (1995: 31–2)

Goodstein also suggests that there is a kind of hypocrisy in the way scientists write up their research, 'describing it as one clear step after the other' whereas the reality is 'You never know what is going on; you cannot usually understand what the data mean. But in the end you figure out what it was all about and then, with hindsight, you write it up' (1995: 31). Yet since the writing up of scientific work is not supposed to be a descriptive reporting of events such as a camera might record, in conforming to the convention, scientists are not being either hypocritical or dishonest. There is nothing inherently untruthful about deliberate editing and selecting, in reporting. All reporting, even that done by the constable in the witness box, necessarily edits out irrelevancies. The constable is not supposed to tell the court everything else he saw at the time of the incident – for example, a child cycling down the street, a jacket in a shop window that he rather fancied. Even those who are sworn to tell the 'whole truth' understand that it is the whole *relevant* truth only that is sought.

Goodstein says:

> It may be permissible to present your best set of data and casually refer to it as typical, but it is not permissible to move one data point just a little bit to make the data look just that little bit better. All scientists would agree that to do so is fraud.
>
> (1995: 32)

Suppose, though, that a scientist fabricates data in the version of a paper he submits for review with the intention of correcting in the final version if, perchance, the data need amending. This was the defence James Urban gave for the fabrication he was found to have committed while researching at Caltech (Roberts 1997). He insisted that it was never his intention to publish fabricated data. His only reason for initially submitting the false data was to speed the review process. Was this dishonest? Was it, assuming his intentions were as he claimed, a minor departure from proper procedure? Was it a trivial lie and as such a harmless deception? Was it like saying 'the cheque is in the post' when you intend forthwith to make that true?

Compare the stratagem that we discussed earlier for fending off an awkward question with an answer which is literally false but which all the same tells enquirers what they really want to know: responding to the 'remote intention' behind a question. Thus the traveller seeking entry to a town and asked if he came from a certain city, believed to be plague-ridden, might answer no falsely yet not be lying if he knew that he was not bringing plague. Here, it might likewise be argued that the remote intention of the reviewers receiving one's data is to make sure that they do not publish false data. Suppose that the submitter does not intend to let that happen, can he meanwhile submit false data without disclosing this and not be lying?

Whether or not such a stratagem is defensible it certainly involves lying, by our definition. A temporary lie is still a lie. Presumably, if one sent a covering letter explaining that the data were still to be confirmed, the reviewers would decline to proceed. But does it matter if *they* are lied to, provided the author of the paper truly intends to amend if need be before publication? We may suppose further that the author confidently expects that the results will confirm the data submitted, in which case even the reviewers are not deceived, except that they are told what will be true as if it were already true. The intent behind such a manoeuvre is not to publish falsehoods but to steal a march on the opposition – it is a form of cheating, a form of queue jumping. Trivial lies (not that these are to be condoned) are supposed not to matter to or for the deceived, but fabricating data even as a merely temporary expedient seems fraught with risk. There would be such a temptation not to amend the data if the results failed to turn out quite as expected. Anyway, cheating is not harmless: it disadvantages those who play by the rules.

What should count as dishonest practice in the conduct of research aside from the obvious cases of faking data, plagiarizing or misappropriating ideas? Goodstein remarks, 'one might argue that, if all scientists rigorously adhered to proper scientific procedure at all times, very little scientific progress would occur' (1995: 25–6). That may be good reason for avoiding inflating the requirement of 'proper scientific procedure' so that it becomes unrealistic to expect it to be strictly followed. Of course, if nothing is done to monitor rules and there are obvious career and financial gains in breaking them, it is already unreasonable to expect people to observe them. Similarly, if something is done which is manifestly inadequate to monitor research, which is plainly a token gesture at monitoring, we should not expect rules to be dutifully observed. Consider, for example, the care given over vetting research protocols for trials on humans and the paucity of follow up. However carefully and sensibly research ethics committees scrutinize patient information sheets, how protective of patients' rights can this be if there is no independent monitoring of how these are presented to patients? In this matter if we simply trust the doctors concerned, are we not falling for the noble scientist myth, in spite of the high financial or career stakes they may have in recruiting patients for trials?

Corner-cutting

Alain Spriet and Therese Dupin Spriet suggest that while there are instances of blatant fraud, much more commonly researchers cheat in little ways – making minor 'corrections', for example, so as to fit a patient within a protocol that excludes anyone weighing over 80 kg – and the patient weighs in at 82 kg. Similarly, one might be tempted to fill in a missing result with a plausible answer (1992: 13–14). According to our account of truthfulness, even 'trivial' lies are not to be tolerated – it is not safe to do so.

Thus, truthfulness rules out such practices as 'trimming' (altering one's data), forging or faking (making up one's data). Whether it also rules out 'cooking' or 'finagling' (selective reporting of one's data – telling only part of the truth) will depend upon codes and declarations, if any, scientists sign up to. Lying is dishonest in science as elsewhere, but deceptions and concealments which do not involve lying (as they would if one were pledged not to deceive or conceal) are not necessarily dishonest. Goodstein worries that requiring scientists to be strictly bound to abide by the rules which define proper scientific conduct may stifle progress, but his examples of the license reputable scientists allow themselves are only of euphemisms and pretences, not actual lying.

He appears to assume that a strict requirement on researchers to be truthful would preclude their engaging in any form of deception, pretence or concealment. He says:

> No human activity can stand up to the glare of relentless, absolute honesty. We all build little hypocrisies into what we do to make life a little bit easier to live. Because science is a very human activity, hypocrisies and misrepresentations are built into the way we do it.
>
> (1995: 31)

We have noted how talk of 'absolute honesty' tends to assimilate honesty (truthfulness) with candour. But these are distinct traits – only the former is plausibly a core virtue. Truthfulness rules out lying, for scientists as much as for anyone else, but it does not rule out pretence or concealment, neither of which need involve deception. Nor does it always rule out intentional deception.

Dishonest pretences

Pretence is dishonest, of course, when it gives the lie to what one promises. Failing to keep one's promise does not necessarily give the lie, but making promises one has no intention to keep (for example, making promises one knows it will be impossible to keep) does give the lie. If doctors profess to be acting in their patients' best interests when in fact they are only pretending, they act dishonestly. David Shimm and Roy Spece maintain that:

> Significant amounts of clinical research are solely to the benefit of science, scientists, society, institutions, and industry and at the expense of subjects who do not realise that their chances of personally benefiting from the research are *extremely* remote.
>
> (1996: 363)

If doctors are committed to putting their own patients' interests first, should they even be in the business of encouraging them to act as martyrs? We 'salve our consciences with the knowledge that informed consent has been given' say Samuel and Deborah Hellman (1991: 1588). But does the rigmarole of obtaining informed consent of subjects in trials ensure that they do realize the extent to which they are being invited to be altruistic?

It is said that randomized clinical trials are justified provided that the doctors who recruit patients are themselves in equipoise: that they do not know which of the treatments or procedures being investigated is better (Lilford and Jackson 1995). That is, after all, why the trial is needed. They are not holding back on helpful information to guide their patients' choices if they simply have no idea which of the alternatives is better. But is not the profession of equipoise often itself a cheat? Is it made plain to the patients being recruited that when their doctors say they do not know, they mean that whatever they personally believe in the light of what they have seen and read does not amount to scientific proof?

> What the physician thinks, suspects, believes or has a hunch about is assigned to the 'not knowing' category, because knowing is defined on the basis of an arbitrary but accepted statistical test performed in a randomised clinical trial.
>
> (Hellman and Hellman 1991: 1586)

Are patients not entitled to have access to the doctor's knowledge *and* opinion? (Hellman and Hellman 1991: 1587).

Patients are likely to suspect that doctors affect equipoise because they are eager to do trials – whether they are motivated merely by the desire to establish what really works or also by personal ambition. Polly Toynbee writes about why she twice refused to join trials. On the first occasion she was invited to join a trial as there was a high family risk of breast cancer. The second occasion arose after she did develop breast cancer. On that occasion she writes:

> I was offered another randomized trial. I would be allocated tamoxifen, tamoxifen and radiotherapy, just radiotherapy or nothing. I was sure my distinguished specialist had a hunch which treatment he thought best. I demanded the benefit of his experience. He would not give it. At this point, any patient wonders whether the imperatives of science are interfering with the doctor's imperative to do the best possible for his patient.
>
> (*The Independent*, 29 May 1996)

Perhaps the Hippocratic ethic that binds doctors to act exclusively in their patients' interests is no longer tenable. The card issued by the General Medical Council to UK medical students listing the duties of a doctor has as item one: 'Make the care of your patient your first concern'. *First* concern, of course, does not necessarily mean *only* concern. All the same, does this duty allow *any* trade offs between the interests of your patient and those of other patients? Perhaps, doctors nowadays should be balancing the needs of other patients against those of their own. But then, if they are truthful, they will need to make it clear (through their professional declarations, for example) that they no longer hold with the Hippocratic notion of unqualified commitment to each of their individual patients. And then perhaps they should drop this talk of the patient's own care being their 'first concern'? Instead, professional declarations could explain to the public that doctors will sometimes see fit to risk doing their patients harm in order to benefit others. And the business of consent getting from patients being entered in trials then should perhaps also be dropped – become more a matter of courtesy, and anxiety-allaying – as one might explain to a young child patient what one is about without seriously seeking the child's informed consent.

Otherwise, the procedure of consent seeking when recruiting patients to trials may often smack of dishonest pretence – especially where the patients being recruited are very seriously ill. What choice have they but to agree, if the only access to a novel 'promising' treatment is through entry to a trial? Even if they could refuse and ask to be given the new treatment outside the trial, what reason have they to believe the formal ritual assurances on consent forms that their care will in no way be compromised if they decline? Is it rational for them to trust their doctors' word? They might be in a position to trust the family GP whom they've known over many years, but if they are in hospital with a serious illness, they may be barely acquainted with the various members of the team attending them (Hellman and Hellman 1991: 1587).

Why do patients with advanced cancer agree to enter Phase 1 trials – trials that do not aim to cure, or yield remission or prolong life, but only to establish the maximum tolerated dose of an anticancer agent? Is it not likely that in many cases they agree only because they are desperate and hope against hope it might benefit them? (Freedman 1996: 330). If those who recruit the patients realize that they are agreeing to enter the trial only because they are deluded, is it not exploiting their desperation and therefore an error to admit them? Here the ritual of informed consent is 'the salve' and a dishonest pretence. Of course, it may be argued that such patients owe some contribution to the scientific quest, since they have surely been beneficiaries of all that has been learned to date. If this is (any part of) the justification for 'inviting' them into trials, honesty requires that it be admitted to. Then the invitation becomes something which patients may be made to understand only asks (calls on) them to do their duty. In that case, there is at least an element of coerciveness in the invitation: it is an invitation that it is uncitizenly to refuse – 'helping' the doctors with their enquiries is rather like 'helping' the police, and the helpers are hardly volunteers.

The 'scientific imperative'

Following the article in the *New England Journal of Medicine* by S. Hellman and D.S. Hellman (1991) which claims that randomized clinical trials 'often place physicians in the ethically intolerable position of choosing between the good of the patient and that of society' was an article by Eugene Passamani, which pointed to the many instances that have come to light of therapies being widely and enthusiastically adopted, only later to turn out to have been ineffective or harmful (1991: 1589–92). An impassioned correspondence on the issue ensued. Whether doctors should put the interests of scientific progress before the best interests of their own patients is an issue we can side-step here.

In passing, though, I do suggest that the idea that randomized clinical trials are indispensable, if knowledge is to advance, trades on a false dichotomy between what we know in consequence of such trials and what we are ignorant about: it ignores the mass of knowledge we have by other, albeit less sure, means. One of the correspondents siding with the Hellmans, Leslie Iffy, noted that Jenner, Semmelweiss and Pasteur advanced scientific understanding without the benefit of randomized clinical trials (quoted by Lantos 1997: 137).[4] In any case, in conducting a randomized trial one has to rely on standard practices and procedures which have not all themselves been tried and tested via randomization.

It is said to be only ethically defensible to mount trials where there is equipoise (genuine uncertainty between the old and the new drug or procedure). Yet, as John Lantos observes, 'If historical data were worthless, we could never be in a state of equipoise because we could never have any idea how the next patient might respond to either treatment'. But of course we do (1997: 143). In our day to day life, we rely on knowledge which is not derived from randomized trials. In medical science, even in recent years, 'much medical progress takes place in the absence of clinical trials' – Lantos gives examples from neonatology and cardiology (1997: 148–50). The conviction that patients who are dying, patients who are diagnosed with cancer, and others, are better off being told 'the truth' is itself not grounded on double blinded randomized trials but on surveys of patients and relatives and on the clinical observations of experienced doctors and nurses.

Hester Elliott describes the following incident where she was upbraided for being unscientific.

> I was telling a group of Sioux people in Poplar, Montana, how to heal ulcers one day, when the local medical doctor and public health officer walked in. Afterwards, they said, I shouldn't have told those people which herbs to use to get rid of ulcers. I said, 'Why is that? I learned about these herbs from another group of Native people. I am only returning to them their own information.'
>
> 'But this hasn't been proved to work scientifically,' said the lady doctor.
>
> 'I don't care,' said I, 'and what's more, neither do they. The ulcers go away.'
>
> 'You are being irresponsible,' they said to me. 'If you really know something that will cure ulcers, you should go through the proper channels and publish and make the information available to all.'
>
> I replied, 'You heard what I said. If you want that to happen go ahead and do it. I haven't got time to re-prove something we all know since time out of mind. I'm too busy cleaning up ulcers'.
>
> (Elliott 1988: 48)

Common sense knowledge is, admittedly, fallible. It is also indispensable – to scientists, no less than to everyone else.

Our concern here, though, is not to resolve the issue of how to reconcile the needs of society to find cures and less toxic treatments with the duties of doctors and nurses to the individual patients in their care, but to clarify what truthfulness requires and permits in the context of clinical research. Truthfulness does not rule for or against putting science needs first or second, but it does rule against doctors and nurses *professing* to put (present, actual) patients first while their research practices show that they do not.

Research which of necessity involves deception of subjects

Sometimes it would be self-defeating to reveal to subjects in advance the purposes of the trial to which they are being recruited. For example, as Allan Kimmel observes,

> We might expect many subjects to 'bend over backwards' to show how accepting they are of members of other races if the subjects are aware that they are participants in a study of racial prejudice.

> (1996: 68)

To avoid distorting the reactions of participants in a study of this kind, its purpose needs to be kept hidden from them until the study is completed. Deception has been a prominent feature of psychological studies, of which Stanley Milgram's obedience study in the 1960s is one of the most notorious and controversial. This study involved deceiving subjects into thinking that they were administering increasingly harmful electric shocks to participants involved in a learning experiment (Milgram 1963).[5] In fact, the real purpose of the study was to see how far subjects would go in obeying the instructions to administer punitive shocks. There is a whole genre of psychological studies, known as 'emergency bystander studies', in which an emergency – for example, a robbery, or a mugging, is faked, to see how bystanders react (Diener and Crandall 1978). Obviously, the aims of such studies cannot be explained to subjects in advance.

Some lines of study involving patients, their relatives or clinical staff may also require that those under observation are either not aware of the purpose of the study or are unaware that they are being observed. Where what is being studied is, for example, patients' compliance with medication instructions, giving advance notice would obviously skew the results. Are deceptive or secret studies involving patients or others in the clinical setting ethically defensible? Do they compromise truthfulness? Can patients or others be adequately informed when they are invited to participate in research if some information about the study they are entered in is deliberately withheld?

Social science researchers claim that deception is a 'methodological necessity' in many important studies: 'An absolute rule prohibiting the use of deception in all research would make it impossible for researchers to carry out a wide range of important studies' (Kimmel 1996: 68). Let us here suppose that is so – and for some clinical studies too. The question then arises whether such studies, however important, are still ethically indefensible, or whether they need not compromise truthfulness provided that they are suitably regulated by codes.

The use of deception in social science studies is said to have reached a peak in the early 1970s. It may not have abated much since:

> In addition to the fact that the frequency of deception has not declined in recent years despite the implementation of more stringent ethical regulations, there is also some evidence that the nature and intensity of the deceptions have also remained relatively unchanged.

> (Kimmel 1996: 78)

Perhaps it is unrealistic to expect the vague wording of codes to constitute a firm bulwark against the conduct of research that is anticipated to yield socially valuable information. On the other hand, the mere fact that many studies continue to involve incomplete disclosure to those recruited as research subjects does not necessarily indicate that the codes are failing to uphold truthfulness. We need here to look more closely at what is allowed – whether, for example, codes distinguish between actually telling lies to subjects (which I maintain would compromise truthfulness) and simply not revealing certain truths about the study's aim (which I maintain need not compromise truthfulness).

The Declaration of Helsinki (1996 version) simply rules that potential subjects must be 'adequately informed of the aims, methods, …'. It does not make explicit if it is all the aims or only some that must be explained. But it directs that where 'the physician considers it essential not to obtain informed consent, the specific reason for this proposal must be stated in the experimental protocol for transmission to the independent committee' (Brody 1998: Appendix I.2, 215).

The Canadian Medical Protective Association's booklet *Consent: A Guide for Canadian Physicians* (1996) states that potential subjects 'must have been given an adequate explanation about the nature of the proposed investigation or treatment'. It says: 'Always a fair explanation must be given' and it upholds the 'reasonable patient standard'. In the experimental situation, it emphasises the importance of full disclosure of risks and benefits. But it does not explicitly discuss the issue before us.

The International Ethical Guidelines for Biomedical Research Involving Human Subjects (Geneva 1993) states that all potential subjects must have been told 'the aims and methods of the research' – again, not specifying whether *all* the aims must be revealed. But it later states that the investigator has a duty 'to exclude the possibility of unjustified deception' (Vanderpool 1996: Appendix F, 504).

The Royal College of Physicians, Research Involving Patients – Summary of Recommendations (1990) says:

> There are some circumstances in which it is justifiable to initiate research without the consent of the patient. Such circumstances do not affect the duty of the investigator to obtain the prior approval of the Research Ethics Committee in the usual way.
>
> (7.64–7.74 in Brody 1998: 318)

All of the above indicate implicitly or explicitly that 'incomplete disclosure' including deception (lying? non-lying?) is sometimes justified – but they offer no guidance as to when or why. The when question was directly addressed in the Belmont Report (1979) (in Vanderpool 1996: Appendix C, 437–48) and dealt with in similar terms later in the Code of Federal Regulations for Protection of Human Subjects (1991) (Vanderpool 1996: Appendix D, 449–83) where the following conditions were put forward as required where incomplete disclosure was proposed:

1 The risks to subjects must be minimal
2 The subjects' rights and welfare must not be 'adversely affected'
3 There are no practicable alternative ways of carrying out the research
4 Where possible full disclosure would be offered subsequently.

The Belmont Report also notes that 'truthful answers should always be given to direct questions about the research' (Vanderpool 1996: 443).

Thus, the Belmont guidelines do not permit lying but do permit deception of subjects who are being recruited into trials. To be sure incomplete disclosure may simply involve concealing information rather than aiming to mislead – though the emergency bystander type studies do involve the latter. But even simply concealing information is deceptive in the consent-seeking context (unless subjects are forewarned): otherwise, the formalities of consent seeking encourage those who are approached to suppose that they are being put in the picture. However, if these guidelines are adopted *and publicized*, then we all know to expect we may sometimes have information kept from us or deceptive tricks played on us when we take part in trials. The deception that is being allowed in these guidelines does not abuse our trust any more than does the use of unmarked cars by the police: *if* we have been warned! And if we do not want to be involved in trials of this kind, we can always ask directly if the particular trial we are being invited to join does involve incomplete disclosure. If we do ask directly, these Belmont guidelines require truthful answers.

The requirement that those who do consent to take part in such trials should be 'debriefed' afterwards is a wise safeguard against abuse. If those who conduct the study know they will have to debrief after, they will be more likely to reflect hard on the question whether what they are putting subjects through is something which the patients will subsequently accept was reasonable. Here too, though, it makes all the difference so far as abuse of trust is concerned whether the debriefers are owning up to having lied to participants or merely to having withheld certain information or played certain deceptive tricks. If debriefers confess to having lied, how are the debriefed to trust that what they are now being told might not also include some lies?

Imagine what might be going on in the mind of a participant who has just left an experiment in which he or she received false feedback about performance on an intelligence test. This participant might think, 'I know I was lied to during the experiment, but I'm not sure when: was the poor score I received on the test really a fake, as the researcher confessed at the end of the study, or did the researcher simply make up a story about the test before I left to make me feel better about receiving such a horrible score?' (Kimmel 1996: 87–8).

The American Psychological Association's 'Ethical Principles of Psychologists and Code of Conduct' (1992) set a standard for deception in research that many other countries have since used as their model (Kimmel 1996: 326). It requires that deception should not be used unless a study has sufficient social value, is not feasible unless subjects are deceived, and only provided that 'psychologists never deceive research patients about significant aspects that would affect their will-ingness to participate, such as risks, discomfort or unpleasant experiences' (quoted in Clarke 1999: 152).

Notice the weasel word 'significant' in the above stipulation: that 'psychologists should never deceive research patients about significant aspects'. 'Significant' for whom – from whose standpoint? 'Significant' is just another word for 'important'. What is insignificant from the standpoint of society at large may be decidedly significant from an individual subject's standpoint. A cost-benefit analysis for building a bridge across a river may include the calculation that a few lives will be lost in the building of it. That cost may be insignificant from the public standpoint, easily off-set by the projected benefits, but hardly so easily from the standpoint of those who are employed to erect the bridge.

The Belmont and Federal guidelines state that the risks to subjects must be 'minimal': another weasel word! Might not a risk be both substantial for the subjects and minimal: the minimum required if the study is to achieve its purpose? With the Milgram study there was the risk not just of immediate distress during the trial but of longer term distress arising from the unpalatable self-insights the study revealed about the participants. What is perhaps most worrisome about the Milgram experiment is the report that when the participants were debriefed they were not, it seems, as disturbed as they should have been (Elms 1982: 236).[6] Arguably, though, we should not take what subjects say when they are debriefed at their word. It might seem rather feeble and pathetic to grumble about the ordeal of the study or the 'inflicted insight' one has received as a result of it, given the social importance of the study.

I suggest that some further additions to the above codes are needed if truthfulness is not to be compromised. The weasel words should be avoided or at any rate it should be made clear that any risks must be insubstantial from the subjects' standpoint. Furthermore, where a study involves the formality of consent-seeking, I would add that potential subjects should be forewarned that the study's aims can only be partially explained at the enrolment stage.

With some studies that necessitate incomplete disclosure, the forewarning could be issued at the very time when consent is sought. With others, alerting subjects to this might itself spoil the study. In the latter case the forewarning would need to be issued generally. Compare how in some circumstances the police can issue warnings to the public that they are using hidden cameras; in other circumstances, they may use them but cannot safely alert those who will be spied upon to this. A notice on the road alerting us to 'Hidden cameras!' does not defeat the police purpose: it may persuade us to drive more sedately than we otherwise might: but that is all the police want of us. If, though, the police are out to catch dope-peddlers, they cannot give notice on the streets where they mount watch: here their aim is to catch the dope-peddlers, not just to encourage them to be more circumspect. But the police make no secret that they are prepared to use covert methods, including hidden cameras to detect such crimes. Their doing so is no abuse of our trust.

Steve Clarke (1999) considers various ways of obtaining 'indirect consent' from subjects: where the subjects are not themselves fully informed but others act as their advocates – who give proxy consent. You might in this way agree, for example, to have a friend or relative fully briefed in advance – someone able to advise if this is something that you, being the sort of person you are, would agree to take part in. There are obvious practical difficulties with this procedure: finding someone you are willing to trust to act as your proxy. Clarke moots the possibility of inviting recruits to rely on ethics committees to act as their proxies. He compares how we are happy to try out a new food product though we do not ourselves know anything much about the chemical ingredients listed on the package, simply because we are assured that the food has satisfied the regulations of our Department of Health.

There is an important disanalogy to note here. A food safety committee has the expertise to pronounce on products and does not need to know anything about the personal quirks of tastes or preferences of individual consumers. Moreover, such a committee can be safely assumed to have no vested interest in new food products being marketed. It is not so clear that research ethics committees (or university ethics committees) do not have a kind of conflict of interest: they are concerned both to protect trial subjects and to help forward scientific research. If it is reasonable to invite people to rely on such committees as their advocates it needs first to be made quite clear whether the committees see their job as one in which the protection of study subjects is something to be balanced against the interests of science, or something which comes first and is not to be weighed against any other interests. There is a world of difference between the stance of a committee that only approves studies if the benefits *to the subjects* are reckoned to outweigh the risks to them and that of a committee that approves studies provided that the benefits to subjects *and others* (the public at large), are reckoned to outweigh the risks to subjects.

Above all, codes that offer guidelines regarding deception in research should pay attention to the difference between deceiving with lies and deceiving without lies. If a study necessitates outright lying it is unethical, however valuable the information it might yield. Concealment of information and use of deceptive tricks on subjects, though, can be justified. Of course, if the concealing and deceiving contradicts the on-going pledge implicit in the informed consent seeking procedure, then the consent seeking becomes a dishonest pretence. That is why it seems so necessary that wherever trials necessitate impartial disclosure and perhaps the use of deceptive tricks as well, honesty requires that those being recruited are forewarned (indirectly, if not directly) of this possibility.

The role of placebos in research trials

Whereas some doctors may be uncomfortable about using placebos as therapy – feeling that it smacks of quackery – using them in research trials is generally felt to be both scientifically and ethically proper (provided certain conditions are observed). Indeed, the use of placebos in research aims to flush out quack remedies, and those who refuse to subject their practices and procedures to the test are considered suspect (Shapiro and Shapiro 1997: 177). From a scientific standpoint it is widely held that concurrent double-blinded placebo-controlled trials yield the most reliable information about a new intervention. The double blinding eliminates unconscious bias of doctors and patients. The placebos 'provide the benchmark for any therapeutic effect' (separating the effect of participating in the trial of a new drug from the effect of the drug itself; also, from the natural healing that occurs over time) (Spiro 1997: 40–1).

Of course, such trials are not always feasible. It is one thing to fool patient and doctor with look-alike pills; quite another to fool not only the patient but the surgeon, anaesthetist, and nurses as well with a fake operation. The theory behind the double blind placebo-controlled trial may be faultless but in practice there can be problems: doctors and patients may sometimes be able to cheat and unblind themselves (though even partial blinding may be better than no blinding) (Shapiro and Shapiro 1997: 174). At any rate, the method may be more reliable than any alternatives – despite the occasional abuses and mismanagement. Let us assume that the scientific case for holding placebo-controlled trials is sound. Where such trials are possible, we will suppose, they are, from a scientific standpoint, the gold standard: in the words of Paul Leber of the Food and Drugs Administration:

> Placebo controls are our surest protection against fads and fashions that come and go in pharmacology, against the reckless claims of therapeutic enthusiasts, and most important against our own mistaken beliefs and prejudices.
>
> (Leber 1986: 32)

But however strong the scientific case for using placebos in research, what about the deception it involves: is this an instance of compromising truthfulness for the sake of science? Does truthfulness permit the kind of compromises involved in using placebos in research trials? Is the deception involved 'honest' deception?

Unlike with the use of placebos as therapy, their use in research can be openly discussed with patients who are being recruited to join trials that are placebo controlled. If they agree to join a trial, they agree to be deceived – they consent to being tricked. Hence, this use of placebos seems easy to justify. Deceiving those who consent does no violence to their right to know: they have formally and informedly waived it. People invited to join such trials may not be in the least put off by the deceptive element. Perhaps, many agree to enter such trials confidently believing that *they* will readily suss out whether or not they are getting the placebo. If they only join the trial in the hope of getting the 'new' treatment, they are free to quit at any time (in theory, that is – in practice withdrawing may not be as easy as it looks on paper).

This consent-based defence for using placebos, does, though, assume that consent is given voluntarily – is uncoerced. We have already questioned whether patients who are acutely ill or who are reeling from the fresh discovery that they have a serious disease are truly free to give or withhold consent. However firmly they are told that they will not be penalized in any way if they decline, is it rational for them to believe such assurances? Even if such assurances are scrupulously honoured and it would be rational to trust them, are such patients emotionally able to be rational?

Consent aside, clinical investigators already are bound (by the Hippocratic *primum non nocere* and by the various codes and declarations) not to invite people to join trials unless they think that being in the trial will not disadvantage them – whatever the risks they must not be thought to outweigh the benefits. The investigator, inviting potential subjects to join the trial, professes to be in a state of equipoise or uncertainty in respect of the treatments or procedures to be compared in the trial.

Explaining just what this equipoise imports is somewhat tricky. Either the investigator obfuscates, affecting to have no opinion whether a new treatment is better or not, or the investigator comes clean, in which case very few people will enrol and doubts arise about the mentality of those who do. If the investigator truly has no opinion as to whether the new might be any better, what is the scientific or moral case for holding a trial? If the new is not promising, why try it? If the investigator thinks, suspects, that the new might be better but seeks proof, and says so, surely many people will (understandably) prefer to take their chances with the new, especially in the case of serious conditions. If they are not allowed access to the new except via the trial, how free is their choice? Are those who volunteer to join a trial, where they could instead simply choose to try the new, just outstandingly good citizens, or are they too bewildered to see where their own interests lie, or are they simply afraid not to do what the doctor 'invites' them to do? As Polly Toynbee says, reflecting on her own dismay at being invited to join a trial when she got breast cancer: 'It is part of one's civic duty to help medicine along, but when your own life is on the line, science takes a back seat' (*The Independent*, 29 May 1996).

Because of the necessity of getting informed consent from trialists, investigators have to confront those whom they invite with their own uncertainties. In order to explain the point of the trial, the standard therapy has to be talked down and the possibilities of the new talked up: but neither too much! Of course, patients can decline the invitation. Even so, they are by then aware, like it or not, of the limitations of what treatments are available. The right to know can easily get converted to a duty to know. Medical paternalism has not after all been expelled, it has just been revamped. The new style paternalism bullies patients into insights about the limitations of knowledge whether they want them or not. It is only a kind of paternalism, though, if patients need to know things for their own good. If, rather, the reason they need to know is for our, the public's good, so that they can be prevailed upon to help advance science, this is not paternalism. But is it exploitation?

Admittedly, there will be some trials where the expression of equipoise can reflect genuine uncertainty without thereby making the trial pointless from the subjects' standpoint: for example, if investigators are wanting to compare two standard treatments. And in such cases patients may be happy to assist. John Lantos observes:

> It may be the case that controlled trials are most useful when progress is slow and we need to distinguish almost imperceptible differences between treatments that are quite similar ...[this]... may also explain why so many randomized trials are done on things that just don't seem to matter very much, like different antibiotics for infections or steroids for septic shock.
>
> (1997: 150)

Is it unethical to use placebo-controlled trials when there is an active standard therapy? From a scientific standpoint the placebo-controlled trial yields more information and is more reliable. Without it, for example, a new drug being compared to the standard may be proven less effective but it will not be known whether it is partially effective and that might be worth knowing – as, for example, if the standard therapy has troublesome side effects. If a trial is to be done, is it unethical not to use the best scientific methods? Sir Austin Bradford Hill, who championed double-blind placebo-controlled trials back in the 1950s and 1960s, quoted with approval an editorial in the *BMJ*, saying:

> In treating patients with unproved remedies we are, whether we like it or not, experimenting on human beings, and a good well-conducted experiment well reported may be more ethical and entail less shirking of duty than a poor one.
> (Shapiro and Shapiro 1997: 168–9)

In similar vein, R.J. Levine, replying to the Hellman criticisms of randomized clinical trials, declares that clinical investigators have a 'duty to maximise social benefit by developing information that will enhance physicians' future capacity to secure the wellbeing of patients' (1991: 72).

Is this alleged duty to 'maximize' a duty that overrides others? That was not the view of Sir Austin. He insisted that the individual patient's interests must always come first: 'The ethical obligation always and entirely outweighs the experimental' (Hill 1963: 1047). But Sir Austin was saying this back in the 1960s. Nowadays, there are many who question the assumption that the obligation to one's patient always overrides other social obligations. The very idea that some obligations, rules or principles are not to be weighed and balanced alongside others is scornfully brushed aside. Jan Narveson, in the introductory remarks to his book, *Moral Matters,* says: 'Be warned: philosophers have come to appreciate that there are probably no rules at all that are plainly to be held in that inflexible manner'(1993: 20). Peter Singer claims that the notion that there are simple rules of morality that allow for no exceptions comes from the Judeo-Christian idea of the moral law. A secular morality will jettison it. (1995: 221) James Rachels observes that 'most philosophers would reject out of hand' the idea that any moral rules are exceptionless (1997: 125).

Thus, it is supposed, doctors' and nurses' duties to their individual patients must be balanced against other duties – like the duty to push forward knowledge of diseases. Beauchamp and Childress (1994), for example, suggest that their four principles and the related rules and rights are all prima facie binding and need to be balanced against each other when applied. They do concede that some duties are 'virtually absolute'- their examples: the duty not to torture or be cruel (1994: 32). I have argued that the duty not to lie is also virtually absolute in medical contexts as elsewhere. However instructive a clinical trial might be, if it necessitates lying to those who join it, it is ethically indefensible. The question of balancing this duty against others should not arise. Doctors and nurses need to commit themselves to a firm and unwavering repudiation of lying. This, though, does not mean that placebos cannot be used in trials, since most trials involving placebos do not necessitate lying. Concealment and deception that does not involve lying can be justified – as, for example, where patients are told when invited to join a trial about the role of placebos in it.

The Declaration of Helsinki firmly sticks to the line adopted by Sir Austin: doctors must never compromise patients' interests in the pursuit of scientific progress: 'the health of my patient will be my first consideration'. Hence, it opposes the use of placebos where there are already effective treatments: 'In any medical study, every patient – including those of a control group, if any – should be assured of the best proven diagnostic and therapeutic method' (Brody 1998: Appendix 1.2, Principle ll.3, 215). But this restriction prevents trials of placebos against remedies which are effective but have troublesome side-effects. Patients may be happy to join such trials – at least where the condition being treated is not itself serious. Baruch Brody points out that a 1996 statement by the American Medical Association steers a middle line between the Helsinki's (and other strict codes) repudiation of using placebos on controls when there is an effective remedy, on the one hand, and the FDA's continued endorsement of such trials except in cases where existing treatments are life-prolonging, on the other hand. The AMA discourages the use of placebo-control groups 'for trials concerning illnesses that produce severe or painful symptoms when effective treatments are available' but it allows their use 'when the standard therapy has a bad profile of side-effects' (Brody 1998: 150).

Since our purpose here is limited to the question of what truthfulness requires in the context of medical research, we need not pursue the question of what trade offs are defensible between the interests of patients and the interests of society. Any of the following different stances are consistent with the account of truthfulness we have adopted:

1 Citizens have an absolute right not to be subjected to medical experimentation except where they give informed and uncoerced consent (the original Helsinki 1964 in Brody 1998).
2 Citizens have a right not to be subjected to medical experimentation except where they (or in the case of legal incompetence, their legal guardians) give informed and uncoerced consent or, if the physician 'considers it essential not to obtain informed consent, the specific reasons for this proposal should be stated in the experimental protocol for transmission to the independent committee' (Helsinki 1996 in Brody 1998).
3 Citizens have a duty to help medical science along and doctors should encourage them to do their duty.
4 Citizens have a duty to support the war against cancer and other serious diseases: there should be medical conscription (and finger-pointing notices should be posted up in surgeries and clinics: 'Your country needs you!').

Any of these stances could be adopted openly, democratically and applied by truthful practitioners. Some people might want to endorse 2 and 3. But are they combinable? Wouldn't the 'encouraging' be coercive? In fact, when we consider some of the trials to which patients do consent, we have reason to wonder how free they felt they were to refuse. It is one thing to agree to enter a trial where you know you might end up taking fake pills, another to agree to enter a trial where you might end up undergoing a sham operation and then having to take dummy-rejection pills thereafter. The *New York Times* reports that 'When Genzyme Corporation of Cambridge, Mass., proposed injecting pig cells into the brains of Parkinson's patients, the [FDA] agency insisted on a placebo design' (Stolberg 1999). Because the patients who got the pig cells needed anti-rejection drugs and antibiotics thereafter and it proved not possible to fake antibiotics, the control group were given real antibiotics. Would anyone freely agree to join such a trial – or only patients desperate for the chance of help not otherwise on offer?

More recently, double-blind trials have been conducted to test the efficacy of fetal-tissue transplantation in patients with Parkinson's disease. It is said that the scientific imperative to adopt double-blind trials of surgical procedures is no less compelling than is the case with testing the efficacy of drugs. History reveals how prone to fashion surgery is – how many procedures fall in and out of fashion (for example: tonsillectomy, Caesarean deliveries). In this particular trial subjects underwent two surgical procedures spaced a week apart, and those on the placebic arm of the trial had a stereotactic frame fitted, a general anaesthetic, skin incision, the drilling of burr holes (though not in their case to penetrate the inner cortex), and identical post-operative care (which included low-dose cyclosporine for six months). To maintain the blinding of investigators, the surgical and evaluation sites were separated. (Freeman *et al.* 1999)

Since those who were recruited to this trial had the placebic aspect fully explained, they all gave *informed* consent. But why did they do so? Had they been offered a choice between joining the trial and simply undergoing the fetal-tissue transplant, how many would have agreed to the trial? Those recruited to the trial were all patients with advanced Parkinson's whose symptoms could not be satisfactorily controlled by drugs. They were promised that if the transplantations proved beneficial, those who'd received the sham surgery would be offered the transplant surgery *for free*. I suggest that if patients with advanced Parkinson's had been able to opt straight off for the unproven therapy that would have been the rational choice. If doctors did not offer that choice, they were putting the interests of science and of society at large before the interests of the patients they were treating. Perhaps that is just what they should have done. But they were not being truthful if they professed to be doing something else.

The US research regulations assist researchers in fudging the nature of the trade off for subjects. In defining what are reasonable risks, it makes all the difference whether the benefits and harms weighed are to one and the same individual (what the subjects in a trial stand personally to gain or lose) or whether the benefits set against the harms include benefits to others besides the subjects. Thus in defence of the Parkinson trial it was urged on the benefits side that: 'The trial will enable thousands to benefit if the treatment works and spare thousands of patients risks and financial burdens if it does not' (Freeman *et al.*, 1999: 991). In other words the trade off contemplated involves weighing the risks to a few (the subjects) against the benefits to the many. Was that spelled out to those invited to join the trial? The

IRBs included among the benefits to *subjects* that they would be contributing to advances in treatment of a disease of great personal interest to themselves. That is undeniable. All the same, were not the circumstances of their choice coercive? If so, was it not untruthful to pretend that they were not?

Truthfulness and the quest for medical knowledge

Just because we look to advances in medical research to combat devastating illnesses and injuries, it is tempting to allow the urgency of the cause to justify corner-cutting over regulatory rules that inevitably impede recruitment. The central safeguard against inroads on trial subjects' rights has been the consent-requirement. That requirement entails two specific duties for researchers when they recruit: that those who are recruited are adequately informed and that they consent freely. Where the patients being recruited are in pretty desperate straits, I have questioned their ability to consent freely. If they are not able to do so, is it not a dishonest pretence on the part of doctors to ignore this fact and still seek their consent? Clearly, much valuable information would be cut-off if doctors were debarred from inviting the seriously ill into trials. Could some other way to include them that did not rely on consent be found? At any rate, I submit that the seeking of consent from people who are not free to say no – or who understandably do not think that they are (however sincerely they are assured that they will not be penalized if they do)[7] – is a dishonest pretence, and one that undermines trust.

The other duty, ensuring that recruits are adequately informed, does not seem, in principle anyway, so much of a problem. So long as we rely on the consent-requirement to protect trial subjects from exploitation in the cause of medical science, the consent seeking has to be taken seriously. That means that researchers must take seriously the duty of adequately informing those recruited. The duty to be truthful with patients whether or not they are being invited into trials already rules out lying to them – but that restriction should not be a serious barrier to medical research. If the duty to be truthful were also to rule out any use of placebos, or any trials in which some information is deliberately withheld from recruits, that would indeed be a major impediment. But we have seen that truthfulness does not rule out concealing or even deceiving, provided those who do the concealing or deceiving do not implicitly or explicitly profess different policies.

Concealing and deception are not in themselves dishonest, but they are if the policy signed up to in public professional pledges suggests that no information is to be concealed. Compare two different pledges that might be made: one promising that on no account will those recruited to trials have any information deliberately concealed from them and another promising that on no account will any information be deliberately concealed that relates to possible risks to the subjects. The former policy would rule out incomplete disclosure to recruits about the purpose of a trial. The latter would not. But the duty to be truthful does not favour the former over the latter. The duty to be truthful, as we have often noted, is not the same as a duty to be open. What the duty to be truthful does require is that those who announce a policy really do mean to follow it.

9   Can doctors and nurses be 'too honest'?

For the habitual truth-teller and truth-seeker, indeed, the world has very little liking.

H.L. Mencken

Moral virtues, as defined by Aristotle, cannot be overdone. Part of what having a virtue involves is having and exercising judgement appropriately. Thus, for example, someone who is courageous, judges well what dangers need to be faced; someone who has good temper, judges well where anger is called for: 'anyone can get angry – that is easy … but to do this to the right person, to the right extent, at the right time, with the right motive, and in the right way, *that* is not for everyone, nor is it easy' (Ross 1954: *Nicomachean Ethics* ll.9). Hence, if we take honesty (and truthfulness as an aspect of honesty) to be a virtue, it does not make sense to suppose one can be 'too honest' or 'too truthful'.

Yet, according to my account of truthfulness, it requires that we repudiate lying. Those who have this virtue, if I am right, do not apply judgement to the question of when to lie. They do not deliberate about the right person to lie to, the right extent to tell lies, the right time, etc. Lying is quite simply off their agenda. Bertrand Russell pokes fun at Aristotle's attempt to fit all the virtues into the scheme according to which exercise of a virtue involves judgement (finding the mean):

> There was once a mayor who had adopted Aristotle's doctrine; at the end of his term of office he made a speech saying that he had endeavoured to steer the narrow line between partiality on the one hand and impartiality on the other.
>
> (1946: 196)

But Russell's jibe is not quite fair to Aristotle. Aristotle notes that some names imply badness – names of passions (his examples: spite, shamelessness, envy) and of (types of) actions (his examples: theft, adultery and murder):

> It is not possible, then, ever to be right with regard to them; one must always be wrong. Nor does goodness or badness with regard to such things depend on committing adultery with the right woman, at the right time, in the right way, but simply to do any of them is to go wrong.
>
> (Ross 1954: *Nicomachean Ethics*, II.6)

Lying (likewise, partiality), I suggest, is another bad type of action. Truthfulness requires that we repudiate lying altogether. But judgement is still needed in the exercise of this virtue – not about *when* to lie, but about other requirements of being truthful which are more complex.

Concealment, pretence and deception (not involving lying) are not, I have argued, bad in themselves. They are not in their nature incompatible with truthfulness. Yet though deception is not as such wrong, there seems good reason to counsel generally against casual deception, if only because people are wont to conflate lying and deceiving and hence to suppose trust is equally abused in either case. Truthfulness does not require that we avoid non-lying forms of deceiving, but it is helped if we take trouble to avoid casual deceiving. Furthermore, concealment, pretence and deception may *all* become not simply inadvisable but plain wrong under certain circumstances: where promises or pledges have been made which rule them out. Truthfulness requires that we take care to avoid making false promises – promises that we do not mean to keep – since false promises are a kind of lie. Therefore we need to use judgement about the practices and policies that we adopt, taking care that these do not give the lie to our pledges.

Resumé: why being truthful matters

We here have taken moral virtues to be traits of character that everyone needs to develop in order to do well, fare well, in life: this is the Aristotelian conception of moral virtues. As we have noted, these traits are strengths that equip us for life. They compensate for our imperfections; they are correctives. They are pervasively relevant, useful: whoever we are, whatever the particular kind of society we inhabit and whatever (ethically defensible) roles we each take on or find ourselves landed with. Now some traits seem easy enough to cast as moral virtues according to these criteria – like good temper (understanding by this, judgement and self-control in relation to anger). Anger is an emotion that everyone is subject to. Everyone needs to learn how to handle it. Similarly, everyone is subject to fear and has to learn how to handle situations that are dangerous or painful. Hence, courage (understanding by this judgement and self-control in relation to fear) seems an easy fit with the criteria.

What about truthfulness, though? Does it fit the criteria? That being truthful is a strength to each one of us is not so easy to see – if it is even true. This idea that truthfulness is a personal virtue alongside good-temperedness and courage may seem especially dubious, if we insist, as I do, that being truthful involves repudiating lying. Are there not many familiar circumstances in everyone's life where telling a lie is needful: sometimes just little fibs that ease our dealings with one another; sometimes bigger 'whoppers' that get us out of serious scrapes – situations where the lie saves a job, secures a promotion, saves a friendship or hard-won reputation? We need here to bear in mind that the motives behind big and little lies need not be in the least self-serving. If truthfulness really does rule out every lie it rules out the lying that is selfless as well as the lying that is self-serving. Can truthfulness so understood be a virtue?

Let us recall the steps by which we have reached the view that truthfulness is indeed a virtue and one that requires that we repudiate telling lies. The case for ranking truthfulness among the moral virtues can be made out simply by establishing the connection between truthfulness and trust. I have hinted at another route to establishing truthfulness as a virtue, connecting it with respect, but I have not attempted to flesh out such a connection here. For our purposes, the former route suffices and it seems much the easier one to trace.

The first step is to point out how important establishing and sustaining trust is: how living communally, in any community, turns on trust being possible and rational. Martin Hollis, in the opening paragraph of his book, *Trust Within Reason*, observes:

> Everday life is a catalogue of success in the exercise of trust. Our dealings with friends and enemies, neighbours and strangers depend on it, whether in homes, streets, markets, seats of government or other arenas of civil society. Would you ask a stranger the time unless you could normally count on a true answer? Could you use the public highway without trusting other drivers? Could an economy progress beyond barter, or a society beyond mud huts, unless people relied on one another to keep their promises? Without trust, social life would be impossible.
>
> (1998: 1)

The second step is to mark the connection between trust and trust in a person's word, since this is where truthfulness comes into the picture. Truthfulness is only one of the pillars that supports trust. We need others. Someone may be wholly truthful but incompetent – hence, not to be relied upon. But the need we have to be able to trust does include the need to trust a person's word – the need for truthfulness. Notice how that comes out in the above quotation from Hollis: that he naturally illustrates the importance of trust with examples of our reliance on truthful communication and that he points up the importance of being able to rely on promises (which it is only rational to do if we can generally take people at their word, i.e. if they are truthful).

Resumé: why we need to teach that lying is always wrong

The third, most contentious and difficult step is to determine what teaching we need to adopt for it to be possible and rational for us to trust each other's word. It is this step that is of crucial importance to our project in this enquiry, since our aim here is to establish what truthfulness requires and permits of us in general and what are the implications for medical and nursing practice. It is easy enough to see that we need to have some teaching against lying. What is not so easy is to establish how stiff a teaching is necessary. If, as I have argued, a very stiff teaching is necessary, it needs to be made plain why a gentler teaching will not work. Let us briefly review the case for the stiff teaching I advocate.

It would seem that if we are under a general duty not to lie, there are only two possibilities: either it is a prima facie duty – one that can be overridden on occasion by other duties, or the duty is absolute – one that binds in all circumstances and is never overridden by other duties. The teaching that the duty is merely prima facie seems too weak a teaching to sustain our trust in one another's word. It puts the duty not to lie on a par with the duty to keep one's promises. We readily accept that there are many circumstances in which we are justified in not keeping a promise and some in which it would actually be wrong to keep a promise. Can we be equally discretionary about our commitment not to tell lies?

I have sided with Augustine and Kant, arguing that trust in one another's word requires that the duty not to lie is taken to be much more strictly binding than is the duty to keep promises. But isn't their absolutist stance that we must never lie too strict? Sissela Bok puts Kant's insistence that the duty is absolute down to his religious fervour. To her it seems plainly unreasonable to rule that lying is always wrong – even to the murderer at the door. Most contemporary philosophers (including prominent Kantian scholars like Christine Korsgaard (1996) and Onora O'Neill (1996: 174) agree with Bok that lying can (on rare occasions) be necessary.

Is there a third way? A possibility here is to seek to soften the simple absolute rule against lying by incorporating some exceptions into the rule. The resultant rule would still be absolute, but less simple. However, we run into difficulties if we try to soften the strict rule against lying: how to do so without inviting further erosion; how to draw a firm but non-arbitrary line between defensible and indefensible lying.

I have argued for a very stiff teaching: that we need to repudiate lying altogether: both lies that are trivial and lies that are serious. Some lies, no doubt, are considered in themselves, trivial. But a teaching which permits us to tell trivial lies is a dangerous teaching – because of the difficulty of making sure that we confine our lies to the trivial, even if that is what we sincerely aim to do. We have noted some of the difficulties surrounding the idea of what is trivial and how in consequence it is easy to make mistakes, thinking that the lie we want to tell is trivial when it is not. Hence, the teaching we need here is one of zero tolerance.

We have considered a number of ways in which a strict rule against lying might be modified, softened, to permit some serious lies: for example permitting lying to those who have no right to know, or to spare others distress, or to save a life. The difficulty, as we have seen, with writing exceptions into the rule against lying is, as MacIntyre puts it, the *ad hoc* nature of the exceptions. Once we start writing in exceptions there seems no firm barrier to our tacking on further ones as need arises. But a firm barrier is needed – or else trust in each other's word becomes impossible. Of course, we can imagine situations where a lie might be told that does no harm to anyone or that does some harm but also averts greater harm (the lies told to spare distress, like the lie Koch told to Thuiller and the lie Sir Isaiah Berlin told to his father; the lies told to save life, like the lie Ed Viesturs told to Rob Hall and the lie Arria told to Caecinna Paetus). But even if any of those lies seems in the very particular circumstances that arose to have been defensible, there is a question about the precedent we set if we defend it. Recall how Sissela Bok defends lying to the murderer at the door: as she says, the occasion is so isolated. Even so, if our willingness to lie only in such circumstances were publicly advocated, would it not undermine people's trust in each other's word? Would it not set a worrisome precedent?

I think it might, depending on how we would justify the exception. As Bok herself goes on to remark, exceptions are liable to get expanded. Hence, the importance of understanding what precedent is being established if we allow any exception. Suppose, then, we agree with Bok that one would be justified in lying to the murderer at the door, it is imperative that the reason why lying here is defensible is made plain – whether, for example, our teaching is that lying is permissible where it is necessary to lie to save a life. Notice that such a stance would have quite significant implications for medical practice. It might be necessary to lie to a patient to prevail on the patient to submit to a life-saving treatment – for example, to promise that you will not transfuse blood though that is exactly what you expect and intend to do. Furthermore, there is the *ad hoc* problem: if it permissible to lie to save a life, why not to achieve some other enormously important benefit – like rescuing the patient from a delusion about bug infestation or weaning a patient off a ventilator?

Just because a teaching that allows lying where the aim is to save life would readily expand to justify very many lies – certainly, in the fields of medicine and nursing, we must reject that teaching as unsafe (subversive of trust). Yet I have myself defended lying in some circumstances: where life and limb are in immediate danger and those endangered are cut off from other means of protection against their assailants. The general obligation we are under not to lie to one another or use violence against one another presupposes that we live in a society where such side-constraints are generally observed, upheld and respected. It would not be reasonable to commit ourselves to acting within the limitations these obligations impose unless we were able to rely on others to protect us against assault. If it turns out that we are being excluded from protection (as Grun was) and have to fall back on our own resources to save ourselves or others against aggression, then we are no longer bound not to lie or not to use violence in self-defence.

Although I allow this defence for lying (parting company here with Augustine and Kant), it does not require us to modify a *teaching* that repudiates lying altogether. Our moral teachings concerning matters of justice (what we owe one another by way of help or non-interference) are designed for members of a society, who live under the protection of the law, who are jointly committed to pursuing their lives within the law, foregoing certain ways of furthering their private aims and concerns (ways that involve using force or fraud) on the understanding that these ways are not tolerated and that though they commit to refrain from such tactics, the state and its officers protect them against deviants. Thus the *teaching* about the duty not to lie can ignore the possibility that one might be cut off from protection as Grun was. Our duties of justice, including truthfulness, are all spelled out against the background assumption that we live in a society that has the will and the way to protect us against direct assault. In other words, I am supposing that justice is a social or community virtue. Its requirements apply to members of a community: not an ideal community in which our rights are always respected and upheld but one in which we can expect at least to have protection against direct assaults on life and limb. I suppose here, like Hobbes, that we are better off in our imperfect communities than in conditions of anarchy and that in our imperfect communities we can make progress, if frustratingly slowly, towards more justice, provided we do not cast aside our fundamental shared commitments repudiating force and fraud that underpin social life.

There is, perhaps, still another way to soften the strict absolute rule against lying, which we have not yet considered. Instead of trying to spell out some exceptions to be incorporated into the rule, it might be thought better to treat the rule as not quite absolute but nearly so. The rule might be said to hold for the most part, but not always. Just when exceptions do arise, it might be said, is something that has to be implicitly grasped and is grasped by those who are wise and experienced. This line might seem to fit well with some of the remarks Aristotle makes about ethics and about the insights to be gained from studying the subject. He is wont to observe that ethics is not an exact science and that the truths to be discovered in ethics, unlike laws of nature, are truths which hold for the most part but not always in every circumstance:

> It is the mark of an educated man to look for precision in each class of things just so far as the nature of the subject admits; it is evidently equally foolish to accept probable reasoning from a mathematician and to demand from a rhetorician scientific proofs.
>
> (Ross 1954: *Nicomachean Ethics*, I.3)

Thus, it might seem to be wrong-headed to try to spell out the exceptions to the rule against lying even though there are (rarely) exceptions to the rule. The rule needs to allow some discretion, some judgement, to accommodate very exceptional circumstances.

I suggest that tempting though this position is, it is not a safe teaching in regard to *lying*. The commitment not to lie is only persuasive and reliable if it is an unqualified and non-discretionary commitment. Anything short of this does not work. Exceptions that are implicit are maybe even more liable to expand and weaken our reliance on the rule. At least if the exception is spelled out there is a possibility that the precedent will be reflected on and that some attempt will be made to fit subsequent exceptions within it. Anyway, whether we do it implicitly or explicitly, when we make an exception we set a precedent.

Trivial lies: implications of the stiff teaching for medicine and nursing

If truthfulness requires, as I claim, that we adopt zero tolerance towards trivial lies, how awkward would this requirement be for doctors and nurses to adopt? Would it compromise the care we expect them to provide? Repudiating the trivial lies may turn out to be much more difficult than repudiating the serious lies. If trivial lies deceive on matters of no importance to or for anyone, they should be easy to give up. Our definition of a trivial lie does not suggest they do not matter to or for anyone at all, only that they do not matter to or for those who are deceived. They may still matter for the tellers of them.

Of course, we need to bear in mind that not everything that we say to one another, knowing it is false, is intended to deceive. We use euphemisms which fool nobody and are not expected to: 'she passed on' when we none of us think she has gone somewhere else. All pregnancies are terminated. But everyone understands that 'termination' of pregnancy no longer refers to women giving birth but is our coded euphemistic way of referring to abortion. There is always the risk, of course, that some people will be fooled by a euphemism: many women who have undergone prenatal screening have believed that the whole point of the exercise really is 'to help baby', whereas that is the point only in respect of a few of the items tested for: for example, testing for hypertension, rhesus, and syphilis (Jim Thornton: 1999).

We have noted too that sometimes what is told or declared is coded speech and not to be taken literally – like the examples (noted in the last chapter) that David Goodstein gives of the language scientists may use in writing up their findings (1995: 31–2). Arguably, telling a patient 'This won't hurt' is also generally understood to be a coded way of saying 'This wont hurt more than you can stand', the hope here being, as Harry Lesser suggests, 'that this is not a lie but a self-fulfilling prophecy' given that doctors and nurses can lessen how much a procedure does hurt by lowering one's expectations (1991: 158).

We have also noted that in some contexts sincerity is not to be taken for granted. Convention requires that you express delight over a present whatever your real feelings. You may brush aside a patient's apology for calling you out in the night with 'No problem!' however unwelcome was the call. These are hardly lies, hence, not clear-cut examples of trivial lies. No one relies on such conventional expressions as indicative of a person's real feelings. It is convenient for everyone that you are able to say things on such occasions that could be sincere but need not be.

Putting aside all these pseudo or borderline examples of trivial lies, what about the residue? Can the caring pragmatist doctor or nurse repudiate the rest? Recall the features of 'trivial' lies on account of which it seems important not to tolerate them:

1   The difficulty of judging if a lie does not matter to or for someone when you cannot ask them;
2   The weasel-word 'minimal', which sounds as if any harm arising from a trivial lie must be slight or negligible whereas in fact what is minimal harm may also be a substantial harm;
3   The risk that lies will be counted as trivial if the intent is to avoid causing distress – as if being harmed is always and only a matter of being made to suffer.

Undeniably, a lie can be a convenient way to resolve a particular predicament – a way to avoid or reduce suffering there and then. If we focus our attention on the immediate consequences, it is tempting to think that the lie is trivial – does not matter for those who are being deceived. Thus, it is tempting to tell a relative that the patient died peacefully whatever the truth of the matter. Thus, it is tempting to play down the painfulness of a procedure that a patient has consented to, bearing in mind how anticipation of pain is likely to make it worse. Thus, it is tempting to lie to a relative as to why a patient will not speak on the telephone (Brewin's example of the irate son refusing to talk to his aged bed-ridden mother).

Yet even if in those situations lies do predictably avoid or reduce suffering, there is a cost in our tolerating such lies: that we undermine trust in the word of doctors and nurses. If it is common knowledge that they are prepared to lie in these sorts of situations, haven't we good reason to suppose that there will be many other situations where too they may see fit to lie? If the medical student who lies that he is a doctor is commended for putting the needs of the patient and her husband first – they needed reassuring – where else will he suppose that the duty not to lie is properly overridden by the duty to reassure? The patient who gets a sick note from her GP so that she can stay at home with her ailing child, may at the time be grateful to the GP for lying on her behalf. But how will this experience affect her trust in the word of her GP in the future? Though these are all examples of well-meaning lies, they set a precedent and one that undermines trust.

Serious lies: implications of the stiff teaching for medicine and nursing

If truthfulness requires, as I claim, that we repudiate serious lies, how awkward would it be for doctors and nurses to conform to this requirement? Serious lies, we have defined as lies that are not trivial – hence, as lies that do deceive people about things the truth of which does matter to or for them. Consider, for example, how you might lie to get round some unreasonable stipulation – one, for example, that debars the patient from a needed treatment (lying to the patient's insurer, perhaps); or one that debars yourself from a promotion or from securing a grant, where a small adjustment about your age, or qualifications, or as to how far advanced your research already is, might be necessary if your application is to be taken seriously. Here, you can hardly suppose that those you aim to deceive would not mind – that if they later found out, *they* would think your lie to have been trivial. Similarly, if you lie to a patient as to why their relative is not after all going to donate a kidney so as to save face for the relative who has changed his mind although tests indicate he would be a good match, you do not suppose that the truth of the matter is of no importance to the patient. Likewise, with lying to children: whether it is about the possibility of cure, the burdens of the treatment they are to undergo or the reason why a parent is not visiting them, the justification for the lie cannot be that the truth does not matter to them.

All the same, there is likely to be a serious and immediate cost if doctors and nurses are unwilling to lie – and the cost may be paid by the patient. Thus, the patient who asks direct questions which those who are put on the spot cannot avoid without lying, may suffer upon hearing the truth. Consider the plight of a woman critically injured in an accident asking after the rest of her family. If she is told the truth, she will certainly suffer; it may even destroy her own will to survive. Compare the lies told by Arria to Caecinna Paetus and by Ed Viesturs to Rob Hall: these were similarly motivated. Less dramatic, but still serious, is the cost to the psychotic patient who refuses to talk to a psychiatrist and who walks away from an effective treatment for a horrible condition, after having quizzed a psychiatrist who will not lie. In the short term, lying can be a real help to a patient. But there are still the long-term costs to be reckoned in. These are costs for the patients themselves if they ever discover that they have been lied to (not that they are bound to resent this, but that their trust in the word of doctors and nurses is bound to be undermined). These are costs for others too, since lies are often witnessed by colleagues or relatives. Even if there are no witnesses, liars set a precedent for themselves that is likely to lead to further lies and hence to an erosion of their own commitment to the duty not to lie.

Truthfulness and discretion

We have been at pains to distinguish truthfulness from openness or candour. Candour, if it is a virtue, does not seem to be an aspect of the virtue of justice (unlike truthfulness). A general readiness to share our thoughts, feelings, attitudes and intentions with one another hardly seems essential to living co-operatively, unlike a general commitment not to lie to one another. Anyway, if candour is a virtue, it must allow reserve. A person who is transparent, who has no reserve, is not to be trusted – not to be trusted with secrets. Whereas lying is wrong even if the motive behind it is wholly honourable, concealing, pretending and deceptive tricks are not wrong *per se* and may be ethically defensible if the motive is honourable or at least not dishonourable. Thus, for example, it can be entirely reasonable to conceal information that others might like to know, provided of course that the way the concealing is done avoids telling lies.

Yet there are circumstances where concealing or pretending or using deceptive tricks is dishonest even if the motive is wholly honourable: namely, where one is pledged not to conceal or pretend or use tricks. As we have already noted, false promises are a kind of lie. Doctors and nurses who aim to be truthful need, then, to consider whether their practices that involve concealing or pretending or deceptive tricks can be squared with the pledges that they themselves make or that the professional bodies to which they belong make. Of course, individual practitioners may not agree with some of the pledges made by the medical or nursing associations to which they belong. But patients are entitled to suppose that they do agree unless they make known their dissent, at least where they not only disagree but do not intend to comply.

Squaring practices with pledges may seem no easy matter. What exactly practitioners are (implicitly) pledged to do or not to do is not obvious, except in the vaguest of terms. People may have heard of the 'Hippocratic Oath' but few will have read it, let alone seen its modern restatements as promulgated by World

Medical Assemblies. Even those who are familiar with such declarations may be quite uncertain of how items are to be interpreted; of what those who make these pledges are actually committing themselves to in practice. Consider, for example, this item, included in the International Code of Medical Ethics (known as the Declaration of Geneva) as agreed to at the 1983 thirty fifth World Medical Assembly: 'A physician shall always bear in mind the obligation of preserving human life'. We can expect that item to be construed differently in different countries and in different generations. Obviously, so: in some countries this pledge is taken to rule out abortion (social abortion at any rate), in others, not.

Those who seek to square pledges with practices face a number of difficulties:

1   What exactly are the pledges implicit in medical (or nursing) practice – and are these known both by practitioners and public even if they are not explicitly promulgated?
2   How are these pledges to be interpreted – given the (arguably necessary) vagueness of their wording?
3   How are they to be applied in a particular context – bearing in mind that traditions vary from one medical specialty to another; and that they shape and are shaped by evolving practices.

Because of the third difficulty we can see that squaring pledges with practices has to be an ongoing project, and one that needs to be carried out in relation to particular (medical and cultural) contexts. What is (or has been) a good fit between pledge and practice in one context may be a bad fit elsewhere. Thus, we should not assume that there has to be some one interpretation that is the correct or more enlightened way for all health professionals everywhere to understand a pledge.

These difficulties notwithstanding, there is a way for health professionals to square their practices with their pledges: namely, by public disclosure of their practices alongside announcement of their pledges. Of course, practices involving concealment, pretence and deceptive tricks cannot be disclosed directly to those on whom they are used – at least not at the time they are used. But their use can be disclosed and explained to the public at large. If we are forewarned about such tactics, we understand that the pledges being made alongside them are not intended to rule these out. Let us note, though, that public disclosure of secretive practices is not the only way to square practices with pledges. An alternative is for health professionals to be circumspect about the pledges that they make.

Squaring practices with pledges

Some of the practices we touched on in Chapter one would seem easy to make an open secret of: putting a sedative in the tea of a patient who is out of control and likely to hurt himself or others; covertly weaning a patient off dependency on a drug or on a ventilator or using hidden cameras to protect child-patients who are suspected victims of parental abuse. None of these tactics need involve telling lies. But they are all practices that only work if not publicised directly to those on whom they are practised. Let us consider some more difficult cases – where public disclosure might cause embarrassment.

'Make the care of your patient your first concern'

As was mentioned in the last chapter, this is the first bullet point duty listed by the GMC in the card summarizing the duties of a doctor that it issues to medical students. What exactly does this undertaking imply? We noted that the correct interpretation must permit doctors to have other concerns besides helping their own patients. It is not, for example, considered remiss for a doctor or nurse to choose only to work part-time – in order, let us say, to make space for a hobby. And clearly when you wait your turn at the GP's surgery you are well aware that you are your doctor's first concern alongside a lot of other people.

Yet does this pledge at least entitle you to expect that when you do get your turn the advice you are given is aimed exclusively at what is deemed to be in *your* best interests? Peter Tate asks how honest it is of GPs to encourage their patients to undergo routine screening – a routine mammography, a colonoscopy, or screening for prostate cancer (1997: 96). If it is a mistake to suppose that getting screened is a way to avoid cancer or to prevent a cancer becoming lethal and if it is obvious that patients only agree to be screened because they assume this is what the screening is for, is it not dishonest of GPs not to put them straight? A policy of sometimes recommending procedures to patients as if these were in their best interests when in fact they were not, could hardly be made public – it could not be openly avowed. It could only be squared with the pledge to make the patient one's first concern if that pledge were qualified – perhaps, to: '*Often* make the care of your patient your first concern'.

How is the pledge to make the care of your patient your first concern to be squared with economizing decisions to offer your patient less than the best? Within a hard pressed public health service, it may be reasonable for doctors 'to try a "second-best" treatment first, and use only the best if that fails' (Newdick 1995: 278). But doesn't truthfulness require that such a policy should be disclosed to patients when they are being prescribed the second-best? Waiting your turn for attention it is obvious that your GP is not exclusively thinking of your best interests, but once you get your turn and your GP is prescribing a drug for you, is it not reasonable to suppose that this is the best available, unless you are told otherwise? If the GP's economizing is reasonable, why need it be kept a secret? So long as doctors persist with the Hippocratic style commitment to make the health of *each* of one's patients one's first concern, any compromises, covert rationing based on age-considerations, for example, seem dishonest.[1] Either the pledge needs to be watered down: at least, to making 'the health of patients generally one's first concern', or the economizing policies that are adopted to offer individual patients less than the best need to be disclosed.

Covert use of the newly dead for training purposes

There may be certain tricky procedures which doctors need to learn and which it would be most helpful for them to try out on the newly dead – like the procedure of endotracheal intubation (ETI) – the placing of a tube in the patient's trachea (the preferred method of managing the airway in patients with life-threatening conditions). Michael Ardagh says that there are no satisfactory alternatives to practicing on the newly dead:

> Virtual reality techniques are not yet practical and animal models have disparate anatomy. Mannequins are considered by many to be too different anatomically, too constant anatomically and too rigid to be of use beyond initial training.
>
> (1997: 290)

Assuming that there are no satisfactory alternatives, there is a good reason to practice on the cadavers of the newly dead. Asking the relatives for their consent is obviously very difficult – is it necessary? One way round this difficulty rather than approaching the relatives, would be to publicize a general policy: announcing that consent will be presumed (and not specifically sought) unless people (patients prior to their death, or their family at the time of death) indicate wishes to the contrary? Would this general presumption of consent suffice to protect individuals' rights? At least, such a policy if publicized, would not, I submit, involve dishonesty though it would involve the deliberate concealing of information that might well upset and distress families. Ardagh notes how in a hospital which instead adopted the policy of seeking proxy consent from families, the policy 'has had the unintended effect of … significantly stifling this important training' – not because relatives were asked and refused, but because doctors were reluctant to ask (1997: 292).

Perhaps many of us would prefer that the practice be allowed, so that doctors can get this valuable training, but on the basis of presumed rather than proxy consent, so that doctors would not need to remind us of the policy when a member of our own family dies. It is surely easier to imagine a society approving such a practice than to imagine its approving another alternative that is said sometimes to be used instead: 'delaying the pronouncement of death during resuscitation in order to teach or practise procedures' (1997: 290). This latter practice would involve dishonesty – lying about the time of death. Of course, the presumed consent strategy with the option available to those who wish to decline participation, itself assumes that the public is informed of the practice – that the practice is an 'open secret'. Ardagh suggests: 'To proceed with presumed consent therefore, we must have a well informed public and preferably a statute to formalise their consent' (1997: 293).

Another way round this problem would be to introduce 'mandated choices': public policy might require individuals to make choices on a variety of issues – such as organ donation (perhaps to be recorded on one's driving license). As Ardagh notes, 'This process informs and honours individual choice, it gives the significant minority the opportunity to decline and it avoids deception' (1997: 293). The presumed consent alternative also avoids deception – though not concealment. But it does require that the public really is informed of the policy and of the rights of individuals and their families to decline involvement.

Stage-managed death

Is it a dishonest pretence to continue to give life support to a patient who is diagnosed (whole) brain dead? Here we need to understand the reason behind the policy: the importance, for example, of 'stage-managing' the death of a child so that the parents are able to take the initiative in deciding that life-support may be withdrawn (Blair and Steer 1997). There need be no pretence, hence nothing dishonest, about meanwhile continuing the life support. It simply allows parents time to be convinced that their child really has suffered an irreversible loss of function of the whole brain. Once parents do accept this and agree that the life support be discontinued, the policy of implementing their wish without undue haste is simply a demonstration of sensitivity, not an indication of dishonest pretence. Surely, this is a policy that should cause no embarrassment if it is publicly acknowledged.

'Covert' withholding or withdrawal of life-sustaining treatments

Is it dishonest pretence to gradually withdraw food from a patient who is terminally ill, or to gradually decrease the oxygen levels of ventilators where the expectation is that the patient will die sooner in consequence? Here we need to ask why the decision to withdraw a life-sustaining treatment is being made and why the decision needs to be carried out in a covert way. One reason for withdrawing a life-sustaining treatment might be that patients make it known that they do not wish such treatments to be continued. Some patients may give advance notice that they do not want to be intubated – patients for example who have terminal lung cancer and respiratory failure. But then why would it be necessary to respect their wishes covertly? Suppose, though, that a patient is not able to take part in a decision but that the relatives, in consultation with the doctors, agree that a life-sustaining treatment is burdensome for the patient – is prolonging a painful dying, if comfort measures fail – the withdrawal then might be done gradually rather than abruptly, not to deceive anyone about what is up but simply out of respect for the sensitivities of the relatives. The mere fact that the withdrawal is done gradually rather than abruptly does not necessarily indicate that there is anything covert about the procedure.

There is of course also the possibility that what is *called* a decision 'not to prolong dying' is mere euphemism for a decision to kill – as, for example, if the patient is not already dying when the decision to withdraw life-sustaining treatment is made. If no one is fooled by the euphemism or meant to be, using it is not dishonest (because then it is not expected, hence, not intended, to deceive). On the other hand, if the point of the euphemism is to disguise what is going on, the pretence may be dishonest: is so, if doctors also pledge on no account to kill their patients.

Dishonest use of placebos

The use of placebos in randomized controlled trials, where patients are informed in advance and freely consent, is not dishonest. The single-blind use of placebos during 'run-in' and 'washout' periods of trials, Martyn Evans points out, is quite another matter.[2] This use is not consented to by those in the trial – one suspects, simply because if they knew they would refuse to take part. However impeccable the scientific case is for having a run-in and washout period – a period free of any active medication, the practice is surely downright dishonest. It is so, because the practice is not common knowledge and because it is hard to see how it could be made so and not be condemned, since its purpose seems to be to by-pass informed consent while pretending to be seeking it. This is quite different from keeping secret some aspect of a trial which would defeat its purpose if divulged to the participants in advance. If instead of giving participants the placebos during the run-in they were simply told they would have no medication for this period, the trial would not be spoiled – except of course that people might refuse to join it. Thus, whereas with trials that necessitate disguise of (some of) the real aims, where participants can be told that some information is going to be withheld but will be given in the debriefing, the single-blind use of placebos is not something investigators would find it easy to debrief on.

Staging the disclosure of risks to patients about to undergo elective surgery

The Audit Commission describes how patients are sometimes only told about some of the significant risks of surgery just before they are operated on. It reports that

> Fifty percent of the urologists in [the study] who treat men with benign prostatic hyperplasia do not mention the risks and complications associated with transuretheral resection of the prostate in the out-patient clinic unless the patient asks about them. Instead, they leave the discussion to the junior doctor who interviews the patient on the ward, to obtain his signed consent just before the operation. This means that the patient first hears of the risks after the decision to operate has been made.
>
> (1993: para. 63)

This surely is a strategy for manipulating consent which should cause embarrassment if made public. When patients are first advised to undergo elective surgery they naturally suppose that the risks and complications they are told about then and there are being fully explained – and not that some more of these will only be divulged to them at the last minute.

Where partial disclosure when seeking consent seems dishonest

The very procedure of seeking informed consent gives people the right to suppose that information is not being withheld on the grounds that were it given one's consent might be withheld. Thus it seems dishonest if parents who were asked to consent to tissue being removed for research purposes during the post mortem examination of their children, were not given to understand that 'tissue' might include parts of organs, even whole organs. The term 'tissue' here would seem to have been used to disguise what was actually intended. What reason could there be for this but to get consent that might otherwise not have been forthcoming? Hence the call for more openness and clarity (*Kmietowicz* 2000).

Extravagant pledges: the right to have 'any risks' explained

Among the rights proclaimed in the Department of Health *Patient's Charter* (1991) is this: 'To be given a clear explanation of any treatment proposed, including any risks and any alternatives, before you decide whether you will agree to the treatment'. If 'any risk' means 'every risk', is that really an ethically appropriate pledge to make? Might not acting on this pledge sometimes result in a patient suffering avoidable harm? To be sure, the legal necessity of getting a patient's consent already runs that risk. But might doctors or nurses be reluctant to disclose a risk, not for fear that consent would be withheld but for fear that the information disclosed might make the procedure even riskier or at any rate more stressful? Peter Baddeley points out how there is a remote risk of perforating the oesophagus when passing a nasogastric tube. He asks: 'Should nurses discuss this risk before undertaking what is an uncomfortable procedure? By doing so, they may increase the apprehensiveness of their patient, the difficulty of the procedure and, therefore, the resulting risk' (1995: 44).

Informing patients with dementia of their diagnosis and prognosis

Will the same openness that is now generally applauded in respect of patients with incurable cancers come to be approved for patients with dementia too? Marek Marzanski notes that the change to more openness in respect of cancer patients was partly precipitated by the need to get consent when new treatment options (radiotherapy and chemotherapy) became available. As he observes, it was only subsequently that it was realised that most cancer patients wanted to know their diagnosis and prognosis. Marzanski moots the possibility that 'a similar change will occur in old age psychiatry after the introduction of new "anti-dementia" drugs' (2000: 111). Meanwhile, though, we should not suppose that truthfulness is compromised if patients with dementia are not volunteered information, provided that they are not lied to.

There can of course be worthy and unworthy motives for withholding information: worthy, if the aim is to spare a patient distress; unworthy, if the aim is to avoid taking the time that might be needed to explain things to a patient who does seem to be wanting to know more. Another rather dubious motive for informing patients might be with a view to seeking their consent to participate in non-therapeutic research: maybe even to seek their advance consent, while they may be still sufficiently competent to give it. This motive for informing patients might even lead to steps being taken generally to screen for dementia with a view to earlier diagnosis. Yet might not such measures and the sharing of information gleaned be detrimental to the patients' own interests? (Berghmans 1998: 36).

Meanwhile a policy of not lying to patients who have been diagnosed and of aiming to share information according to their individual needs and wishes is one that can be publicly acknowledged. It requires no compromise of a pledge of truthfulness towards patients. Thus doctors should refuse to lie to patients with dementia – even if relatives suggest this. But doctors may reasonably listen to what relatives advise about how much information a patient might welcome, granted that individual patients may differ in their attitudes and inquisitiveness and that relatives may often be better placed than doctors to speak for patients who are not altogether able to speak for themselves.

The test of public disclosure

We have surveyed some secretive practices that might seem difficult to square with pledges: some of these practices are perhaps already open secrets; some of the others could become so. But the point of making an open secret of a covert practice is not that this ensures that the practice is ethically defensible. The point of public disclosure is simply to avoid untruthfulness. A practice may still be unjust, though it is not untruthful. Justifying medical and nursing practices requires more than simply matching them to the pledges that are made.

Of course, we should not suppose wherever we find that pledges and practices do not square up that we have uncovered an instance of untruthfulness. Discrepancies may not be noticed. Lying is by definition intentional deception. Likewise, a false promise: it is a promise that we do not intend to keep. That is not, though, to suppose that we must be *thinking about* our lying when we lie. Compare how we make the appropriate moves behind the wheels of our cars, signalling (intentionally) to turn, and the like, without necessarily thinking about it. Wittgenstein asks: 'To what extent am I aware of lying when I lie? Just in so far as I don't "Only realise it later on", and all the same I do know later that I was lying' (1967: s.190). Untruthfulness cannot happen by accident. Discrepancies may be concealed and need studying to determine if they really are such. Hence, promises or pledges that turn out not to fit in with practices may still have been made sincerely.

Doctors and nurses can be 'too open'

Openness, a readiness to share all one knows or believes, all one's attitudes and expectations, is incompatible with the duties of doctors and nurses – most obviously with their duties to keep confidences. Indeed, keeping confidences can sometimes necessitate more than simply not revealing. One may need to take steps to conceal, to pretend, or even to use some deceptive trick (like equivocating or evading questions). Francis Bacon (in his essay 'Of Simulation and Dissimulation') observes: 'He that will be secret must be a dissembler in some degree ... no man can be secret, except he give himself a little scope for dissimulation, which is, as it were, but the skirts, or train of secrecy' (1825: 19).

Confidences aside, there may be other good reasons for withholding information from patients (or relatives). You do not have to volunteer to the patient who is a smoker, who has a persistent cough, laryngitis, and a fever that the diagnosis of lung cancer crosses your mind. If the patient says to you, 'I hope you're not thinking I've got lung cancer!' you do not have to rejoin, 'Why that is precisely what I'm thinking!' But nor do you need to lie, 'Certainly not!' There are many ways of parrying awkward questions and the motive for doing so need not be unworthy.

Though the duty not to lie is absolute and the duty to inform (where it applies) is prima facie, it does not follow that breach of the former duty is always a greater enormity than breach of the latter. If evidence is to hand that patients are harmed if bad news is kept from them, then it is inexcusable for those who should know this to persist in secretive ways. It is no defence that they take care to avoid lying. Truthfulness requires that. But doctors and nurses have other duties besides the duty to be truthful: for example, the duty of care. A surgeon tells a patient that the operation 'went well': meaning, it went well from the surgeon's standpoint (no hitches), only, not from the patient's standpoint (not all the malignant tissue could be removed). This is an evasively vague reply, but not a lie, but it is intended to deceive. Nowadays, it is usually inexcusable to respond evasively in this context, since there is plenty of evidence that patients are better off being told straight (though sensitively), despite the bleak implications. But it is not always inexcusable to speak evasively – not with patients who indicate that they do not want to know if the news is bad.

10 Truth and trust
Medical ethics today and any day

The first rule is to speak the truth; the second is to speak with discretion

Pascal

In the Introduction to the BMA's practical guide to doctors, *Medical Ethics Today*, it is said that 'The fundamental principles observed by the medical profession remain constant but their application to newly evolving situations requires debate' (BMA 1993: xxiii). Is truthfulness one of these fundamental principles that has always been observed by the medical profession? I have argued that it should be – if we understand truthfulness as a basic commitment not to lie. Yet it is often remarked that honesty, including truthfulness, hardly gets explicit mention in codes or in writings on medical ethics until quite recent times. What has been a constant theme until quite recently is the need for secrecy. The importance of being circumspect about what patients are told, of not disclosing information that might dash hopes, seems a well-entrenched and long-standing tradition. Recall Hippocrates:

> Perform [these duties] calmly and adroitly, concealing most things from the patient while you are attending to him. Give necessary orders with cheerfulness and sincerity, turning his attention away from what is being done to him; sometimes reprove sharply and emphatically, and sometimes comfort with solicitude and attention, revealing nothing of the patient's future or present condition.
>
> (*Decorum*, Hippocrates, quoted in Kennedy and Grubb 1989: note 54, 231).

Is the current 'Western' emphasis on the patients' right to know something to be explained as an adaptation of long-standing principles to new circumstances? In part, perhaps. Certainly, there are options nowadays that doctors can offer patients which are novel: for example, the possibility of being fed by tube, of resuscitation being attempted, or of donating one's vital organs when one dies. Patients can only have a say in such matters if they are put in the picture of what may be in store. On the other hand, the choice of whether to tell patients that they are terminally ill is not a new option. Here we might ask whether secrecy was always a mistake, or whether the 'Western' preference for openness with the terminally ill is better in certain sorts of cultures but not necessarily better *per se*. In this final chapter, I will distinguish what on the matter of 'truth-telling' seems to be basic, and fitting for medical practice to observe anywhere, any day, and what is derivative, and fitting for medical practice to observe in some places, at some times.

Two very different kinds of duty

We need here to take note of certain differences between the duty doctors (and health professionals generally) are under not to lie and the duty they may be under to inform. The former duty, I have argued is a basic, general duty – one of the duties of justice that everyone is under. The latter duty, I have argued is derivative – from duties of care and from patients' rights of autonomy. Thus the latter duty, but not the former, is role-dependent.

Some duties derive from rights, others are more basic – they generate rights but do not presuppose them (Gormally 1994: 40). Suppose I promise you to feed your cat, Clementine, while you are away on holiday. I have a duty (towards you, though Clementine is the beneficiary) derived from the right (your right, not Clementine's) created by the promise. But you can release me from the promise, in which case I am no longer duty-bound. Here the right is prior to, is the source of, the duty. The duty is cancelled if the corresponding right is waived. The duty to inform is a case in point. Contrast the duty you are under not to lie to me – or not to subject me to torture – these are duties that seem more basic than the rights I have on account of them. I cannot release you from these duties by waiving my right. These are duties you owe not to me particularly but to anyone (Kant would say, 'to humanity') : they are basic duties of justice that are prerequisites to living tolerably in peace with one another.

The duty not to lie, the duty 'to tell the truth'

We have noted that it is quite misleading to rephrase the teaching, 'Never lie!' as 'Always tell the truth!' – because of the ambiguity of the latter expression. Sometimes people mean by the latter simply, 'Never lie!' (Only tell the truth!); sometimes they mean, rather, 'Always disclose – be open!' which is, of course, quite another thing. As we have seen, Kant is a stout defender of 'truth-telling' in the former sense but not in the latter. Because of this confusion over what 'truth-telling' means, it is misleading to refer to the duty not to lie as the duty to 'tell the truth'. It is often said that doctors and nurses regularly face conflicts of duty (and have to weigh one against the other). A favourite illustration of the kinds of conflicts they face: 'A physician has to determine whether to tell the truth or break a confidence. He cannot do both, yet each of two moral rules commands his allegiance' (Beauchamp and Childress 1989: 39). Certainly we can expect conflicts to arise from time to time between the duty to keep a confidence and a duty to inform (disclose). But is it so obvious that conflicts will arise forcing a choice either to breach a confidence or to tell a lie? Usually there are other ways of preserving confidences – such as keeping silent. Moreover, I have argued, as does Kant, that deliberate deception (lying aside) is not *per se* untruthful. Francis Bacon commends 'dissimulation in seasonable use' (1825: 21). One such use is to protect confidences.

If the duty not to lie is as important for being able to trust a doctor's or nurse's word as I have claimed, is it not strange that it did not receive more attention in times gone by? Nowadays it does get attention – but maybe not so much on its own account but more as a kind of afterthought – something obviously not to be tolerated if patients have a right to information. But we have seen that the practice of lying to patients was not altogether ignored in writings on medical ethics in earlier centuries.

What is most contentious in my account of lying, is, of course, the claim that the duty is absolute, permitting no exceptions, no discretion. The notion that the duty applies so tightly is roundly dismissed by most philosophers. Henry Sidgwick observes:

> Many moralists have regarded this [the rule 'to speak the truth'], from its simplicity and definiteness, as a quite unexceptionable instance of an ethical axiom. I think, however, that patient reflection will show that the view is not really confirmed by the Common Sense of mankind.
>
> (1962: 315)

Sidgwick treats this duty as one that derives from a right that can be forfeit or suspended. He defends benevolent lying to children, to invalids and generally to those who have no right to know the information they seek. Most contemporary philosophers will agree with Sidgwick: if not with the particular exceptions he proposes, at least with the general claim that common sense must permit us some exceptions or discretion. I will not here repeat the reasons why, on the contrary, I think that common sense should confirm the strict repudiation of lying – why I think that any qualifications would destroy trust.

The idea that lying should be totally repudiated can easily be made to look silly if one defines 'lying' more broadly than I have done. Arnold Ludwig observes: 'Honesty may be a noble ideal, but it has little value in the life and death struggle for survival and security. Man has little choice in the matter – he must lie to live' (1965: 215). But then (as we noted in Chapter 4) those who insist on the routine need to lie tend to include a lot more than I have done in the definition. When we turn to Ludwig's definition of lying we find that it includes 'any type of behaviour which deviates from truth' (1965: 215).

Is it, unrealistic to insist that the duty not to lie is exceptionless even if we under-stand lying to include no more than 'asserting what one believes to be false in order to deceive someone'? How can we be obliged to do what we know to be impossible? Is it not obvious, even if we do not routinely lie, nor need to, that we do all the same tell lies from time to time? Is it not itself a dishonest pretence to commit ourselves to rules we cannot expect to follow? But what I am arguing for is the need to *resolve* not to lie. To resolve is not the same as to predict. One may sincerely resolve, yet foresee and predict occasional lapses. (Christians are supposed to acknowledge that they trespass daily, and seek forgiveness, and yet to resolve not to trespass.)

Moreover, we may reasonably be prepared to forgive and excuse some lapses, bearing in mind how difficult it can be to avoid lying in some situations, especially where one is caught off guard. Recall Kant's observation, 'Who has his wits always ready?' (1964: 95). To excuse, though, is not to justify.

Andrew Thorns tells of a predicament he faced when as a junior doctor he was working in 'rural Africa'. One of his duties there was to act as the local police surgeon.

> I remember a young boy, probably in his teens, being brought to me by the police. I forget what he was accused of, but the punishment was to be beaten by a stick. As police surgeon I was required to sign a document certifying that he was fit enough to receive punishment.
>
> (Thorns *et al.* 1998: 939)

Thorns relates that on the one hand he considered this form of punishment to be 'brutal' and wrongful, and his signing the paper would seem to condone the action; on the other hand, he could not 'show disrespect for local law'. What Thorns did was to listen to the boy's chest and then lie, saying that the boy had a chest infection and so was not fit enough to be beaten. To carry the situation off he had to administer a dose of antibiotics. Thorns implies that had a similar situation occurred again, he would have acted differently: 'a second time I would be more prepared' (Thorns *et al.* 1998: 939).

One thing this incident reminds us of, aside from the way in which we may be suddenly put on the spot and have no time to think things through, is that doctors and nurses do sometimes face situations where basic humanitarian rights are not being recognized. I have argued that the teachings we need in medical ethics are teachings that presuppose living in a community where the authorities are willing and able to protect people's basic rights. That, one hopes, is the normality. But doctors and nurses working in some countries – especially anywhere that is war-stricken – cannot make this cosy assumption. Relief agencies like the Red Cross or Médecins Sans Frontières, have to work out what stance to adopt where their doctors and nurses might be, or appear to be, implicated in meting out punishments, such as sharia punishments in Afganistan (amputation of feet or hands).

Was Thorns' lie not only excusable, given that he was put on the spot and had not been forewarned, but justifiable? The one kind of case in which I have defended lying is where a person is threatened with serious assault – like Grun, like the case of a murderer at your door. If racist thugs break into a hospital intent on killing some of your patients, you are entitled to lie to protect them. But Thorn faced not thugs, but police, presumably acting in accordance with local law. Was the local law, according to which a beating was not a cruel punishment, one that Thorns had any obligation to respect? If this, perhaps, any, form of corporal punishment is cruel and degrading, then Thorns would have had no obligation to show respect: indeed, it would have been wrong to do so. But not every law that is unenlightened violates a basic human right. Our obligation to respect the law does not hold merely if the law is faultless. We may 'respect' a law in the sense that we do not disobey it, while at the same time expressing our dissent and unwillingness to be involved in its enforcement. Sometimes this may be a more (or even the only) effective way of achieving reform.

The duty to inform

This duty, I have claimed, is not a duty we owe one another generally, but it arises for doctors and other health professionals because of other duties they take on: the duty of care and the duty to respect their patients' autonomy. I have argued that how much information is owed as a matter of good care can be expected to vary according to context and case. Perhaps some of the insights in regard to dying patients and the kind of isolation they endure when information is kept from them, will turn out to hold good for dying patients in all cultures. At any rate, on the matter of sharing information – the scope of this duty in so far as it derives simply from the duty of care – doctors and nurses should be entirely pragmatic (evidence-based). Where sharing information can be shown to help patients, openness is fitting; where sharing information can be shown to hinder patients' well-being, secrecy may be fitting.

But the other source of this duty, the duty to respect patients' autonomy, might seem to impose a universal obligation on doctors to share information with their patients. The question whether patients benefit or suffer if information is shared requires us to look to the evidence – to find out what patients want and need. Whatever the evidence suggests, it may be said, don't doctors anyway have a (prima facie) duty to share information, a duty that is independently based – based on patients' right to have their autonomy respected? Should we then insist that openness, the readiness to share information with patients, is something that is fitting for medical practice to observe anywhere, anytime?

Respect for autonomy

Let us take a closer look at this duty to respect patients' autonomy. The discovery of this duty has been generally hailed as a major advance in medical ethics:

> Medical paternalism has been found inappropriate for contemporary medical practice. It is considered to be at odds with the principle of individual autonomy, which has emerged as a paramount value in Western nations.
>
> (E.H.W. Kluge 1993: 140)

But what does observance of this principle or duty involve? Does it rule out deliberate withholding of information and the various concealing, pretending and deceptive tricks that I have defended (for example, covertly weaning a patient off dependency on a drug or on a ventilator)?

Understanding of what this duty might involve is not helped by the fact that the concept of autonomy as it occurs in contemporary philosophical debate is itself ill-defined. Etymlogically, it means self-rule and it was originally used in respect of Greek city-states. It has since come to be used of individual people – people who are in some sense supposed to take charge of themselves. In contemporary discussion it is used sometimes to refer to a capacity (for self-rule, for making one's own decisions, being independent) and sometimes to refer to a right (to exercise the capacity – making one's own decisions). Some of the things said of autonomy seem to refer to something else again. Thus, in discussion of a case (in the Appendix of Beauchamp and Childress) a nurse observes: 'It is important to maximise autonomy whenever possible' (1994: 514). What can this mean? It neither makes sense to talk of maximizing a capacity nor of maximizing a right.

Should we understand the duty to respect patients' autonomy as a duty to respect their capacity or a duty to respect their right? The idea that respect is owed to a capacity is hard to make much sense of. Doctors need to take care not to injure or impair capacities: that is part of the general duty to do no harm, but the importance of respecting patients' autonomy is meant to be a recent discovery. The importance of not injuring people's rational capacities (bound up with their ability to make choices and form opinions) is surely no new idea. It would seem, then, easier to make sense of this duty to respect autonomy in relation to the idea of a right that patients have. This right is the new discovery.

What is this right? Beauchamp and Childress explain this as a right that patients have to form their own views and make their own choices. We noted the implausibility of a claim that patients have a right to hold any views whatsoever, make any choices whatsoever, and the insignificance of a claim that patients have a right to hold some views and to make some choices. Champions of the right to have one's autonomy respected are very ready to concede that the right is merely prima facie: a right to be independent so long as we do not interfere with others' rights to be independent; a right which we are entitled to waive and may forfeit. Once these accommodations are allowed, the right may seem to have very unclear boundaries – and consequently be very difficult to know how to respect.

Be that as it may, let us suppose that patients do have a prima facie right to make their own choices, a right that doctors (and nurses) must respect. Does respect for this right imply an obligation to share information with patients – hence not to go in for concealing, pretending or deceptive tricks? Notice that withholding information (or otherwise restricting a patient's choices) does not harm a patients' *capacity* for acting autonomously. When Bertrand Russell was imprisoned, his liberty was constrained, but not his capacity for forming views, or making choices. (It was while he was incarcerated that he wrote *An Introduction to Mathematical Philosophy*.) But is it a violation of patients' rights to attempt, by withholding information, to influence their choices? It is if you have promised to be open – to fully inform. But is that a promise you should make? Is that promise already implicit in the duty to respect patients' autonomy – or is it enough that you aim to adequately inform? I have argued that patients are owed adequate information, not full information. What is 'adequate', I have argued, is something that has to be judged according to context and case.

One of the bullet point duties listed in the card nowadays issued to UK medical students by the GMC is: 'listen to patients and respect their views'. With the 'listen to patients', I have no quarrel. But what exactly does the latter requirement mean: 'respect their views'? Does respect their views mean that one should not challenge them or seek to change them? Certainly doctors should be civil towards patients, but that is separately itemized: 'treat every patient politely and considerately'. Thus the instruction to 'respect their views' must imply something additional. Suppose that your patients' views are standing in the way of their recovery from or avoidance of serious illness: do you not owe them a duty to correct their views. Suppose your patients' views are, if uncorrected, likely to cause harm to others: the pregnant woman who does not think her drug taking will harm her baby; the elderly patient who does not believe that he is no longer fit to continue driving his car. Suppose the patients' views result in precious health resources going to waste: the recipient of a kidney transplant who does not comply with medication and is likely to end up needing another transplant. Presumably, the instruction to respect patients' views is intended to be qualified by the other duties listed on the card: respect their views when these do not interfere with their own or other people's health or safety. But why would doctors be minded to challenge or change their patients' views except in pursuance of their other duties?

There is, as we have noticed, a sinister side to the association of respect for patients with respect for their autonomy: the implications for those patients who do not have autonomy. Those who lack the capacity to be autonomous (babies, the senile, the comatose, the deranged), lack the right to exercise it. Hence, it may easily be supposed that these patients are not owed respect in any sense. If what entitles patients to respect is merely their capacity or right to exercise autonomy, those whose capacity cannot be restored are likely to be marginalized as non-persons:

> Fragility and vulnerability, rather than being seen as appropriate parts of life from the cradle to the grave, become obstacles to be overcome by the self-sufficient man or woman. The *successful* patient is always the one who transcends patienthood.
>
> (Campbell 1991: 105–6)

Mill and individual liberty

Interestingly, John Stuart Mill, who inveighs against paternalist encroachments on individual liberty, does not make use of the notion of 'autonomy' in *On Liberty*. Perhaps the two notions, 'liberty' and 'autonomy' come to much the same thing: [1] where we are thinking of people's rights to make their own choices, however unwise or silly – provided, of course, they are only harming themselves. But notice how, in the context of *patients'* choices, the likelihood is that the choices they make will affect others, often deeply. Patients who reject advice and persist in risky habits may not only compromise their own future liberty of action but also that of their families, who end up caring for them. Patients who do not comply with medication or other restrictions on their habits after expensive operations will require further procedures. That is costly for them – also, for others, unless their health care is privately funded. Of course, when Mill says, 'Each is the proper guardian of his own health'(1962: 138) he is not supposing that society will foot the medical bills arising from people's wayward self-neglect.

Mill is a firm believer in the educational benefit to be had in learning from one's own mistakes. But where the choices individuals make can impinge momentously on the lives of others, we may be justified in denying them that particular benefit. Even if in some situations we suppose that patients' choices will not significantly affect others, we may still hesitate to defer to their right to make their own mistakes, if, for example, there is no way of retrieving the harm they may do themselves. Consider how, for example, a patient who refuses to co-operate in rehabilitative exercises may be permanently more crippled in consequence. Would a physiotherapist not be justified in cajoling, coaxing and being circumspect in talking about future prospects (without actually lying) in order to overcome the patient's resistance?

Mill's arguments against paternalism are mainly directed against imposed conformity – the 'despotism of custom' (1962: 200) and its crimping of individualism and eccentricity: 'He who lets the world, or his own portion of it, choose his plan of life for him, has no need of any other faculty than the ape-like one of imitation' (1962: 187). But the physiotherapist who cajoles a patient into doing painful exercises, and who evades questions about the amount of mobility the patient can realistically expect to recover, need not be trying to impose conformity, merely to help the patient salvage some degree of mobility. Mill observes: 'If a person possesses any tolerable amount of common sense and experience, his own mode of laying out his existence is best, not because it is best in itself, but because it is his own mode' (1962: 197). Yet he goes on to note that not everyone is always able to draw on common sense and experience: not a child, not someone who is delirious nor someone 'in some state of excitement or absorption incompatible with the full use of the reflecting faculty' (1962: 229). A patient who has suffered a severe stroke or other disabling injury may be in just such a state of absorption – and in need of more than non-judgemental information-giving. Anyway, Mill approves of paternalist advice, instruction, encouragement and persuasion. It is only the attempt to *compel* compliance to which he takes strong exception (1962: 206, 226).

Patients do have certain basic rights liberty rights that are not automatically forfeit if they make choices that are likely to harm themselves or others. But these rights are no new discovery: the right to refuse a treatment is enshrined in the common law (according to which 'battery', unconsented-to touching, is a crime). Yet it may be argued that this right is being violated in an underhanded way, where doctors or nurses circumvent being faced with refusals by withholding information that might deter their patients from consenting. 'Underhand' perhaps suggests not just concealing but doing so where that is against the rules. Professing to be informing fully about possible risks and complications when one is deliberately concealing something is dishonest – it is a lie. But need doctors so profess: and should they?

The trend towards greater frankness and fuller disclosure, especially when doctors seek consent for invasive procedures, may have much to do with the law and the increase of legal actions against doctors. It can be seen as one aspect of defensive medicine:

> The idea is that if you let the patient in on all the information you have, if you make the patient feel as if the two of you are making all of the important decisions together – or even that you are turning these decisions over to the patient – then you can scarcely be asked to shoulder the blame yourself when things come out wrong. The patient's lawyer can still ask whether you let the patient know all the risks of the procedure, but you will have an answer: Yes. We discussed the risks and the alternatives in detail. In fact, you could even say, the patient, given all the relevant information, was the one who made the decision and chose the treatment.
>
> (Konner 1993: 18)

Rather than smugly applauding the Western trend as an improvement over older traditions, we should ask if this trend is not largely symptomatic of a deterioration of public trust in doctors (whether or not merited). At any rate, we should not suppose that doctors in earlier times, who saw fit to dwell on benefits, and to breeze over possible harms, of the operations they recommended, were less truthful, just because they were less open.

The legal duty to inform

Doctors in 'Western' countries nowadays do indeed have a legal duty to seek informed consent – which means they must do more than explain 'in broad terms' the nature of the procedure they are recommending. But this requirement that they explain more – in the case of operations, that they discuss risks, possible complications and alternative options – is not derived from patients' rights against battery but from their rights against negligent treatment. Negligent treatment is treatment that falls below proper standards of care. Thus, the legal duty to give full information is derivative from the duty of care, not from some basic liberty right. How much information is owed as a matter of care is naturally something that needs to be worked out in relation to the particularities of a case.

I suggest that the moral right to fuller information is likewise simply derivative from the duty of care. Thus the duty to inform patients has two independent sources. One source is the duty of care. Here how much information should be offered or withheld depends on what is found to serve the caring aims (which can be expected to vary from case to case). Standards are likely to need continual adapting in the light of new evidence and new possibilities. The other source is the duty to respect patients' liberty to refuse treatments. The patients' right here is a fundamental 'human' right against assault. The obligation it demarcates is a constant (and no new discovery). Obviously there are qualifications – some special circumstances in which unconsented-to touching is not a violation of this right, but we can ignore these here as they are not germane to our theme.

Patients as partners?

It would not be fair, though, simply to dismiss the trend towards openness and the sharing of information as if it were fuelled only by fear of litigation. The more high-minded motivation is the concern to make the right decisions for patients and the recognition that making the right decision may depend on finding out the patients' own views and preferences. The opening words of *Medical Ethics Today* describe the 'therapeutic partnership':

> The relationship between doctor and patient is based on the concept of part-nership and collaborative effort. Ideally, decisions are made through frank discussion, in which the doctor's clinical expertise and the patient's individual needs and preferences are shared to select the best treatment option.
>
> (1993: 1)

It is this recognition of the authority patients should have not just over whether or not to accept what is recommended, but over what it is suitable to choose, that marks a significant change in the doctor-patient relationship: and why it is said that 'respect for patient autonomy has become a core principle of modern medicine' (BMA 1993: 321).

But should this recognition lead us to condemn medical paternalism as no longer appropriate for contemporary medical practice? What about patients who do not want 'frank discussion'? Should they be made to engage in it willy-nilly: for their own good? If so, medical paternalism is still necessary: only, whereas it used to take the form of withholding information the patient was better off not knowing it will now take the form of sharing information the patient does not want but is better off knowing.

Is there not, anyway, still a place for medical paternalism where circumstances are not ideal: as, for example, with the patient who needs to do the painful exer-cises in order to recover some degree of mobility after a stroke? As I have argued, it is not at all clear that Mill's objections to paternalism would tell against the physiotherapist who is in no hurry to put the patient straightaway fully in the picture, spelling out how limited are the long term prospects.

Nor, I suggest, is it obvious that Kant would have any objection to the physio-therapist's paternalism in such a case. Kant objects to 'using' people as mere means to our own ends, as if they did not have ends of their own. But the nurse's aims in withholding information are not at all self-serving or inattentive to the presumed wishes of the patient. Kant illustrates children's need for discipline with the following analogy:

> The trees in the forest discipline each other; they cannot obtain air for growth in the spaces between them, but only up above, so they grow tall and straight; but a tree that is open is not restricted and so grows crooked, and then it is too late to train it. So it is with man. Trained early he grows up straight along with his fellows; but if he is never pruned, he becomes a crooked tree.
>
> (1930: 249–50)

By the same analogy Kant might well approve of the physiotherapist's paternalistically motivated circumspection. A tree that was tall and straight but has suffered an injury may need a temporary support if it is to recover and not become permanently misshapen.

A teaching for all time?

The teachings that prevail these days in regard to truthfulness may have the effect of making doctors and nurses less trustworthy than in times gone by. Though the teachings emphasize the duty to be truthful, they confuse truthfulness with frankness and openness (as if the duty to be 'honest and open' is one duty). Since it is so obviously impossible, and anyway improper, to be frank and open always, the teachings in effect encourage a discretionary attitude both to frankness and, since it is not clearly distinguished, to truthfulness. The upshot is that the duty to be truthful turns out to be merely one desirable alongside other desirables – a prima facie duty to be weighed against others. Thurstan Brewin, as we noted at the outset of our study in Chapter 1, commenting on the change of attitudes between the 1950s and 1990s in 'Western' countries in favour of disclosing to patients 'every risk, grim diagnosis and prognosis' remarks: 'Yet the actual practices have changed less than the rhetoric' (1996: ix). This is hardly surprising, given that the rhetoric is so ambivalent.

Hence, for all the 'Western' disapproval of the secrecy that doctors used to permit themselves, and get away with, the current teaching permits not only secrecy but lying. If I am right, the teaching that is needed should repudiate lying altogether. This is a teaching for all time. It is so because it is the only teaching that is adequate to sustain trust in the word of doctors and nurses. That trust is and always has been a necessary supporting pillar of the covenant between the patient and the health professional. That is the essence of truthfulness as a virtue. Those who have this virtue are committed to avoid lying and they have the strength of will and shrewdness to act accordingly in the main. Success requires shrewdness of judgement as well as strength of will – for example, the ability to anticipate being caught off guard, and to learn from such experiences.

We need not suppose that those who have this virtue never lie, only that they intend never to lie: that is their ongoing aim. (We need not suppose that having a virtue implies perfection.) The aim itself is not unrealistic, though it seems so if we confuse truthfulness with openness, and sweep into our definition of lying all forms of secrecy. We have noted how the expression 'tell the truth' invites this kind of confusion – how it encourages us to suppose that either we do not tell the truth (lie) or we do tell the truth (disclose all we know). Since doing the latter is plainly often ridiculous, it seems we have to permit ourselves sometimes to do the former: lying is sometimes necessary. But this is a false dichotomy. Very often we have other options (like refusing to speak) and recourse to these need not be any kind of betrayal of trust or threat to it. On the contrary, trust is supported not only by our commitment not to lie but also by our caution about what we disclose. Pascal, properly construed, got it exactly right: 'The first rule is to speak [only] the truth; the second is to speak with discretion'.

Notes

1 Truthfulness in medical and nursing practice

1 The consultant was found not guilty of professional misconduct but was made to give a formal undertaking that this sort of action would not occur again. No action was taken to modify the 'sentence' on the nurse. John M. Kellett (1996) 'A nurse is suspended', *British Medical Journal,* 313: 1250.
2 Hereafter, when I speak of 'rights', let it be understood that I am speaking of 'moral' or 'ethical' (not in this book differentiated) not 'legal' rights – unless otherwise indicated.
3 'The term "informed consent" came into common use only after 1960, when it was used by the Kansas Supreme Court in *Nathanson* v. *Kline,* 186 Kan. 393, 350, p.2d. 1093 (1960)'. Bok (1978: 233).
4 The *Committee on Publication Ethics (COPE) Report 1998* recommends that an independent agency be established in the UK to monitor standards and to counter what it perceives as a growing problem of research misconduct (reported in *British Medical Journal* 1998: 316, 1695).

2 Noble lies and therapeutic tricks

1 Melvin Konner describes how at the Saitama centre in Japan, which is committed to maintaining patients' hope for a good outcome, 'the (hospital) staff routinely review together the lies they have told to different patients, in order to maintain a consistent pretence' (1993: 5).
2 Quotation taken from Henry E. Siegerist 1961: 308.
3 All quotations from Plato are taken from the translations in John M. Cooper (ed.) 1997.
4 All quotations from Gregory are taken from Laurence B. McCullough (ed.) 1998.
5 All quotations from Rush are taken from Dagobert D. Runes (ed.) 1947.
6 All quotations from Percival's *Medical Ethics* are taken from Chauncey D. Leake (ed.) 1927.
7 All quotations from Hutcheson's *A System of Moral Philosophy*, vols I and II, originally published in 1755 are taken from the facsimile edition by Bernhard Fabian, 1969.
8 In England, *Chatterton* v. *Gerson* [1980] 3 W.L.R. 1003 and *Sidaway* v. *Board of Governors of the Bethlem Royal and the Maudsley Hospital* [1985] 2 W.L.R. 480 and in Canada, *Reibl* v. *Hughes* (1980) 114 D.L.R. (3d) 1.
9 Admittedly, a little further on in this document is entered the following reservation: 'When it is not medically advisable to give such information to the patient, the information should be given to an appropriate person ....'

3 Why truthfulness matters

1 Not Francis Bacon: 'If it be well weighed, to say that a man lieth, is as much as to say, that he is brave towards God, and a coward towards men. For a lie faces God and shrinks from man' (1825: 5).
2 Cf. St. Augustine: 'The mouth that lieth slayeth the soul' (On Lying: 390).
3 All quotations from Aristotle (384–22 BC) are taken from the translation by W.D. Ross (ed.) *The Nichomachean Ethics of Aristotle,* London, Oxford University Press, 1954.
4 See Peter Geach, *The Virtues*, Cambridge, Cambridge University Press, 1977, p. 13.

4 What truthfulness requires

1 'The trouble is that in cases such as that of the murderer at the door it seems grotesque simply to say that I have done my part by telling the truth and the bad results are not my responsibility'(Korsgaard 1996: 150).
2 Interestingly, as we have already noted, one of Augustine's *objections* to softening the strict rule against lying is just that doing so renders one powerless in the face of evil – because then one can be bullied into doing all sorts of evil things under the threat that unless one complies the bully will do something worse. Bernard Williams' example of Jim and the Indians illustrates the point (in *Utilitarianism: For and Against*, J.J.C. Smart and Bernard Williams, Cambridge University Press, Cambridge, 1973).
3 But notice that we do not always lie in order to get someone to do something. Often we lie simply to conceal something we do not want others to know about us – for example, something that we have done or failed to do. Not all lies are manipulative. Berlin's lie to his father was not manipulative.

5 The teaching we need to preserve truthfulness

1 The only writer I have found who departs radically from the mainstream view and who like me maintains that the duty not to lie should apply without exception to health professionals is Joseph Ellin (who, incidentally, is, like myself, a philosopher, not a health professional) ('The solution to a dilemma in medical ethics, *Westminster Institute Review*, 1: 3–6, 1981). By a somewhat different route, he reaches the same conclusion as do I regarding the duty not to lie. But he applies this duty only to health professionals – not, as I do, to everyone.

7 Deceptions and concealments in medical and nursing practice

1 We will discuss the use of placebos in research in the next chapter.

8 Dishonesty in medical research

1 In Sinclair Lewis's novel, *Arrowsmith*, New York, Harcourt, Brace & World, 1925, Rippleton Holabird nimbly climbs the career ladder to fetch up as Director of a prestigious research institute in New York. Max Gottlieb, the unworldly scientist, short on people-skills, unwisely takes on the Directorship for a time and goes mad; another scientist, Terry Wickett, who is in the Gottlieb mould, resigns from the Institute, frustrated by the pressures therein that distract him from his own pure quest and attempts to carry on his studies, living hermit-like in the backwoods of New England. Arrowsmith strives to combine both the purity of the scientist's quest with a life outside the lab – with some hard consequences for him and those dear to him.
2 These and other examples of fraud in recent biomedical research are described by Gerald Dworkin in 'Fraud and Science', in Berg and Tr35øy (1983: 65–74)
3 This case is described in W.J. Broad and N. Wade, (1982) and in David J. Miller (1992)

4   Admittedly, Jenner's own methods hardly pass muster from an ethical standpoint nowadays – testing his vaccine on an eight year old child and on his own 10 month old son by infecting them first with cow-pox and then inoculating them (repeatedly over a number of years) with purulent matter directly from a small-pox pustule of an actively sick person.

5   Cf. Stanley Migram, *Obedience to Authority*, New York, Harper & Row, 1983.

6   Alan C. Elms observes: 'The remarkable thing about the Milgram subjects was not that they suffered great persisting harm, but that they suffered so little, given the intensity of their emotional reactions during the experiment itself', ('Keeping deception honest: justifying conditions for social scientific research stratagems' in Tom L. Beauchamp *et al.* (eds) *Ethical Issues in Social Science Research*, Baltimore, The Johns Hopkins University Press, 1982, p. 236).

7   The promise may be sincere in that those who make it do not *intend* to disadvantage those who say no. That is not to say that those patients who do say no will not be at a disadvantage all the same.

9 Can doctors and nurses be 'too honest'?

1   According to a report in the *Sunday Telegraph*, many patients who need renal dialysis are denied it because of the expense. 'Decisions on which patients should be denied dialysis are made on the basis of age, with doctors reporting that some are only in their fifties. One doctor said last week: "very few are told the reason they are not receiving the treatment as there seems little point in upsetting them" ' (Martyn Halle and Ian Cobain, 'Kidney patients "condemned to die" through cash shortage' 5 March 2000).

2   In 'Justified deception? The single-blind placebo in drug research' *Journal of Medical Ethics*, 26, 3: 188–93.

10 Truth and trust: medical ethics today and any day

1   'Clearly' they do, according to Raanan Gillon: in 'Autonomy and consent', in Michael Lockwood (ed.) *Moral Dilemmas in Modern Medicine*, Oxford, Oxford University Press, 1985, pp. 111–25.

Bibliography

American Hospitals Association (1973) 'Statement on a Patient's Bill of Rights', *Hospitals*, 47: 41.

American Psychological Association (1992) 'Ethical principles of psychologists and code of conduct', *American Psychologist,* 47, 1597–611.

Amundsen, D.W. and Ferngren, G.B. (1983) 'Evolution of the patient-physician relationship: antiquity through the renaissance', in E.E. Shelp (ed.) *The Clinical Encounter*, 14: 3–46 Dordrecht: D. Reidel.

Ardagh, M. (1997) 'May we practise endotracheal intubation on the newly dead?' *Journal of Medical Ethics*, 23, 5: 289–94.

Atiyah, P.S. (1981) *Promises, Morals, and Law*, Oxford: Clarendon Press.

Audit Commission (1993) *What Seems to be the Matter: Communications between Hospitals and Patients*, London: HMSO.

Bacon, Francis (1825) *Essays* in B. Montagu (ed.) *The Works of Francis Bacon*,1, London: William Pickering (originally published in 1597).

Baddeley, P. (1995) 'A doctor's view' in V. Tschudin (ed.) *Ethics: the Patient's Charter*, London: Scutari Press.

Baier, A. (1990) 'Why honesty is a hard virtue', in O. Flanagan and A. Oksenberg Rorty (eds) *Identity, Character and Morality*, 259–82, Cambridge, MA: MIT Press.

Barnes, J.A. (1994) *A Pack of Lies*, Cambridge: Cambridge University Press.

—— (1979) *Who Should Know What?* London: Penguin.

Beauchamp, T.L. and Childress, J.E. (1994) *Principles of Biomedical Ethics*, New York: Oxford University Press.

Beecher, H.K. (1959) *Experimentation in Man*, Springfield, II: Charles C. Thomas.

Belmont Report (1979) reprinted in H. Y. Vanderpool (ed.) *The Ethics of Research Involving Human Subjects: Facing the 21st Century*, 437–48, Frederick, MD: University Publishing Group.

Berghmans, R.L.P. (1998) 'Advance directives for non-therapeutic dementia research: some ethical and policy considerations', *Journal of Medical Ethics,* 24, 1: 32–7.

Berg, K. and Trานøy (eds) (1983) *Research Ethics*, New York: Alan R. Liss.

Blair, A.W. and Steer, C.R. (1997) 'Your child is brain dead', in C.R.K. Hind (ed.) *Communication Skills in Medicine*, London: BMJ Publishing Group.

BMA (1993) *Medical Ethics Today: its Practice and Philosophy,* London: BMJ Publishing Group.

Bok, S. (1978) *Lying*, Hassocks, Sussex: Harvester Press.

Brewin, T.B. (1977) 'The cancer patient: communication and morale', *British Medical Journal*, 2: 1623–7.

—— (1993) 'How much ethics is needed to make a good doctor?' *The Lancet*, 341: 161–3.

—— and Sparschott, M. (1996) *Relating to Relatives, Breaking Bad News, Communication and Support*, Abingdon, Oxford: Radcliffe Medical Press.

Broad, W. and Wade, N. (1982) *Betrayers of the Truth*, New York: Simon and Schuster.

Brody, B.A. (1998) *The Ethics of Biomedical Research*, New York: Oxford University Press.

Brody, H. (1980) *Placebos and the Philosophy of Medicine*, Chicago, IL: Chicago University Press.

—— (1983) 'Deception in the teaching hospital', in D. Ganos, R.E. Lipson, G. Warren and B. J. Weil (eds) *Difficult Decisions in Medical Ethics*, New York: Alan R. Liss.

—— (1997) 'The doctor as therapeutic agent: a placebo effect research agenda', in A. Harrington (ed.) *The Placebo Effect*, Cambridge, MA: Harvard University Press.

Bronowski, J. (1977) *A Sense of the Future*, Cambridge, MA: MIT Press.

Cabot, R.C. (1903) 'The use of truth and falsehood in medicine: an experimental study', *American Medicine*, 5: 344–9.

—— (1938) *Honesty*, New York: Macmillan.

Campbell, A. (1991) 'Dependency revisited: the limits of autonomy in medical ethics', in M. Brazier and M. Lobjoit (eds) *Protecting the Vulnerable*, London: Routledge.

Canadian Medical Protective Association (1996) *Consent: A Guide for Canadian Physicians*, Ottawa: Canadian Medical Protective Association.

Christie, B. (1999) 'Panel needed to combat research fraud, *British Medical Journal,* 319: 1222.

Clarke, S. (1999) 'Justifying deception in social science research' *Journal of Applied Philosophy*, 16: 151–66.

Cliffe, L. Ramsay, M. and Bartlett, D. (2000) *The Politics of Lying: Implications for Democracy*, Basingstoke: Macmillan.

Code of Federal Regulations: Protection of Human Subjects (1991) reprinted in H. Y. Vanderpool (ed.) *The Ethics of Research Involving Human Subjects: Facing the 21st Century*, Frederick, MD: University Publishing Group.

Cook, S. (1981) *Second Life*, New York: Simon and Schuster.

Cooper, J.M. (ed.) (1997) *Plato's Complete Works*, Indianapolis, IN: Hackett.

Day, D.O. (1998) 'The initial therapeutic stage: trust', in T.F. Parnell and D.O. Day (eds) *Munchausen By Proxy Syndrome*, Thousand Oaks, CA: Sage Publications.

Declaration of Helsinki 1996 (1998) reprinted in B.A. Brody, *The Ethics of Biomedical Research*, New York: Oxford University Press.

Department of Health (1991) *The Patients' Charter*, London: Department of Health.

Diener, E. and Crandall, R. (1978) *Ethics in Social and Behavioral Research*, Chicago, IL: University of Chicago Press.

Dworkin, G. (1983) 'Fraud and science', in K. Berg and K.E. Tranøy (eds) *Research Ethics*, New York: Alan R. Liss.

—— (1988) *The Theory and Practice of Autonomy*, Cambridge: Cambridge University Press.

Dyer, O. (1998) 'GP found guilty of forging trial consent forms', *British Medical Journal*, 317: 1475.

Ekman, P. (1985) *Telling Lies*, New York: W.W. Norton & Co.

Elliott, D. and Stern, J.E. (eds) (1997) *Research Ethics: A Reader*, Hanover, NH: University Press of New England.

Elliott, H. (1988) 'The reformation of health care is under way!', in D.E. Young (ed.) *Health Care Issues in the Canadian North*, Edmonton: Boreal Institute of Northern Studies.

Ellin, J.S. (1981) 'The solution to a dilemma in medical ethics', *Westminster Institute Review*, 1: 3–6.

Elms, A.C. (1982) 'Keeping deception honest: justifying conditions for social scientific research', in T.L. Beauchamp, R.R. Faden, R.J. Wallace Jr and L. Walters (eds) *Ethical Issues in Social Science Research*, Baltimore, MD: The Johns Hopkins University Press.

Evans, M. (2000) 'Justified deception? The single-blind placebo in drug research', *Journal of Medical Ethics*, 26, 3: 188–93.

Fabian, B. (ed.) (1969) *Collected Works of Francis Hutcheson*, vol. VI, Hildesheim: George Olms (originally published in 1755).

Faden, R.R. and Beauchamp, T.L. (1986) *A History and Theory of Informed Consent*, New York: Oxford University Press.

Fairbairn, G. (1987) 'Responsibility, respect for persons and psychological change', in S. Fairbairn and G. Fairbairn (eds) *Psychology, Ethics and Change*, London: Routledge & Kegan Paul.

Feinberg, J. (1983) 'Legal Paternalism', in R. Sartorius (ed.) *Paternalism*, Minneapolis, MN: University of Minnesota Press.

Foot, P. (1978) *Virtues and Vices*, Oxford: Basil Blackwell.

—— (1982) 'Moral relativism', in J.W. Meiland and M. Krausz (eds) *Relativism*, Notre Dame, IN: University of Notre Dame Press.

—— (1985) 'Utilitarianism and the virtues', *Mind*, XCIV: 196–209.

Freedman, B. (1996) 'The ethical analysis of clinical trials: new lessons for and from cancer research', in H.Y. Vanderpool (ed.) *The Ethics of Research Involving Human Subjects: Facing the 21st Century*, Frederick, MD: University Publishing Group.

Freeman, T.B., Vanter, D.E., Leaverton, P.E., Godbold, J.H., Hauser, R.A., Goetz, C.G. and Olanow, C.W. (1999) 'Use of placebo surgery in controlled trials of a cellular based therapy for Parkinson's disease', *New England Journal of Medicine*, 341, 13: 988–91.

Fried, C. (1978) *Right and Wrong*, Cambridge, MA: Harvard University Press.

Ganos, D., Lipson, R.E., Warren, G. and Weil, B.J. (1983) (eds) *Difficult Decisions in Medical Ethics*, New York: Alan R. Liss.

Geach, P.T. (1977) *The Virtues*, Cambridge: Cambridge University Press.

Gillon, R. (1985) 'Autonomy and consent' in M. Lockwood (ed.) *Moral Dilemmas in Modern Medicine*, Oxford: Oxford University Press.

—— (1995) 'Covert surveillance by doctors for life-threatening Munchausen's syndrome by proxy', *Journal of Medical Ethics*, 21.3: 131–2.

Gisborne, T. (1797) *An Enquiry into the Duties of Men*, vol. II, London: B. and J. White; and Cadell and Davies.

Goodstein, D. (1995) 'The fading myth of the noble scientist', in N.J. Pallone and J.J. Hennessy (eds) *Fraud and Fallible Judgement*, New Brunswick, NJ: Transaction Publishers.

Gormally, L. (1994) (ed.) *Euthanasia, Clinical Practice and the Law*, London: The Linacre Centre for Health Care Ethics.

Griffin, M.T. and Atkins, E.M. (eds) (1991) Marcus Tullius. Cicero, *On Duties,* trans. E.M. Atkins, Cambridge: Cambridge University Press.

Griffith, D. and Bell, A. (1996) 'Commentary treatment was not unethical', *British Medical Journal*, 313: 1250.

Hackett, T.P. (1976) 'Psychological assistance for the dying patient and his family', *Annual Review of Medicine*, 27: 371–8.

Harrington, A. (1997) *The Placebo Effect*, Cambridge, MA: Harvard University Press.

Hellman, S. and Hellman D.S. (1991) 'Of mice but not men. Problems of the randomized clinical trial' *New England Journal of Medicine*, 324: 1585–9.

Hill, A.B. (1963) 'Medical ethics and controlled trials', *British Medical Journal*, 1: 1043–9.

Hilts, P.J. (1997) 'The science mob: the David Baltimore case – and its lessons', in D. Elliott and J.E. Stern (eds) *Research Ethics: A Reader*, Hanover, NH: University Press of New England.

Hippocrates (1961), *Decorum*: all quotations taken from Siegerist (1961).

Hobbes, T. (1909) *Hobbes's Leviathan*, Oxford: the Clarendon Press (reprinted from the edition of 1651).

Hollis, M. (1998) *Trust Within Reason*, Cambridge: Cambridge University Press.

Hooker, W. (1849) *Physician and Patient*, New York: Baker and Scribner.

Hume, D. (1888) in L.A. Selby-Bigge (ed.) *A Treatise of Human Nature*, Oxford: Clarendon Press (originally published in 1739).

—— (1975) in L.A. Selby-Bigge (ed.) *Enquiry Concerning the Principles of Morals*, Oxford: Clarendon (originally published in 1777).

Jones, J. (1999) 'UK watchdog issues guidelines to combat medical research fraud', *British Medical Journal,* 319: 660.

Jonsen, A.R. and Toulmin, S. (1988) *The Abuse of Casuistry*, Berkeley: University of California Press.

Kant, I. (1923) On a Supposed Right to Tell Lies from Benevolent Motives, Appendix in *Kant's Critique of Practical Reason and Other Works on the Theory of Ethics*, trans. T.K. Abbott, London: Longmans, Green and Co (originally published in 1797).

—— (1930) *Lectures on Ethics*, trans. Louis Infield, London: Methuen & Co (originally published in 1924 and based on students' lecture notes from 1780–81).

—— (1964) *The Doctrine of Virtue, Part ll of The Metaphysics of Morals*, trans. M.J. Gregor, New York: Harper Torchbooks (originally published in 1797).

—— (1979) *The Conflict of the Faculties*, trans. M.J. Gregor, New York: Abaris Books (originally published in 1798).

Kellett, J.M. (1996) 'A nurse is suspended', *British Medical Journal*, 313: 1249–51.

Kennedy, I. and Grubb, A. (1989) *Medical Law: Text and Material*, London: Butterworth.

Kerr, P. (ed.) (1990) *The Penguin Book of Lies*, London: Viking.

Kimmel, A.J. (1996) *Ethical Issues in Behavioural Research*, Cambridge, MA.: Blackwell.

Kluge, E.H.W. (1993) *Readings in Biomedical Ethics: A Canadian Focus*, Scarborough, ON: Prentice Hall Canada Inc.

Kmietowicz, Z. (2000) 'Relatives to be told if organs are to be retained after postmortem', *British Medical Journal*, 320: 821.

Konner, M. (1993) *The Trouble with Medicine*, London: BBC Books.

Korsgaard, C.M. (1996) *Creating the Kingdom of Ends*, New York: Cambridge University Press.

Krakauer, J. (1998) *Into Thin Air*, London: Pan Books.

LaFollette, M.C. (1995) 'The role of the social sciences in the analysis of research misconduct', in N.J. Pallone and J.J. Hennessy (eds) *Fraud and Fallible Judgment*, New Brunswick, NJ: Transaction Publishers.

Lantos, J.D. (1997) *Do We Still Need Doctors?* New York: Routledge.

Leake, C.D. (ed.) (1927) *Percival's Medical Ethics*, Baltimore, MD: The Williams & Wilkins Company.

Leber, P. (1986) 'The placebo control in clinical trials (a view from the FDA)', *Psychopharmacology Bulletin,* 22: 30–2.

Lesser, H. (1991) 'The patient's right to information' in M. Brazier and M. Lobjoit (eds) *Protecting the Vulnerable*, London: Routledge.

Levine, R.J. (1991) 'Comment re: "Ethics and statistics in randomized clinical trials"' *Statistical Science*, 6: 71–4.

Lilford, R.J. and Jackson, J. (1995) 'Equipoise and the ethics of randomization' *Journal of the Royal Society of Medicine*, 88: 55–9.

Ludwig, A.M. (1965) *The Importance of Lying*, Springfield, II: Charles C. Thomas.

McCullough, L.B. (ed.) (1998) *John Gregory's Writings in Medical Ethics and Philosophy of Medicine*, Dordrecht: Kluwer Academic.

McCullough, L.B., Jones, J.W. and Brody, B.A. (1998) *Surgical Ethics*, New York: Oxford University Press.

MacIntyre, A. (1981) *After Virtue: a Study of Moral Theory*, Notre Dame, IN: University of Notre Dame Press.

—— (1995) 'Truthfulness, lies, and moral philosophers: what can we learn from Mill and Kant? In G.B. Peterson (ed.) *The Tanner Lectures on Human Values*, 16: 309–61 Salt Lake City, UT: University of Utah Press.

MacKinney, L.C. (1952) 'Medical ethics and etiquette in the Early Middle Ages: the persistence of Hippocratic ideals', in *Bulletin of the History of Medicine*, xxvi: 1–31.

McLean, S. (1989) *A Patient's Right to Know*, Aldershot: Dartmouth.

Macready, N. (1997) 'US doctors lie to help patients', *British Medical Journal*, 315: 148.

Mancuso, M., Atkinson, M.M., Blais, A., Greene, I. and Nevitte, N. (1998) *A Question of Ethics*, Toronto, ON: Oxford University Press.

Marzanski, M. (2000) 'Would you like to know what is wrong with you? On telling the truth to patients with dementia', *Journal of Medical Ethics*, 26, 2: 108–13.

Merton, R.K. (1968) *Social Theory and Social Structures*, New York: Free Press.

Milgram, S. (1963) 'Behavioral study of obedience', *Journal of Abnormal and Social Psychology*, 6, 4: 371–8.

—— (1983) *Obedience to Authority*, New York: Harper & Row.

Mill, J.S. (1962) 'On Liberty' (originally published in 1859) in M. Warnock (ed.) *Utilitarianism: John Stuart Mill*, London: Collins.

Miller, D.J. (1992) 'Plagiarism: the case of Elias A.K. Alsatbi', in D.J. Miller and M. Hersen (eds) *Research Fraud in the Behavioral and Biomedical Sciences*, New York: John Wiley & Sons.

Miller, R.B. (1995) 'Moral sources, ordinary life, and truth-telling in Jeremy Taylor's casuistry', in J.F. Keenan and T.A. Shannon (eds) *The Context of Casuistry*, Washington DC: Georgetown University Press.

Mixon, D. (1987) 'Deception, self-deception and self-determination', in S. Fairbairn and G. Fairbairn (eds) *Psychology, Ethics and Change*, London: Routledge & Kegan Paul.

Mondeville, H. de (1977) 'On the morals and etiquette of surgeons', in S.J. Reiser, A.J. Dyck and W.J. Curran, (eds) *Ethics in Medicine: Historical Perspectives and Contemporary Concerns*, Cambridge, MA: MIT Press.

Narveson, J. (1993) *Moral Matters*, Peterborough, ON: Broadview Press.

Newdick, C. (1995) *Who Should We Treat?* Oxford: Clarendon Press.

Nyberg, D. (1993) *The Varnished Truth: Truth Telling and Deceiving in Ordinary Life*, Chicago, IL: University of Chicago Press.

—— (1996) 'Deception and moral decency,' in P.A. French, T.E. Uehling, Jr and H.K. Wettstein (eds) *Midwest Studies in Philosophy: Moral Concepts*, vol. xx, Notre Dame, IN: University of Notre Dame Press.

O'Neill, O. (1996) *Towards Justice and Virtue*, Cambridge: Cambridge University Press.

Osuna, E., Perez-Carceles, M.D., Esteban, M.A. and Luna, A. (1998) 'The right to information for the terminally ill patient', *Journal of Medical Ethics*, 24, 2: 106–9.

Pallone, N.J. and Hennessy, J.J. (1995) *Fraud and Fallible Judgement*, New Brunswick, NJ: Transaction Publishers.

Pang, M.S. (1999) 'Protective truthfulness: the Chinese way of safeguarding patients in informed treatment decisions', *Journal of Medical Ethics*, 25, 3: 247–53.

Pappworth, M.H. (1967) *Human Guinea Pigs: Experimentation on Man*, Boston, MA: Beacon Press.

Passamani, E. (1991) 'Clinical trials – are they ethical?' *New England Journal of Medicine*, 324: 1589–92.

Patterson, J. and Kim, P. (1991) *The Day America Told the Truth*, New York: Prentice Hall Press.

Plato (1997) all quotations taken from John M. Cooper (1997).

Porter, D. and Porter, R. (1985) *Patients and Practitioners*, Cambridge: Cambridge University Press.

—— (1989) *Patient's Progress*, Stanford, CA: Stanford University Press.

President's Commission for the Study of Ethical Problems in Medicine and Biomedical and Behavioural Research (1982) *Making Health Care Decisions*, 1, *Report*, Washington DC: US Government Printing Office.

Rachels, J. (1997) *Can Ethics Provide Answers?* Lanham, MD: Rowman & Littlefield.

Ramsay, L.E. (1997) 'Commentary: placebo run-ins have some value', *British Medical Journal*, 314: 1193.

Ramsey, P. (1970) *The Patient as Person*, New Haven, CT: Yale University Press.

Randall, F. and Downie, R.S. (1996) *Palliative Care Ethics: a Good Companion*, Oxford: Oxford University Press.

Rawls, J. (1971) *A Theory of Justice*, Cambridge, MA: Harvard University Press.

Reid, R. (1974) *Microbes and Men*, London: BBC.

Roberts, L. (1997) 'Misconduct: Caltech's trial by fire', in D. Elliott and J.E. Stern (eds) *Research Ethics: A Reader*, Hanover, NH: University Press of New England.

Ross, W.D. (ed.) (1954) *The Nicomachean Ethics of Aristotle,* trans. W.D. Ross, London: Oxford University Press.

Runes, D.D. (ed.) (1947) *The Selected Writings of Benjamin Rush*, New York: Philosophical Library.

Russell, B. (1946) *A History of Western Philosophy*, London: George Allen and Unwin.

Ryan, C.J., de Moone, G. and Patfield, M. (1995) 'Becoming none but tradesmen: lies, deception and psychotic patients', *Journal of Medical Ethics,* 21, 2: 72–6.

St Augustine, Bishop of Hippo (1847) 'On lying' and 'To Consentius: against lying' trans. Rev. H. Browne in *Seventeen Short Treatises*, Oxford: John Henry Parker.

Saunders, Dame C. (1994) 'The dying patient', in R. Gillon (ed.) *Principles of Health Care Ethics*, West Sussex: John Wiley & Sons.

Senn, S. (1997) 'Are placebo run-ins justified?' *British Medical Journal*, 314: 1191–3.

Shapiro, A.K. and Shapiro, E. (1997) *The Powerful Placebo*, Baltimore, MD: The Johns Hopkins University Press.

Shimm, D.S. and Spece, R.G. (1996) 'An introduction to conflicts of interest in clinical research', in R.G. Spece, D.S. Shimm and A.E. Buchanan (eds) *Conflicts of Interest in Clinical Practice and Research*, New York: Oxford University Press.

Shklar, J.N. (1984) *Ordinary Vices*, Cambridge, MA: Harvard University Press.

Shorter, E. (1993) 'The history of the doctor-patient relationship', in W.F. Bynum and R. Porter (eds) *Companion Encyclopedia of the History of Medical Ethics*, 2: 783–800, London: Routledge.

Sidgwick, H. (1962) *The Methods of Ethics*, London: Macmillan & Co.

Siegerist, H.E. (1961) *A History of Medicine*, vol. 2, New York: Oxford University Press.

Silverman, W.A. (1998) *Where's the Evidence?* Oxford: Oxford University Press.

Singer, P. (1995) *Rethinking Life and Death*, Oxford: Oxford University Press.

Smart, J.J.C. and Williams, B. (1973) *Utilitarianism For and Against*, London: Cambridge University Press.

Solomon, R.C. (1993) 'Deception and Self-Deception in Philosophy', in M. Lewis and C. Saarni (eds) *Lying and Deception in Everyday Life*, New York: Guilford Press.

Sommerville, J.P. (1988) 'The "new art of lying": equivocation, mental reservation, and casuistry,' in E. Leites (ed.) *Conscience and Casuistry in Early Modern Europe*, Cambridge: Cambridge University Press.

Southall, D., Plunkett, C.B., Banks, M.W., Falkov, Adrian F. and Samuels, M.P. (1997) 'Covert video recordings of life-threatening child abuse: lessons for child protection', *Pediatrics*, 100: 735–60.

Spiro, H.M. (1986) *Doctors, Patients, and Placebos*, New Haven, CT: Yale University Press.

—— (1997) 'Clinical reflections on the placebo phenomenon', in A. Harrington (ed.) *The Placebo Effect*, Cambridge, MA: Harvard University Press.

Spriet, A. and Dupin-Spriet, T. (1992) *Good Practice of Clinical Drug Trials*, (trans. Robert Coluzzi and J. Young) Basel: Karger.

Stolberg, S.G. (1999) 'Sham surgery returns as a research tool', *The New York Times*, 25 April.

Surbone, A. (1992) 'Truth telling to the patient', *Journal of the American Medical Association*, 268: 50–4.

Tate, P. (1997) *The Doctor's Communication Handbook*, Abingdon, Oxon.: Radcliffe Medical Press.

Thorns, A., Lloyd, G., Szukler, G. and Welsh, J. (1998) 'White lies' *British Medical Journal*, 317: 939–41.

Thornton, J. (1999) *Should Health Screening be Private?* London,: IEA Health and Welfare Unit.

Tomasi, J. (1991) 'Individual rights and community virtues', *Ethics,* 101, 521–36.

Tooley, M. (1972) 'Abortion and infanticide', *Philosophy and Public Affairs*, 2: 37–65.

UK CC (1989) *Exercising Accountability,* advisory document, London: United Kingdom Central Council for Nursing, Midwifery and Health Visiting.

Valmana, A. and Rutherford, J. (1997) letter in *British Medical Journal*, 314: 300.

Vanderpool, H.Y. (ed.) (1996) *The Ethics of Research Involving Human Subjects: Facing the 21ˢᵗ Century*, Frederick, MD: University Publishing Group.

Warnock, G.J. (1971) *The Object of Morality*, London: Methuen & Co.

Watson, J.D. (1980) *The Double Helix: a personal account of the discovery of the structure of DNA*, New York: Atheneum.

White, D.M.D. (1997) letter in *British Medical Journal*, 314: 299.

Wittgenstein, L. (1967) *Zettel*, G.E.M. Anscombe and G.H. von Wright (eds) trans. G.E.M. Anscombe, Oxford: Blackwell.

Index